LETTING YOURSELF "OFF THE HOOK"

It's a simple truth that even the most begrudging grudge-holder must one day admit: hard feelings are often hardest on those who cannot—or will not—forgive. That is why those who have hurt us seem to have moved on, leaving us mired in our blame, anger, and bitterness. Until now.

In this much-needed antidote to the agony of repressed emotions, we learn to recognize forgiveness for what it is: not a sign of weakness but of profound emotional strength. And in the pages of this singular guide we discover the simple secret to making peace with the past: that only through the process of forgiving others can we ever truly forgive ourselves.

"Explores an ingredient that is essential to spiritual growth. Sid and Suzanne Simon bring the rare combination of vitality and gentleness to the recovery field."
—**Stephanie S. Covington, Ph.D., L.C.S.W.**
author of *Leaving the Enchanted Forest*

"Offers ordinary people like you and me the necessary strategies for letting go of our hurts. *Forgiveness* will be an experience you will treasure."
—**Rev. Leo Hoar, Ph.D.**
professor and campus minister, Springfield College

"Unique and important. The Simons have translated an important psychological and religious concept into a practical program for enhancing human relationships and personal growth. Their work is moving, profound in its implications and universally applicable."
—**Dr. Howard Kirchenbaum**
senior fellow, The Sagamore Institute

"Unfailingly convincing . . . [a] knowledgeable, dispassionate look at the process of truly letting go."
—**Booklist**

SIDNEY B. SIMON has authored or co-authored seventeen books, including the bestselling *Values Clarification* and *Getting Unstuck*. He has held the post of professor of psychological education at the University of Massachusetts at Amherst.

SUZANNE SIMON coordinates the Incest Survivors Support Group at the University of Massachusetts' Every Woman's Center. Together, through their popular "forgiveness workshops," the Simons have helped thousands of people release the pain of unhealed wounds.

Forgiveness

How to Make Peace with Your Past and Get on With Your Life

DR. SIDNEY B. SIMON
AND SUZANNE SIMON

WARNER BOOKS

A Time Warner Company

Passage from *Quotes* by Harvey Jackins, published by Rational Island Publishers, Seattle, WA.

Copyright © 1990 by Dr. Sidney B. Simon and Suzanne Simon

Produced by The Philip Lief Group, Inc.

All rights reserved

Warner Books, Inc., 1271 Avenue of the Americas, New York, NY 10020

 A Time Warner Company

Printed in the United States of America

First trade printing: November 1991

10 9 8 7 6 5 4

Library of Congress Cataloging-in-Publication Data

Simon, Sidney B.

    Forgiveness / by Sidney B. Simon and Suzanne Simon.
      p. cm.
    ISBN 0-446-39259-6
    1. Forgiveness. I. Simon, Suzanne, 1947–   . II. Title.
  BF637.F67S56 1990
  155.9′2—dc20

89-40467
CIP

Cover lettering by Bernard Maisner
Cover design by Julia Kushnirsky

To my wife, Suzanne. In truth, there would be no book without her. It is her story, her pain and anguish, her courage, and her beauty that gave birth to the ideas in this book. She is a partner's partner, a co-author's co-author, and a consummate reclaimer of life, a very model of what healing looks like and can be. I love her.

Sidney B. Simon

To my father, who gave me the reason to learn forgiveness; to my mother, who believed my story; my sister, who supported the healing of it; my brother, who spoke up about it; my daughter, who accepted me despite it; and to Sid, my loving husband, who always believed in me and knew that I could and would rise above it.

Suzanne Simon

CONTENTS

ACKNOWLEDGMENTS

The ideas presented in this book grew out of an on-going healing process that included the help, guidance, and support of many people in my life. I wish to acknowledge them now.

My sincere thank you and deep appreciation to Jeanette McIntosh, Latifa Amdur, Marion McIntire, Verena Smith, Payasa Tree, Stephanie Nurenburg, Joan Schneider, and Carol Drexler—gifted women healers who, each in their own way, shared their inner wisdom and with their professional expertise guided, supported, comforted, and gently pushed me in all the right ways.

My heartfelt thanks to Trenda Caron, Laraine Pincus, Loretta Eazarsky, Robin Moulds, and Kim Kautz, friends who loved me through the hard times and celebrate now the joy I have found.

Thank you to my mother, sister, brother, daughter, and former mother-in-law. They all came through when I most needed them.

I offer the deepest and most tender appreciation to my sister. Without her invaluable support and love I'd still be stuck in denial. She gave me the first inkling that I didn't have to "go it alone," and she was there every single step of the way.

A special appreciation to my mother, who perhaps had the most to lose by the publication of this book, but who said, "If our family experience can help even one other person, then it needs to be told." It already has, Mom.

I am eternally grateful to the many Survivors who struggle daily to free themselves from their own painful pasts. I celebrate their *will* to survive. They continue to be powerful role models for me.

And to Charlie Kreiner and Carol Drexler, a heartfelt appreciation for the *on-going* healing work we are doing. Their wisdom, skill, compassion, and vision keep me on the right track.

Suzanne Simon

Both of us wish to acknowledge John Simon, who did the very first editing of the manuscript, and who did it with tenderness, insightfulness, and impeccable skill. Susan Meltsner added immeasurably to this book. She came to a forgiveness workshop we gave and then waved her magic wand and art to shape the final book. Jamie Rothstein gave consistent wisdom and support in her editing. Cathy Hemming, that rustler in cowgirl clothes, always nourished and supported us. Joann Davis, our editor at Warner Books, never wavered in her belief and encouragement as to how powerful this book was to be.

We can't help but give acknowledgment to the Epson Computer Company, Wordperfect, the word processor of choice, and Don Lesser, our computer guru. This book comprises some of the first words we ever wrote on the computer, after years of typewriter drudgery. Our gratitude is boundless, especially since we never had a hard-disk crash or lost a single word of the manuscript due to any computer error or contrariness.

A heartfelt thanks to all those workshoppers who attended our many forgiveness workshops here in the United States, Europe, and Greece. From their experiences we honed our ideas, the developmental stages, and the theory presented in this book. Some of their stories illuminate the pages. Their spirit guided us throughout the writing. Their healing helped our own.

Finally, we owe an enormous debt to all five of our children. Each in their own way nudged, noodged, and snuggled us forward on this project. Thanks, John, Douglas, Julianna, Matthew, and Carie.

Sidney B. Simon
Suzanne Simon

Forgiveness

INTRODUCTION

The world is round and the place which may
seem like the end may also be the beginning.
                              —Ivy Baker Priest
                                Green Grows Ivy

We stood around the casket, my brother, my sister, and I, gazing down at what remained of the man whom we had always loved but sometimes hated, whom we tried to respect but for so many years feared and avoided. He barely resembled the formidable giant who wielded so much power over us when we were children. He had been seriously ill for a long, long time.

I cannot tell you what my brother and sister were thinking as they stood beside me in that dimly lit funeral parlor. I, however, was remembering the man who adored my mother, who would lean over to kiss her outstretched arm while she poured his coffee and played footsie with her under the dinner table. I was thinking about the man who had been a skilled craftsman, an imaginative storyteller, an avid reader, and an exceptional gardener. And with this last talent in mind, I broke the silence.

"I thought we could bury these with Dad," I said, reaching into my pocket to retrieve a gift I tearfully bought soon after receiving the news of his death. Both my brother and my sister laughed out loud when they saw what I held, a half-dozen packets of

1

seeds, the very same kind our dad planted each spring for as far back as any of us could remember. Reminiscing about our dad's prize tomatoes and how no salad had ever tasted quite as good as the ones made from the vegetables he grew, we tucked the seed packets into his pockets and around his body. Sharing a joyful moment in the midst of an otherwise solemn occasion, we smiled affectionately and chuckled as we whispered to each other about visiting our father's grave and finding a magnificent garden growing on it. We did not defame this man who was our father. We celebrated him.

Yes, this was a fitting send-off for a man who cultivated the tastiest tomatoes on Long Island. But it was also much more than that. It was a tribute to the healing his children had done during the years preceding his death.

You see, when we were young, Dad came into our bedrooms and sexually molested us. At other times, he exploded into violent rages, lashing out at us in anger and frustration. Yes, this man did some horrible things to us when we were children, and we had not forgotten that.

In fact, had our dad died three or five or ten years earlier, we might have stayed away from his funeral altogether, and if, out of duty, we had attended it, we would not have been able to see anything good in him. We could not have acknowledged that there was more to him than the abuse he perpetrated or that we were more than the victims of his abuse. Instead of tranquillity and affectionate laughter, there would have been bitter tears and stone-cold silence, resentment, pain, anger, regret. We might have condemned him to rot in hell and condemned ourselves to more years of hiding, hating, and hurting. But instead, we walked away from his coffin knowing that he would rest in peace and even more important, that we would go on living at peace with ourselves.

What made the difference for us? Forgiveness.

Perhaps you are shaking your head in disbelief right now and wondering how anyone could truly forgive something as unspeakable as incest. You may even be asking yourself why anyone would want to. The truth is that we did not want to or set out to forgive. All we ever wanted was for pain from the past to stop interfering with our lives and our happiness in the present. To accomplish that, my sister, my brother, and I, each in our own way, worked through our pain and let go of it.

We did not and never will forget what had happened to us. We did not and never will condone our father's actions. Nothing could alter the fact that how he treated us was no way to treat little kids. Yet, before our dad died, according to our own needs and our own time frames, each of us reached a point where we no longer needed to make him pay for what he had done. We stopped expecting him to make up for it. We stopped using incest as an excuse for everything that was wrong with our lives. And we stopped waiting for our parents to give us as adults what we did not receive from them as children. We let go. We healed. And yes, we forgave.

This ending in Suzanne's life marked the beginning of our work in the area of forgiveness. We were already co-leading the personal growth workshops we offered together. But soon after her father's death in July of 1984, we started to take a closer look at the process Suzanne went through in order to heal the psychological wounds she sustained during childhood and to forgive the man who had inflicted them. At the time, we suspected that forgiveness might be the missing "peace" that so many of the people we encountered in our workshops and seminars were so desperately trying to achieve. Six years later, we are more convinced than ever that it is.

We have all been hurt. Lingering in the cobwebbed recesses of our mind is at least one memory—but more likely many memories—of parents who expected too much or too little, were overprotective and overbearing, distant and unaffectionate, absent or abusive; memories of teachers who belittled and berated us or labeled us a slow learner or a troublemaker, kept us after school for something we did not do or set us up as an example for the rest of our class; memories of being teased and taunted on the playground, chosen last in gym class, or left standing alone in a corner during junior high school dances. Some of us encountered prejudice, discrimination, or insensitivity because of our race, religion, or disabilities. Others were hurt when we were the subject of vicious gossip, passed over for a promotion, rejected by a lover, or betrayed by a friend.

Yes, we have been hurt. As far back as childhood or as recently as last week, you may have experienced the sting of rejection, ridicule, humiliation, deception, disappointment, or abuse. *This book is about healing those wounds*.

Of course, you may think that you have already done that in many cases. You may believe that you recovered from most of those old injuries and injustices years ago, that your painful or disappointing past experiences no longer affect you, and that may be true. We *can* heal our wounds to the point that they no longer interfere with our lives. But take a closer look at your life as it is today.

Can you list the ways your life would be better if only something that happened in the past had never happened at all?

Do you hold grudges and harbor bitter or resentful feelings toward your parents or siblings, refusing to speak to them or having a strained relationship with them at best?

Did you swear you would treat your children differently from the way you were treated as a child but find yourself hitting, screaming, nagging, or doing and saying many of the same things your parents did or said to you?

Do you frequently feel empty inside, perhaps filling the emptiness with alcohol or drugs, by overeating, working eighteen hours a day, gambling, or shopping until your credit card bills are sky high?

Do you sometimes feel as if you are reenacting your past, playing the same old scenes in new settings with new actors standing in for the parents, lovers, former spouses, friends, or bosses who originally hurt you?

Do new relationships fail to get off the ground because you fear that new friends or lovers will hurt or reject you as others have hurt or rejected you in the past?

Have you built walls to keep people from getting close enough to hurt you, only to discover that you are trapped behind those walls, feeling lonely, isolated, and alienated?

Do you approach any new challenge—whether a job interview or a blind date—expecting to fail or to be disappointed—because you have failed and been disappointed so often in the past?

Do you do the bare minimum to get by at work; keep track of your spouse's wrongdoings and review the entire list each time you argue; walk around with your ''dukes up,'' ready to do unto others *before* they can do unto you?

Do you simply not feel whole? Even though you don't know quite what it is, does *something* seem to be missing from your life?

If you answered ''yes'' to one or more of these questions, chances are that you are still hanging on to something that once hurt you, and it is, in turn, hanging on to you—like the proverbial albatross around your neck, weighing you down, holding you back, and keeping you from liking yourself, enjoying your life today, or looking forward to the future. *This book is about recognizing that connection between the past and the present, wrapping up unfinished business and putting it behind you once and for all.*

If what you have done and continue to do because you were hurt has made a negative difference in your life—and we have never known it not to—you made a wise decision when you picked up this book and began reading it. *This book is about letting go and moving on.*

Many of the ideas you will find here grew out of our exploration of Suzanne's personal struggle to heal and forgive. However, they are also an extension of Sid's pioneering work in the areas of personal growth, values clarification, and self-esteem. For more than twenty-one years, his courses at the University of Massachusetts; workshops and seminars conducted throughout the United States, Canada, and Europe; and his books (such as *Values Clarification* and *Getting Unstuck*) have helped countless men and women improve their sense of self-worth and make positive changes in their lives. Yet in spite of all the progress these people made and no matter how many obstacles to change they dismantled, they still got stuck and they still told us that they felt something was missing from their lives.

We began to wonder if the grudges, resentments, self-defeating habits, and everything else that goes along with *not* forgiving and *not* making peace with the past were the ultimate barrier to a healthy, productive, and satisfying life. Believing they were, in the fall of 1985 we presented our first forgiveness seminar at the Kirkridge Conference Center in Bangor, Pennsylvania. There, and at the many forgiveness seminars we have conducted since then, we have learned that forgiveness is indeed a matter of enormous importance to people of all ages and from all walks of life. We learned as much about forgiveness as we taught, and in this book we share the ideas and suggestions that have evolved over the past five years from our own and many other people's experiences. The tears, laughter, anger, and honesty of those seminar participants testified to the resiliency of the human spirit and the capacity to heal and forgive that each of us has—no matter how we were hurt or how those painful past experiences have altered the course of our lives.

Although you may not have been hurt by incest the way Suzanne was, whether or not they meant to, many different people have indeed hurt you—your parents, siblings, teachers, childhood playmates, grown-up lovers, and others. *This book is about forgiving the people who hurt you, not as a favor to them, but so you can let go of the pain and get on with your life.*

As Suzanne will tell you, she did not forgive for her father's sake or because it was the proper "Christian" thing to do:

No, I forgave because that is what I needed to do to feel whole, to like myself, and to rid myself of the excess emotional baggage that was weighing me down and holding me back. I wanted peace of mind, and I could not have it as long as I was stymied by unfinished business from my past and expending most of my energy nursing my unhealed wounds. I was not happy with myself or my life. I thought that maybe, just maybe, I could do more and be more than I was. And so I chose to heal.

This book describes a healing process that has worked in our own lives as well as in the lives of thousands of other men and women. You will read some of their stories on the pages of this book. It's not that we (or they) are saints. We are not endowed with forgiving natures that border on the superhuman. We simply got tired of living in pain from the past and became willing to try something new. You can do that, too. Regardless of how you were hurt or what you have done because you were hurt, you have the inherent wisdom and the inner resources to heal your wounds and create a better life.

Like the people you will read about in this book, you can re-create your life, rebuild your self-esteem, and find the inner peace that has eluded you—if you are willing to work your way through an ongoing healing process that helps you to:

- acknowledge that you were hurt and what you have done because you were hurt;
- get rid of guilt and shame and stop taking all of the blame for everything that ever happened to you;
- stop playing the victim who wallows in self-pity, indulges in self-destructive behavior, lashes out at innocent bystanders, goes through life expecting the worst, or perpetually repeats the past;
- unload your anger and indignation;
- recognize that in spite of it all you did survive, that you developed personal strengths and compassion as a result of your past experiences;
- put the past in its proper perspective, neither dwelling on it nor forgetting it, but rather seeing it for what it is—a part of who you are but not all of what you are.

At the end of the road that many have traveled before you and many others are traveling now lies something you may have never known before, something you may have been looking for in all the wrong places throughout your life, something each and every one of us deserves—peace of mind, joy, hope, and a future that can be whatever *you* want it to be. But please do not think that forgiveness or the healing process that leads you to it is an instant miracle cure for all that ails you. The path you choose when you choose to heal is long, difficult, and even painful at times. Completing unfinished business and letting go of pain from the past takes time. It takes hard work and lots of it. Even though the ride may take you over rough terrain and through many a long, dark tunnel, we believe it is well worth the price of admission. We invite you to climb aboard, turn the page, and continue the journey you no doubt began a long time ago, by leaping the first of many hurdles you will encounter—the fear and skepticism you may feel when you consider the prospect of actually forgiving someone who hurt you.

CHAPTER ONE

FORGIVENESS

Forgiveness is not a new idea. Throughout our lives, parents, teachers, and religious leaders have urged us to:

> forgive and forget;
> let bygones be bygones;
> turn the other cheek;
> kiss and make up.

"To err is human, to forgive divine," we were told time and time again, until we were left with little doubt that forgiveness was a virtue, the good, honorable, and morally correct thing to do. Yet there is something disturbing about the prospect of actually forgiving the real people who caused us real pain. It is liable to make our stomach churn, our pulse quicken, and our palms sweat; to cause indignation and resentment to rumble to the surface. More often than not, instead of feeling loving, benevolent, and willing to forgive, we find ourselves thinking: "Wait a second, I'm the injured party here. Why should I do all the work? Why should I forgive *them*? They should be apologizing to *me*!"

That statement certainly sums up Elise's feelings about forgiving her sister Megan. Elise was a thirty-three-year-old high school English teacher, married and the mother of eight-year-old twins, when we met her, and her feud with Megan, two years her junior, had been going on for decades. In fact, according to Elise, Megan had been a thorn in her side since the day she was born. "Megan was one of those babies everyone 'oohed and ahed' over all the time," Elise explains. "She was adorable, she knew it, and she played it for all it was worth." Elise's mother dressed the two girls identically, but blond, blue-eyed Megan drew admiring looks and words of praise while gangly Elise with her mousy coloring and freckled face, heard, "Isn't that sweet, you're wearing the same outfit as your sister."

When the two girls were young, they went everywhere together. "Mom's idea, not mine," Elise sighs. "Megan was my little shadow. I couldn't get rid of her, and if my friends and I didn't do what she wanted, she nagged and whined or threw a tantrum."

Things only got worse as the two girls grew older. Megan, apparently well aware of her older sister's less-than-loving feelings, became a ruthless "tattletale and attention grabber," keeping an eye on Elise and reporting anything she did that might displease their parents. "Then she'd follow up by telling them something wonderful that she did that day," Elise bristles. "It was the perfect one-two punch. I looked like the bad seed, and she was, as always, the little angel." But what really got to Elise was that Megan, who had plenty of her own boyfriends, flirted shamelessly with the few boys Elise dated. "I still see red when I think about one guy whom I really liked, and she knew it," Elise fumes sixteen years after the fact. "Megan did her little number on him, and he spent half the night talking about how gorgeous she was. The next day at school he came up to me and said, 'I hope you don't mind, but I'm going to ask your sister out.' Do you think Megan, knowing how I felt about the guy, told him to take a hike? Of course not. She went out with him and came into my bedroom afterward to 'compare notes' about what a great kisser he was, knowing full well he'd never even kissed me."

As you can see, the injuries and injustices Elise believed she had suffered because of Megan could fill a list a mile long, and Elise is unwilling to let go of any of them. "Every potentially happy moment in my life, Megan took away from me," Elise concludes, "right down to showing up on the night before my wedding, announcing that her latest boyfriend had gotten her pregnant and getting everyone so upset that they didn't even care that I was getting married. She's been one up on me since the day she was born. So why should I be the one to give up what's left of my pride and dignity by forgiving her?"

Elise equated forgiveness with:

giving up;
giving in;
wimping out;
admitting defeat.

If such thoughts come to mind when *you* consider the prospect of actually forgiving someone who hurt you, then forgiveness is likely to seem as unappealing to you as it did to Elise. Chances are that you, like she, have been engaging in ongoing psychological warfare with your siblings, parents, children, present or former spouses, and anyone else who ever hurt you. They fired the first shot, and the running battle has continued ever since. Over the years you battled back with words and with silence, with acts that caused pain and acts that induced guilt, face to face and by physically and emotionally removing yourself from the battleground. At times you fought to win, hoping to finally get the upper hand and show them how it feels to be hurt by someone they love. But mostly you fought to keep from losing any more than you had lost already. You hold your ground by holding on to the pain you suffered at the hands of these enemies, by *not* forgiving them for what they have done. The ultimate irony is that in many cases, they aren't even aware of your misery, and while you are turning yourself inside out, they don't feel a thing.

Like Elise, Warren, a thirty-five-year-old building contractor, has yet to find a convincing reason to forgive his father for treating him like ''the invisible kid'' throughout his childhood. ''My father made it very obvious that he wished I'd never been born,'' Warren claims, and as melodramatic as it might sound, his perception was not entirely inaccurate. His father was a first-year medical student when Warren's mother became pregnant, and they married because ''that was considered the honorable thing to do back then.'' Warren still shudders when he recalls the arguments he overheard as a young boy, fights between his mother and father that ''always got around to my father reminding my mother that she tricked him into marrying her by getting pregnant with me.

''I figured that if I tried hard enough, I could earn his love,'' Warren continues. ''That there had to be something I could do to get him to pay attention to me and act the way fathers were supposed to act.'' Unfortunately, nothing Warren did brought about the father/son relationship he so desperately wanted. He studied hard and did well in school, but that did not impress his father. He went out for sports, but his father was always "too busy" to attend the athletic events in which Warren participated. "Once I spent a whole semester in wood shop making him these ornately carved bookends, and all he said was, 'What are they supposed to be?' "

Warren's parents divorced when he was fifteen, and his father remarried immediately. Old wounds festered, and new ones were inflicted when his father and stepmother had three children in rapid succession and Warren spent holidays "watching them be the family I always wanted to have. My dad treated his new kids exactly the way I had been dying for him to treat me."

At twenty-one Warren gave up all hope of winning his father's love. He dropped out of college and went into the construction business with the man his mother had married. He married and had children of his own, all the while making sure to avoid his father. This was easy for Warren to do, since, with the exception of a card at Christmastime, his father made no effort to keep in touch with him.

With each passing year, Warren became more resolute about shutting his father out of his life just as he had once been shut out of his father's life, so much so that when Warren's father had a heart attack two years ago, Warren did not call or visit his father in the hospital. In fact, he and his wife had "the worst argument of our entire marriage," because he learned that she had sent his dad flowers and a get-well card.

"We still fight about my dad," he sighs. "Since the heart attack he's been calling us, inviting us to his house, saying he wants to get to know his grandchildren. My wife talks to him because I won't, and then she starts in about how we should patch things up. But I keep telling her there's nothing to patch up. There's nothing between us, and there never was. She dragged me to your seminar so I could learn to forgive him. But why should I do that? Because he's getting old and wants to see his grandchildren? Well, that's too bad. He should have thought of that before. He made his bed, let him lie in it."

Warren associates forgiveness with:

forgetting;
absolving;
condoning;
letting the "bad guys" get away with the rotten things that they
    have done.

You too will be reluctant to forgive if, like Warren, you subscribe to the theory that forgiving lets the ''bad guys'' off the hook, that it allows them to get away without having to suffer for what they have done. And most of us do indeed believe that the people who hurt us should pay for the pain they caused, that they *deserve to be punished, not forgiven*. What's more, because we were the one they hurt, we feel obliged to mete out that punishment, which we do by *not* forgiving them, by continuing to resent them and snipe at them, by not speaking to them and generally refusing to readmit them to the human race.

Hardest of all is continuing to see them on a regular basis and forcing ourselves to act as if nothing is wrong—all because we don't know how to confront them with our anger. If we were to unlock the prison gates and let them out, we fear that we would be shirking our responsibility to ''make them pay.'' If we forgave them, we believe we would be betraying ourselves and negating or minimizing the impact of the pain they caused us. Obviously, when seen in this light, forgiveness is unlikely to top the list of priorities in our lives.

Of course, many of the people we meet do not react to forgiveness as vehemently as Elise and Warren did. Indeed, some have what might be described as a nonreaction, insisting that there is nothing for them to forgive. For instance, Marcy, who attended one of our forgiveness seminars with her mother, a recovering alcoholic, came up to us during a break and said, ''I really don't understand any of this. What's done is done. I can't go back and change the fact that my parents were alcoholics. My dad is dead. My mom doesn't drink anymore. So what's the point of digging up all this old stuff? It's only going to complicate my life and make me remember things I'd rather forget.''

Pursuing a similar line of thinking, a colleague of ours who is quite frank about expressing his conviction that teaching forgiveness is ''hogwash,'' says, ''You'll turn everyone into benign, benevolent zombies. They'll all be too blissed out to function in the real world, where you need a good, strong suit of armor to make sure you don't get eaten alive.''

This perspective reflects the idea that attempting to forgive the people who hurt you will:

open up a Pandora's box;
send you plunging into an emotional abyss;

force you to relive unpleasant experiences and admit how badly
   you were hurt in the first place;
leave you vulnerable to being hurt again.

If you feel this way about forgiveness, for one reason or another,
we think you might just be afraid to forgive. Perhaps anger, bitterness,
and resentment serve as a barrier that protects you from pain, anxiety,
and self-doubt. Or you may believe that any move you make to
forgive the people who once hurt you will unleash a tidal wave of
frightening emotions and mind-boggling questions. For perhaps the
first time in decades, you will be forced to seriously consider
the magnitude of old injuries and injustices as well as acknowledge the
damaged life you have led because of them. You will have to admit
you were hurt and examine the details of how, when, and why you
were hurt. What's more, you may have to give up the attitudes and
behaviors that have protected you from being hurt again. From this
vantage point, forgiveness is a frightening concept indeed, and most
of us prefer to avoid rather than openly embrace the things we fear.
   Even for those of you who picked up this book feeling ready to
forgive, feeling willing and even anxious to get rid of your grudges
and heal your old wounds, forgiveness is not easy. It is not easy to
do, and the thought of doing it is not easy to accept. If it were, you
would have done it by now. But the fact is you haven't, and one of
the reasons you haven't is that *not* forgiving provides you with certain
payoffs or illusions:

• **The illusion that if this hadn't happened, you'd have a
  "perfect" life.**
  Not forgiving provides a readily available explanation or
  excuse for anything and everything that is wrong with you
  and your life. If only things had been different and you had
  not been hurt when and by whom you were hurt, you would
  be so much better off than you are now. But since those bad
  things did happen and you cannot alter the fact that they
  happened, how can you (or anyone else) expect you to be any
  way but the way you are? At one time or another, most of us
  have used this line of thinking to get us off the hook. If we do
  heal and forgive, we will not be able to use it anymore.

• **The illusion of being good.**
  Not forgiving helps you define who you are. You are the

victim of some injury or injustice. And although this may make you feel less lovable and capable than nonvictims, you are comforted nonetheless by the fact that you are one of the good guys—since the people who hurt you are obviously the bad guys. Once you forgive, the world can never again be defined in such black-and-white terms. You will have to accept and deal with shades of gray.

- **The illusion of power.**
  Not forgiving helps you compensate for the powerlessness you felt when you were hurt. In fact, while keeping the people who hurt you locked away in the prison of your mind, you feel practically omnipotent, since no one can make you forgive or force you to stop holding a grudge.

- **The illusion that you won't be hurt again.**
  Not forgiving protects you from being hurt again by the people who originally hurt you and by new people in your life. By keeping the pain alive, your eyes peeled for potential danger, and your guard up, you reduce the risk of ever again being rejected, deceived, abused, betrayed, or otherwise injured.

But are the benefits of not forgiving worth the price you pay for holding grudges, harboring resentments, and hanging on to pain from the past? Is having a handy excuse not to try for more worth never having more because you did not try? Is being an innocent victim as fulfilling as being a survivor, or is that sense of power you get from holding a grudge as satisfying as having the power to make your own choices? And is protecting yourself from possible pain worth missing out on life's real pleasures? We do not think so. We believe that the life you have now and can keep by *not* forgiving is not nearly as full and fulfilling as the life you could create by letting go of the pain and making peace with the past.

What Forgiveness Is Not

- **Forgiveness *is not* forgetting.** By forgiving the people who hurt us, we do not erase painful past experiences from our memory. Nothing we have done so far has been able to turn back the clock and remove the unpleasant incidents from our life history, and forgiveness will not do that, either. We cannot forget, nor should we. Those experiences, and even the pain they caused, have a great deal to teach us, both about not being victimized again and about not victimizing others.

• **Forgiveness *is not* condoning.** When we forgive, we lessen the past's impact on our present and future, but this does not alter the fact that the injuries and injustices we experienced were painful and unfair when they occurred originally. By forgiving the people who hurt us, we are not saying that what was done to us was acceptable or unimportant or "not so bad." It was bad. It did hurt. It has made a difference in our life. In fact, true forgiveness cannot occur while we are in any way denying, minimizing, justifying, or condoning the actions that harmed us.

• **Forgiveness *is not* absolution.** Many of us who were raised in the Catholic religion regularly confessed our sins and then received absolution. We performed whatever penance the priest suggested, and the slate was wiped clean until we next sinned, confessed, and were absolved. Many of us still associate forgiveness with this sort of absolution, but that is not what we are expected to do when we forgive the people who hurt us. We do not "let them off the hook." We do not absolve them of all responsibility for their actions. They are still responsible for what they did and must make their own peace with the past.

What's more, "I absolve you" are words spoken from atop our mountain of self-rightousness and demonstrate that we have not yet healed our wounds or let go of pain from the past. They let us play God, a benevolent God this time rather than a punitive one, but still a God who judges and then condemns or absolves the sinner. Absolution is just another way to be "one up" on the people who hurt us. And that is not forgiveness.

• **Forgiveness *is not* a form of self-sacrifice.** Forgiveness is not gritting our teeth and tolerating the people who hurt us. Plastering a smile on our face and "making nice" is not forgiving. Forgiveness is not swallowing our true feelings and playing the martyr, saying it's all right when it is not or getting by somehow in spite of the pain. The "grin and bear it" approach to forgiveness makes life less joyful and more difficult. Actual forgiveness has the opposite effect and cannot be undertaken halfheartedly. We either forgive or we don't. Being honest about the fact that we are not ready to forgive yet is better for us in the long run than pretending to forgive.

• **Forgiveness *is not* a clear-cut, one-time decision.** No matter how sincerely we want to let go of the past and move on with our life, we cannot expect to wake up one morning, think, "Okay, today's the day I'm going to forgive someone who hurt me," and then blithely do it. We cannot make a five-year plan that designates the first Tuesday of every third month as a forgiveness day or finish reading this book, make a list of people who have hurt us, and systematically forgive them. Forgiveness just doesn't work that way. It cannot be forced. Forgiveness is what happens naturally as a result of confronting painful past experiences and healing old wounds.

> *Forgiveness is a way of reaching out*
> *from a bad past and heading*
> *out to a more positive future.*
> —Marie Balter

Marie Balter had plenty to forgive. Born to an unwed, alcoholic mother who could not take care of her, Marie was placed in foster care at age five and later adopted by a couple whose severe disciplinary measures included locking her in the cellar. By age seventeen Marie was virtually paralyzed by depression and suffered muscle spasms, choking, hyperventilation, and hallucinations, which doctors misdiagnosed, labeling her a schizophrenic. In 1947 she was committed to a state mental hospital, where she remained for the next seventeen years. They were years of utter hopelessness and despair. There were times when Marie could not eat or move and times when she contemplated suicide.

Finally, in the early sixties, doctors reevaluated Marie's condition and determined that she was not schizophrenic but instead suffering from depression and a panic disorder. With appropriate treatment and the help of friends and mental health workers, Marie was released from the hospital in 1964.

At age thirty-four Marie had to decide what to do with her life, and she had every reason not to do much with it at all. After all, she had been abandoned and abused, locked away. from the world, and robbed of seventeen years of "normal" living. She had every right to feel angry and bitter, sad and hopeless; to take it easy and live day to day, expecting little and settling for whatever she got. But that is not what she did.

Marie married, earned a bachelor's degree from Salem State College and a master's degree from Harvard. She worked with psychiatric patients, lectured, and wrote her autobiography, which in

1986 was made into a television movie starring Marlo Thomas. Then in 1988, when Marie was fifty-eight years old, she returned to the institution where she had been confined for so many years—not as a patient this time, but as the hospital's community affairs director. In an Associated Press article announcing her appointment, Marie Balter explained her triumph over enormous adversity in this way: "I would not have grown one bit," she said, "if I had not learned to forgive."

When Marie Balter attributed her triumph over adversity to forgiveness, she did *not* mean that she pushed painful memories out of her mind or pretended that they never happened; decided that painful past experiences were insignificant or justifiable; swallowed her feelings and went on in spite of them; or just woke up one morning and decided all was forgiven. But what *did* she mean? If forgiveness is not any of the attitudes and behaviors we already listed, what *is* it?

What Forgiveness Is

• **Forgiveness is a by-product of an ongoing healing process.** Many of us grew up believing that forgiveness was an act to be performed or an attitude to possess, and the reason that we could not forgive was that we were not trying hard enough. But what really keeps us from forgiving the people who hurt us is that we have not yet healed the wounds they inflicted.

Forgiveness is the gift at the end of the healing process. We find it waiting for us when we reach a point where we stop expecting "them" to pay for what they did or make it up to us in some way.

• **Forgiveness is an *internal* process.** It happens within us. It is a feeling of wellness and freedom and acceptance. Those feelings can be ours at any time, as long as we *want* to heal and are willing to try.

• **Forgiveness is a sign of positive self-esteem.** It is no longer building our identity around something that happened to us in the past, realizing that there is more to us and more we can do. The past is put into its proper perspective, and we realize that the injuries and injustices are just a part of our life and just a part of who we are rather than all of us.

The religions in which we were raised presented forgiveness as a moral obligation. To be considered "good" and worthy, we were supposed to "turn the other cheek" and forgive our enemies. We believe, however, that *forgiveness is instead our moral right*—a right to *stop* being hurt by events that were unfair in the first place. We claim the right to stop hurting when we can finally say, "I'm tired of the pain, and I want to be healed." At that moment, forgiveness becomes a *possibility*—although it may not become a reality for quite some time.

• **Forgiveness is letting go of the intense emotions attached to incidents from our past.** We still remember what happened, but we no longer feel intensely angry, frightened, bitter, resentful, or damaged because of it. Forgiveness becomes an option once pain from the past stops dictating how we live our life today and we realize that what once happened to us does not have to determine what will happen to us in the future.

• **Forgiveness is recognizing that we no longer *need* our grudges and resentments, our hatred and self-pity.** We do not need them as an excuse for getting less out of life than we want or deserve. We do not need them as a weapon to punish the people who hurt us or keep other people from getting close enough to hurt us again. We do not need them as an identity. We are more than a victim of injury and injustice.

• **Forgiveness is no longer wanting to punish the people who hurt us.** It is no longer wanting to get even or to have them suffer as much as we did. It is realizing that we can never truly "even the score," and it is the inner peace we feel when we stop trying to.

• **Forgiveness is accepting that nothing we do to punish *them* will heal *us*.** It is becoming aware of what we did because we were hurt and how these attitudes and behaviors have also hurt us. It is deciding that we have simply done enough hiding and hurting and hating and that we do not want to do those things anymore.

• **Forgiveness is freeing up and putting to better use the energy once consumed by holding grudges, harboring resentments, and nursing unhealed wounds.** It is rediscovering the strengths we always had and relocating our limitless capacity to understand and accept other people and ourselves. It is breaking the cycle of pain and abuse, ceasing to create new victims by hurting others as we ourselves were hurt.

• **Forgiveness is moving on.** It is recognizing that we have better things to do with our life and then doing them.

This is what Marie Balter meant when she said she was able to grow because she forgave. She and the people you will read about in this book were able to forgive because they made a concerted, ongoing effort to examine and heal their wounds, to clean up the unfinished business in their lives, to let go and move on. They changed their attitudes and behaviors, pushed through their fears, and gave up their grievances and condemning judgments. And you can do those things, too—not as a favor to the people who hurt you or because someone once told you that forgiving was the good or right thing to do—but for yourself, for your own health, happiness, and emotional well-being.

Forgiveness Is Something You Do for *You*

When Marie Balter overcame the obstacles placed in her path by a "bad past," when she healed her wounds and let go of the pain, she was not doing anyone any favors. She did not turn her life around to please her mother, reassure her adoptive parents, or give the mental health system a shining example of their ability to rehabilitate mental patients. No, what Marie Balter did, she did *for herself*. She forgave and put the pieces of her life back together so that *she* could feel proud, so *she* had a reason to get up each morning and something to look forward to when she went to bed each night.

And that is what forgiveness is all about—working through the unfinished business, letting go of the pain and moving on *for your sake*. You forgive so that you can finally get rid of the excess emotional baggage that has been weighing you down and holding you back; so you can be free to do and be whatever you decide instead of stumbling along according to the script painful past experiences wrote for you.

To date, the people who hurt you have not made up for what they did to you, and even if they wanted to, they probably could not really do that. Think about it. In all the years that you have been holding grudges and harboring resentments, has anyone who once injured you or treated you unfairly ever offered an apology that *actually relieved your pain*? Have they ever done anything that actually compensated for injuries and injustices you suffered, the good times you missed, the life you led?

Like Elise, you may be waiting for the day when your siblings, parents, children, spouses, or friends will come to you on bended knee apologizing profusely and begging your forgiveness. But if that day came, it would not be enough. It would not relieve your pain or evaporate your resentment. It would not change your life or make you happier, healthier, and more at peace with yourself. *You* are the only one who can do that.

All the years you have waited for them to "make it up to you" and all the energy you expended trying to make them change (or make them pay) kept the old wounds from healing and gave pain from the past free rein to shape and even damage your life. And still they may not have changed. Nothing you have done has made them change. Indeed, they may never change. Inner peace is found by changing yourself, *not* the people who hurt you. And you change yourself *for yourself,* for the joy, serenity, peace of mind, understanding, compassion, laughter, and bright future that you get. These are the rewards *you* can receive. The people you forgive benefit, too—but that is not why you forgive them.

However, make no mistake about it, you will have to work for these things. You will have to work long and hard to heal your wounds and make peace with your past. There are no short cuts, no ways around the fact that *forgiveness is possible if and only if you commit yourself to an ongoing healing process.*

The Healing Process

Healing is a personal process, influenced by:

- the specific ways you were hurt, when, and by whom;
- how you reacted to the injuries and injustices you experienced—including what you came to believe about yourself and what you did because you were hurt;
- your present circumstances—both the positive and negative aspects of your life today, the problems you may be experiencing and the insight, resources, and emotional support you have right now;
- your own personal vision of inner peace and what you want your life to become.

These are the jigsaw puzzle pieces of your life. Although many people have accumulated some puzzle pieces that are similar to your own, no one else has all of the same pieces you do, and no one else has fit their pieces together to form a picture that is identical with your own. You have different gaps to fill in order to complete your puzzle, different pieces to discard because they no longer fit you. So your healing process will not be exactly the same as anyone else's. Although the purpose of the journey—to attain peace of mind and improve the quality of life—is something we all have in common, for each of us the journey itself will be somewhat different.

However, even though each of us will move through the healing process in our own way and in our own time frame, we all will pass through six stages of healing:

1. *Denial*. This is the stage in which we attempt to play down the impact or importance of painful past experiences and bury our thoughts and feelings about those experiences.

2. *Self-blame*. While in this stage, we try to *explain* what happened to us by assuming we were somehow responsible for the injuries and injustices we suffered, decimating our self-esteem as we work overtime to convince ourselves that we would not have been hurt *if only* we had been different or had done things differently.

3. *Victim*. In this stage, we recognize that we did not deserve or ask for the hurt we received. We are well aware of how we were damaged by painful past experiences, so much so that we wallow in self-pity, expect little of ourselves, indulge ourselves at the expense of those around us, or lash out at everyone and anyone who ''crosses'' us.

4. *Indignation*. In this stage, we are angry at the people who hurt us and at the world. We want the people who hurt us to pay and to suffer as we have. Our tolerance is virtually nonexistent, and our self-righteousness is at an all-time high.

5. *Survivor.* Finally, at this stage, we recognize that although we were indeed hurt, we did in fact survive. Our painful past experiences took things away from us but gave us things as well. We become aware of our strengths and welcome the return of our compassion, sense of humor, and interest in matters other than the pain. We bask in the knowledge that, all things considered, we did the best we could.

6. *Integration*. In this stage, we are able to acknowledge that the people who hurt us may have been doing the best they could, too, that if we are more than our wounds, they must be more than the inflictors of those wounds. With this

knowledge, we can release them from prison and reclaim the energy we used to keep them there. We can put the past in perspective—without forgetting it—let go of the pain, and get on with our lives unencumbered by excess emotional baggage.

When summarized in this way, the six stages of the healing process—which will be described in more detail later in this book—seem clear cut, leaving the impression that you move from one to the other in a linear fashion, one step after the other. But that is not how the process actually works. Healing happens in fits and starts, when you are standing still as well as when you are taking giant leaps forward. It also involves moving backward at times, to a former stage for a short while.

In fact, your healing process began the instant you were hurt. Although much of what you have done since you were hurt and much of what you go through in the early stages of the process may not feel good or be considered healing, they eventually bring you to a turning point, the point at which you decide that you are tired of hurting and want to heal. And that is also why the experiences that hurt you and even the worst of what you did because you were hurt—which are the subjects of the next two chapters—are part of the healing process, part of the journey that will ultimately lead you to feel whole, at peace with yourself and others, including the people who hurt you.

CHAPTER TWO

HOW HAVE WE BEEN HURT?

I was six years old when my father first sexually molested me. I was hurt when it happened, continued to be hurt, and unwittingly hurt myself for many years afterward.

My reactions were similar to those of many other men and women who were abused during childhood, raised in alcoholic or otherwise dysfunctional families, or hurt in other ways at crucial times during their lives. I found it difficult, if not impossible, to trust people and felt unsafe, insecure, and powerless. I was weighed down by guilt and shame because, at some very basic level, I believed I was responsible for what had happened and was convinced that I was somehow cursed, that there was something about me that drew unwanted attention to me.

The sexual abuse continued until I was twelve, and during those years my mother had no idea what was happening in her home. Because my father had been disabled by a back injury, my mother had to work, and it was when she was at work that the abuse occurred. She truly did not know about it, and I did not tell her. I believed that the knowledge would destroy her. My wish to protect her from the truth did not keep me from ''firing'' her from her job as my mother, however. Because I decided that I could not talk to her about the abuse and because any other subject seemed unimportant in comparison, I stopped talking to her about anything. We lived together as housemates, but I did not accept her attempts to nurture me and I did not give her any reason to feel connected to me as her daughter.

Essentially, I engineered my own abandonment. I lost my father because he abused me, and I severed my ties to my mother because she—through no fault of her own—could not help me.

Suzanne was hurt by incest, and she is not alone. Recent surveys show that one in three girls and one in seven boys are sexually molested during childhood, with the majority of abuse being perpetrated by parents or other familiar and trusted adults. If, like Suzanne, you were sexually abused as a child, there can be no doubt that you were indeed hurt by that experience. And even though the abuse itself may have ended long ago, chances are that you still feel its effect today.

But incest survivors are not the only ones who have been hurt or need to heal old wounds.

You may be reading this book because you *were* abused sexually, physically, or emotionally. Or you may be reading it because you were raised by alcoholic parents or because your marriage self-destructed and ended in divorce. Maybe you got scapegoated because of your religious beliefs or the color of your skin or were teased, taunted, and discounted because you were fat, smart, poor, or walked with a limp. The exact nature of painful past experiences is not the issue here. To compare old wounds is as fruitless as comparing whether it is worse to be blind or to be deaf, to lose an arm or lose a leg. Regardless, something is missing, and adjustments must be made.

No one has to make a movie of the week about the way *you* were hurt in order to validate the pain you felt. You were there. The injury or injustice was real. It really happened, and it had a real impact on your life. If something that once hurt you—even if it wasn't something as "sensational" as incest—still affects you in any way, it is a hurt to be reckoned with, a hurt that needs to be healed.

Yes, we have all been hurt. And if you want to heal and forgive, you must acknowledge that fact, examining what and who hurt you so that you can face and fix the problems that are created by coping with old wounds. Toward that end, in this chapter we review the top eight hits on the "hurt" parade—disappointment, rejection, abandonment, ridicule, humiliation, betrayal, deception, and abuse, as well as the ways these types of pain from the past are carried into the present.

Disappointment

When Darlene was eight years old, her parents got divorced—a devastating event in and of itself, made more so by the fact that it occurred in the 1950s when divorces were much less common than they are today. Darlene's mother retained custody of Darlene—the couple's only child—and her father was given visitation privileges every other Saturday. Darlene, who had been, as she puts it, "the classic Daddy's girl," looked forward to each weekly visit, but unfortunately her father did not always show up.

"The first time he missed a visit was horrible," she says, recalling the incident in detail more than thirty years after the fact. "I had the whole day planned in my mind. I had even made him a present in art class and had it all wrapped and ready to give to him." When Darlene's mother told her that her father called to say he couldn't make their visit, Darlene at first did not believe her. "I told her that my daddy wouldn't do that to me and refused to move from the front step, which was where I always waited for him." After it became apparent that her father really wasn't coming to get her, Darlene got angry—at her mother. "I screamed at her and said it was all her fault, that she had been mean to my father and forced him to stay away. Then I stormed up to my room and stayed there for the rest of the day."

The next day Darlene's father called, apologized, and promised he would never disappoint her like that again. Darlene immediately forgave him, and "everything was rosy," until he missed another visit and another and another.

"He always had an explanation," she says. "He always went out of his way to make it up to me. But he didn't stop doing it. And you see, I *really* wanted to believe he wouldn't do it again, so every time he missed a visit I was devastated." By the time she turned ten, Darlene was convinced she could not count on her father. She no longer planned to see him and, in fact, began intentionally making other plans for "his" Saturdays. "By the time I hit my teens, I hardly saw him at all," she explains. What's more, firmly planted in Darlene's mind was the idea that "you couldn't trust people to do what they said they would, because if you did, you were setting yourself up to be disappointed."

Disappointment is the inevitable outcome of *not* getting something that you want, are looking forward to, or expect. And since, in reality, we do not always get what we want, we all have at one time or another been disappointed. Of course, not every unfulfilled wish, dashed hope, and unmet expectation made a lasting impact on our lives, but some—like Darlene's disappointment over her father's missed visits—did.

For one thing, some disappointments simply hurt more than others. Sometimes you want something so badly—a promotion, for instance, or a certain job, a marriage proposal, or a pregnancy—that you are devastated when you do not get it. Sometimes you are so sure that something will turn out a certain way that you are taken completely off guard when it doesn't. In addition, when the job you didn't get was given to someone less qualified or a promotion was given on the basis of favoritism instead of merit or your sister gets pregnant so easily while you have a fertility problem, the unfairness of the situation makes the disappointment more painful. In each of these instances and others, disappointment does hurt—a lot.

Rejection

"Steve was my first lover," says Melinda, a twenty-eight-year-old restaurant manager. "And he was the first guy I was ever really deeply in love with."

When they met at a Catskill Mountains resort where they both had summer jobs, Melinda was seventeen and Steve was twenty. "He said he fell in love with me the first time he saw me," she recalls. "It took me longer, but not much." Two weeks after they met, they were spending every free moment together.

By coincidence, they lived only ten minutes apart in Connecticut and continued seeing each other for several weeks after the summer season ended. Then Melinda left for college. "I had chosen a school in the Midwest long before I met Steve, but the plan was for me to get through the year and then transfer to a school back East." During the first semester, they wrote letters every day and worked full-time jobs to pay for long-distance phone calls and as many flights to see one another as they could arrange. By spring, however, Steve's letters had dwindled to one per week, and when Melinda got home at the end of the school year, Steve informed her that he wasn't going back to the resort as planned, admitting he had been seeing someone else for the past few months.

"He said I wasn't around when he needed me," she says,

recounting their tearful confrontation. "That in a lot of ways I just wasn't able to meet his needs at all. I didn't know what he meant by that exactly. Did he mean sexually? I thought so since I was pretty inexperienced and the other girl definitely wasn't. Was he saying I wasn't supportive, that I was too career-oriented or selfish? I didn't know. I didn't ask. I just went home and cried. I was a mess."

Steve was torn. He wasn't sure what he wanted, and Melinda, hoping he would decide in her favor, went through three "nightmarish" weeks of seeing Steve in the afternoons while his other girl friend worked and then "sitting home at night wondering what she had that I didn't.

"He finally made his choice," Melinda sighs. "And it wasn't me. I never knew his actual reasons, but they didn't really matter, I guess. The bottom line was that I was the one he let go. I was the one who wasn't good enough somehow." "Not good enough" remained the bottom line of Melinda's self-image for a long, long time, reinforced by a series of ill-fated relationships with men on the rebound that Melinda now realizes "had rejection written all over them before they even began."

Being rejected by a lover, a spouse, a job interviewer, a peer group, a parent, or anyone else *always* hurts. Rejection severs a tie that is meaningful to us and that hurts. Rejection creates loss—the loss of love, friendship, or something else we wanted to get or would have preferred to keep—and that hurts. But what really cuts to the quick—and hangs around to haunt us—is the implicit message that almost always accompanies a rejection, the implication that we are, to use Melinda's words, "not good enough somehow."

If an article you wrote is rejected by the school newspaper or a national magazine, the first thought that comes to mind is that you don't write well enough. The explanation for being cut from the football team is clear and simple—you were not athletic enough. You were not talented enough, so you were not cast in the class play. You were not lovable enough, so your parents neglected you or preferred your younger sister over you. And when a spouse or lover rejects you, you can think of dozens of ways you were not good enough—not good enough in bed, not good enough as a breadwinner or a housekeeper, not supportive enough, not attentive enough, and on and on. The "not good enough" message is replayed in your mind like an endless tape loop, keeping alive the memory of rejection and the pain it caused.

Abandonment

Similar to rejection because it, too, breaks an emotional bond between us and an important person in our life, abandonment is a devastatingly painful experience, and the fear of abandonment is a powerful force in the lives of many of us.

"I was one of those babies you read about in the papers," Sandy explains. "My mother bundled me up, pinned a note to me, and left me on somebody's doorstep. When my parents sat me down at age five and told me I was adopted, I wasn't surprised. Somehow I already knew. I had always felt different, like I didn't fit."

That feeling grew stronger as Sandy got older. "My adoptive parents were good to me. They treated me the same way they treated their own kids," Sandy says. "But something was missing, something inside me. It's an eerie feeling, really. When I was little I used to wonder a lot about what my real mother looked like. Did I look like her? Did I have brothers or sisters somewhere who looked like me? I had these 'Prince and the Pauper' fantasies, where I'd meet my identical twin—who was wealthy and privileged, adopted like me except by royalty or movie stars—and we'd change places. I was always dreaming about having someone else's life, because mine never seemed real to me."

During her teens, Sandy acted out her alienation, her sense of being utterly alone in the world. "I was the ultimate misfit," she says, chuckling morbidly. "I dressed all in black. I wrote bleak poems and drew nightmarish landscapes. Any conversations I had at home consisted of grunts and one-word answers, and my only friends were the other outcasts, the poor kids and the crazy ones and the ones who were into drugs."

At their wits' end, Sandy's parents took her to a therapist. "I drove him crazy," she recalls. "Week after week I'd sit there staring at the walls, ignoring his questions, refusing to say anything at all." Finally the therapist came right out and asked her why she was wasting his time. Perhaps Sandy had been waiting for that particular question, or maybe she was finally ready to share some of the load she had been carrying. This time she answered. "I told him that was what I was—a waste of time, a mistake, someone who never should have been born. If he wanted proof, I'd show him my adoption papers. Because as far as I was concerned, being dumped on someone's doorstep proved beyond a shadow of a doubt that you weren't worth a damn."

Although they might not use the same words, thousands of adoptees share Sandy's sentiments. Despite adoptive parents who loved them and did the best they could to raise them, their sense of abandonment remains. To be left, to have ties to someone completely and irrevocably severed, causes enormous pain. The wounds fester, poisoning the abandoned with pervasive feelings of self-doubt. There must have been something about them that led their parents to abandon them, they reason, for no parent would put a child up for adoption unless that child was unlovable, worthless, or somehow deficient. No amount of reassurance, no explanation, completely convinces them that they were not at fault. And even when they do let themselves "off the hook," as Sandy eventually did, a certain emptiness remains. "I began searching for my real mother a couple of years ago," Sandy says. "Because I want to feel whole, and I'm not sure I can until I know who my mother is and why she gave me up."

A sense of abandonment, a bewildering mix of anguish and anger, may also follow the death of a loved one. You can say logically that your father or mother, grandparent or spouse, did not die so they could hurt you, yet you do indeed feel abandoned, left behind with your grief, left alone to face life without that person in it.

Less dramatic, perhaps, but still painful is the sense of abandonment you felt when childhood friends moved away or inexplicably moved on to a different group of friends that did not include you. And many of you have felt abandoned when close friends fell in love or got married. Their priorities changed. They devoted more time and emotional energy to their lover or spouse, and you were left out, left behind, while they moved on without you.

Whatever form it takes, abandonment leaves pain and emptiness in its wake. And when someone physically or emotionally "goes away" forever, the piece of us that goes with that person leaves an empty space that is exceedingly difficult to fill. Indeed, as it did for Sandy, the empty feeling, the pain, the unanswered questions, and the bitterness can last a lifetime.

Ridicule

Thirty-five-year-old Patricia is a successful businesswoman who lives alone in New York City. Although she dresses fashionably and is slender and attractive, when Patricia looks in the mirror she sees a clumsy, overweight child who was chosen last for gym class relay races, teased and laughed at by her classmates, and called "Fatty Patty" by her brother and all the kids in her neighborhood. "Fatty Patty" wore chubby-chick clothes and did not date during high school or college. Her older brother used to claim they did not need a garbage disposal because they had her, and her sister teased her about shopping for school clothes by suggesting she visit "Omar the tentmaker." Patricia never got used to being ridiculed, but she did learn to defend herself against it. She rewrote the Golden Rule and did unto others *before* they could do unto her.

Unfortunately, "Fatty Patty" lives on inside grown-up Patricia. To this day she believes that the people she meets are silently judging and laughing at her. She lets no one get close enough to hurt her, cutting them down with her sharp tongue and pushing them away with barbed comments and brutal sarcasm.

Ridicule is defined as "the act of making someone the object of scornful laughter; to make fun of; mock; deride." But if you have ever been ridiculed, you don't need a dictionary to tell you what it means. You can still hear that scornful laughter ringing in your ears, still recall those mocking words, and still feel the sting of derision and criticism.

Maybe you were called names like "fatty" or "faggot," "sissy" or "butterfingers," "weakling," "cry-baby," or "teacher's pet." Maybe the labels were racial or ethnic slurs like "nigger," "kike," "wop," "spic," or "chink." Perhaps you were laughed at for being poor or shy or disabled in some way. We and almost everyone we know have been singled out and made to feel different or deficient by someone at some time in our lives.

And we have not forgotten. People like Patricia who were ridiculed for being fat still feel fat and think they look fat long after the real fat is gone. People who were labeled clumsy or stupid or incorrigible still see themselves that way. No one has to mock them for it anymore because they mock themselves, thinking or even saying aloud, "I am so stupid!" "What a klutz I am!" and "Look at me—I can't do anything right!" If you doubt that ridicule is a long-lasting hurt, just examine your sore spots. Almost every one of them can be traced back to a put-down from the past.

Humiliation

Ridicule and humiliation—hurt pride and dignity—often go hand in hand. For who can be ridiculed without feeling humiliated? Many of you may have also been humiliated by teachers who called you stupid or hopeless or held you up as an example for the rest of the class *not* to follow. Your pride and dignity may have been hurt by parents who dressed you in unstylish clothes or cut your hair by putting a bowl on your head or sent your older brother to chaperone your dates. Perhaps you have been chewed out in front of your co-workers, embarrassed by your children in public places, mortified by alcoholic parents who created scenes at parties or in front of your friends, or utterly humiliated by being "the last to know" that your spouse was having an extramarital affair. And if you have ever "made a fool of yourself," you know that humiliation sometimes leaves wounds that were self-inflicted.

For instance, when Melinda recalls the untimely demise of her relationship with Steve, she remembers a good deal more than the pain of being rejected. "I humiliated myself beyond belief," she says. "I swallowed my pride during those three weeks when he saw me during the day and her at night, but I lost every shred of dignity and self-respect when he said it was really over between us. I cried. I begged—on my knees, even. I called on the phone but hung up when he answered and then called back to apologize for calling and hanging up. He got a job delivering pizzas, and one time I even went to a friend's house and ordered one so I'd get a chance to talk to him face to face. It only went on for a week or two, but still when I think of the things I said and did, I just cringe."

Like Melinda, when we recall the humiliating moments in our lives, we still cringe. As youngsters we may have been told that "sticks and stones may break my bones, but names will never hurt me," but the truth of the matter is that name calling as well as other forms of ridicule and humiliation *did* hurt us. They attacked something we had done or, worse yet, some integral facet of who we were, and we recoiled from the pain. Like a medieval knight protecting a castle under siege, we fortified the defenses around that particular area of vulnerability or built sky-high walls to keep people from getting close enough to in any way hurt us again. Many of us still use those defenses and hide behind those walls today.

Betrayal

On the night of her senior prom, Sara "went all the way" with her steady boyfriend, Tom, whom she had been dating since her sophomore year of high school. The following Monday, Sara was heading out of the girls' locker room when she spotted Tom and a group of his friends gathered in the hallway. She walked toward them and to this day wishes she hadn't, because she overheard a conversation that dealt her a horribly painful blow.

"I hear you scored on prom night," someone said.

Someone else patted Tom on the back and chimed in, "So you finally wore her down, huh?"

"Are you kidding?" Tom bragged. "She couldn't wait. She had her prom gown off before I was finished locking the motel room door."

Sara felt as if she had been slapped in the face. Tears welled in her eyes, and her heart pounded furiously. She had been betrayed.

Betrayal is a sharp, stabbing pain that sends shock waves throughout the body. You too may have felt that pain and remember it well. A boyfriend or girl friend may have shared intimate details of your relationship with others the way Tom did. Or perhaps you were betrayed by a friend who told other people a secret you shared, even though you asked that the information be kept in confidence. You may have been betrayed by co-workers who gossiped and spread rumors about you or felt betrayed when your former spouse portrayed you as "the bad guy" to your kids. Or, as Suzanne was, you may have been betrayed by a parent whom you trusted implicitly but who shattered that trust by abusing you or acting explosively or unpredictably (or for no apparent reason at all). Although it did not occur in Suzanne's case, if you reported sexual abuse to your mother or another adult and that person did not believe you, you suffered a double betrayal.

When betrayal occurs, we can almost hear a bond of trust snap and feel the pain rush in. We might feel as if we'd been slapped in the face—the way Sara did—or socked in the gut or, to quote one of our friends, as if we were "falling down a deep, dark hole, tumbling over and over like Alice on her way to Wonderland." It is a long way up from the bottom of that hole, and some of us have not made it out yet.

Deception

Like betrayal, deception damages your ability to trust. However, when you are deceived and lied to, you find it difficult not only to trust other people, but to trust your own judgment as well.

For some of you lies took the form of broken promises—like those Darlene's father made after each missed visit. He would never do it again, he said. But he always did, and Darlene learned not to believe him. Unfortunately, as is often the case with deception, Darlene generalized her experience and had a hard time telling whom, if anyone, she could believe or count on.

Like Melinda, many of you heard lovers, spouses, parents, and others assure you that nothing was wrong when you could sense or actually see and hear that something was. In fact, secrecy and deception were not the exceptions but rather the rule in some families.

"My father had affairs," says Betsy. "And my mother always knew about them. There was always tension hanging in the air, even though they both went out of their way to put on this lovey-dovey act for our benefit. But we weren't stupid. We may not have heard exactly what they were saying, but we couldn't help hearing them fight late at night. And when Mom all of a sudden got up from the dinner table and went into the bathroom, we knew she wasn't running the water to wash her hands. She was trying to keep us from hearing her cry.

"I can't speak for my sisters, but I always thought our whole 'happy family' routine was a lie—only I could never prove it because we all pretended there was nothing wrong. Sometimes I thought I was crazy. And sometimes I thought I was the problem no one would talk about."

Deceptions that involve denying real problems and keeping family secrets do indeed leave you feeling "crazy." You don't know what to believe. You do not know what is safe to say and what isn't. And you certainly have one heck of a time trusting your own judgment.

You can also see the psychological side effects of deception by considering the growing number of people being victimized by the "great American dream"—the one that promises success and prosperity to anyone who is willing to work hard to achieve it. Thousands of people are hurt by this deception because the truth of the matter is that there is only so much room at the top, that racism and sexism still keep many doors closed to many people, that factories close down or layoffs occur and people who worked hard all their lives find themselves unemployed and disenfranchised. "We did what we were supposed to do, and look where it got us," they think resentfully. "What did we do to deserve this?" they wonder as grief overwhelms them. Bitterly they question why such bad things have befallen them when they tried so hard to be good. And the only answer they can grasp is that they were not good enough, did not try hard enough, or were unfortunate enough to be born black or female or into a family that encouraged them to pursue the same blue-collar work their fathers had done before them.

As you can see, every lie comes with a long list of questions, and at the top of that list is "Why? Why did they lie to me, and why did I believe them?" No one gives you a satisfactory answer to that question, and sadly, the answers you come up with on your own are almost always self-defeating. You get angry at the people or "systems" that lied to you, but you also become furious with yourself—for trusting the people who deceived you and for being too "stupid, gullible, or naive" to figure out that you were being deceived in the first place. Drawing such conclusions can and does do untold damage to self-esteem.

Abuse

In recent years, the pervasive problems of child abuse and domestic violence have gained widespread recognition. Countless books have been written about them. Television movies have been made about them. Hardly a day goes by without an article about abuse appearing in the newspaper. When a particularly horrifying case of abuse captures the attention of the national media, we are literally bombarded with detailed accounts of children who were beaten by their parents, wives who were battered by their husbands, or the extreme lengths a teenage girl went to in order to stop the sexual abuse she had been experiencing for many years. We read these stories or watch these television movies and try to fathom the nightmare these abuse victims must have lived through. But those of us who have been abused ourselves do not have to wonder what it might have been like—we know.

Some of you were physically abused—beaten, burned, shaken, thrown across rooms, tied to your beds, or locked in closets. Some of you were sexually molested—fondled, raped, photographed, or forced to perform acts you neither understood nor wanted to perform. Many of you were emotionally abused—neglected, ignored, or told again and again that you were stupid, crazy, evil, worthless, that you were responsible for your parents' misery, that they wished you had never been born. Some of you were abused as children. Others among you were battered or degraded as adults by your lovers or spouses. And more of you than you might imagine went straight from abusive childhood homes into abusive adult relationships.

Regardless of the form it takes, when it happens, or how long it lasts, abuse *hurts*! Some of you have physical scars that bear witness to the bodily injuries you sustained. You may still jump when you glimpse an abrupt movement from the corner of your eye or flinch when you are touched in a certain way or have flashbacks during lovemaking.

But abuse does more than physical damage. It shatters our sense of trust. After all, we implicitly trusted the people who hurt us. We knew instinctively they were the ones who were supposed to care for, protect, and unconditionally love us—but their actual behavior hurt us, scared us, and demonstrated repeatedly that they must not love us at all. If we could not trust the most important people in our lives *not* to hurt us, then whom could we trust?

Abuse damaged our self-esteem, for who but the lowest of the low would be treated the way we were treated? Abuse bombarded us with negative messages about ourselves—and we believed them. After all, we were just children. Certainly our parents knew more about these things than we did. Why would our parents tell us that we were bad, worthless, incompetent, and so on if it wasn't true? And sometimes the abuse itself, sexual abuse in particular, left us feeling dirty, damaged, and different from every other human being on the planet. We could tell no one our horrible secret, yet we often felt as if everyone knew and thought less of us because of it.

In addition, abuse leaves its victims with an enormous burden of guilt and shame. Plagued by unanswered and unanswerable questions, we may still wonder about what we might have done to cause the abuse and what we could have done to prevent or stop it. When the abuse occurred we felt powerless, out of control, and a pervasive sense of powerlessness may still possess us. Or perhaps we feel an overwhelming need to control every aspect of our lives and all the people in it. These feelings too are the long-lasting results of abuse.

We Have All Been Hurt—but Does It Matter?

Every single hurt we have sustained over the years is not a big deal. If every name you were called, every test you failed, or every disappointment you experienced still affected you, you would be too paralyzed by pain to get out of bed in the morning.

Clearly, some painful past experiences no longer influence your life. You have indeed gotten over them. On the other hand, there are a few hurts that you still hang on to. You know which ones they are by the way you feel when you think of them. The important hurts do not go away on their own. They do not go away even when you truly want them to leave you alone and do everything you can to forget or ignore the pain. Just as Melinda came to believe she was not good enough, just as Darlene went out of her way not to be disappointed, just as Sandy could not feel "whole" because her mother had abandoned her as an infant, you too may still suffer from the hurt you first felt years ago—and that is why the old, even ancient, wounds do matter. Until you heal them, they will go on influencing the quality of your life.

The size of your wounds does *not* matter, however. It is absolutely pointless to compare how you were hurt with how someone else was hurt. Just listen to how ridiculous it sounds to say, "I shouldn't feel bad about being physically abused because I was never sexually molested," or, "I guess I should be glad my parents only hurt me by getting divorced instead of hurting me by being alcoholics." What happened to somebody else did not hurt you. What happened to you did, and if it hurt, it hurt.

Also, it does *not* matter that the same experience would not hurt you today. It isn't happening today. Yes, it may seem silly to feel your stomach churn and your heart pound over something that happened to you in the third grade. But telling yourself that you are foolish to still feel the pain does not make it hurt less. In fact, the negative things you say to yourself usually make old wounds hurt more.

It *does* matter that you were hurt—regardless of how or when. That painful or disappointing experience really happened. You can try to deny its effect on you, avoid thinking about it, or ignore the emotions it provokes. You can try to run away from it, turn it upside down or inside out, or bury it under work, food, sexual activity, or drinking and drug use, but the memories remain in your mind and the emotions well up unexpectedly and often. They are a force to be reckoned with—as are the mixed emotions you may feel about the people who hurt you.

Who Hurt You?

At the beginning of our forgiveness seminars, we ask the participants to help us make a list of people who have hurt them in the past or are hurting them now. The list gets pretty long and usually looks something like this:

We have been hurt by:

Parents
Lovers
Spouses (former and present)
Children
Stepchildren
Brothers and sisters
Grandparents
Friends
Co-workers
Employers
God
Teachers
Preachers
Peers and playmates
People of the opposite sex or other races and religions
Just plain strangers
Whole systems (schools, government, criminal justice system,
        and so on) and the media
Ourselves

You may be able to add to this list, and certainly it would grow much longer if you named the specific people who have hurt you. We are also struck by the fact that each time we ask an audience to make a list, the same people top it—parents, spouses, lovers, and children—giving credence to that song about always hurting the one you love.

You do not need a Ph.D. to figure out why these people are the ones who hurt you deeply and often. They are the people whose love, approval, and acceptance you treasure. They are the ones with whom you have shared the most intimate facts of who you are. What's more, you do not expect them to hurt you. There is always an element of shock when they do, and the shock waves reverberate straight through to your soul.

When Parents Hurt You

We certainly do not intend to make parents the "heavies" in this book. We are parents ourselves and know all too well how difficult a job raising children can be and how minimally we are prepared for the awesome responsibility we assume when we become parents. We shudder to think that every single problem in our children's lives will someday be laid at our doorstep. We know we did the best we could under the circumstances. Most of your parents also did the best they could, but unfortunately—in their case and ours as well—that just may not have been good enough. The truth of the matter is that many and perhaps all of us really were hurt in some way by our parents.

Of course, unless your parents were seriously mentally ill—and sadly, some of them were—they did not intentionally set out to hurt you. They did not wake up in the morning and ask themselves, "Let's see. How can I hurt my child today?" Although it sometimes seems as if they did, your parents probably did *not* consciously and maliciously devise a plan to harm you and then carry it out skillfully. In fact, some parents had only the best of intentions, *but they hurt you anyway.*

For instance, your mother or father may have truly wanted you to "live up to your potential." Unfortunately, in their efforts to mold and shape you into the best son or daughter you could possibly be, they constantly bombarded you with negative criticism. You may have tried hard to please them, to wring from them some small word of praise, but no matter what you did or how well you did it, you were told you could do even better. In addition, parents who only wanted to make sure you did not get hurt overprotected you or always seemed to be one step ahead of you pointing out the dangers in your path, inadvertently teaching you to fear new people and new experiences. And parents who thought they were helping you to have a better life than their own pushed you to be what *they* wanted you to be, negating your uniqueness and discounting *your* interests, hopes, and dreams.

But please don't think we are making excuses for the parents who hurt you. They may have had your best interests at heart—but what they actually did caused pain and misery. Many of the things your parents did—comparing you with your older siblings, for instance, or leaving you to take care of your younger brothers and sisters, or making you wear hand-me-down clothes that other children made fun of—they did unknowingly.

Some of the pain you suffered—when your parents argued, lost their jobs, got divorced, or died—certainly was not directed toward you or intended to hurt you, but it did.

And of course, there were also some things that your parents did to you that they simply *should not have done*. They should not have abused you—physically, sexually, or emotionally. They should not have dragged you into bars or gone on three-day drinking binges leaving you and your siblings to fend for yourselves.

We believe that parents get top billing on the list of people who have hurt us, not just because so many of our parents have caused us pain—regardless of how or why—but also because the wounds they inflicted tend to be the deepest and the hardest to heal.

Why is that? Well, first of all, when our parents hurt us, we were usually too young to fully comprehend what was happening to us or adapt to the situation in healthy ways. In addition:

- The wounds inflicted by our parents often threatened our very survival, attacking the innermost core of who we were and jeopardizing our sense of trust, safety, security, and self-worth.
- The damage done to us—and remember that damage need not have been as blatant as physical or sexual abuse—occurred at a time when we were learning vital lessons about how to live in the world and relate to other people. What we learned from the most influential role models in our lives—our parents—became the foundation for all of our future attitudes, beliefs, and behaviors. Some of us, because of what happened in our childhood homes or what we missed out on during childhood, were left with a cracked and crumbling foundation on which to build our lives.
- At some level we knew that *parents are not supposed to hurt their children*. When our parents hurt us, we recognized instinctively that something was terribly wrong. Not only

were we at a loss to explain what was happening, but also we did not want to believe it was happening. We quickly absolved them and blamed ourselves. We denied that the painful experience happened at all or went to great lengths to make sure it didn't happen again or did not hurt us as much the next time. The way we adapted to hurtful circumstances *served us at the time*. The adjustments we made in attitude and behavior helped us survive. Problems have arisen, however, because many of us still think and act the way we did back then—*even though it no longer serves us and may even hurt us now.*

This last statement, which applies to any way we were hurt by anyone, is why what we have done and continue to do because we were hurt has made a difference in our lives. What kind of difference? The next chapter answers that question, giving us a glimpse at the walking wounded all too many of us have become.

CHAPTER THREE

THE WALKING WOUNDED— WHAT WE HAVE DONE BECAUSE WE WERE HURT

The Monk and the Woman

Two Buddhist monks, on their way to the monastery, found an exceedingly beautiful woman at the riverbank. Like them, she wished to cross the river, but the water was too high. So one of the monks lifted her onto his back and carried her across.

His fellow monk was thoroughly scandalized. For two hours he berated him on his negligence in keeping the rule: Had he forgotten he was a monk? How did he dare touch a woman? And worse, carry her across the river? What would people say? Had he brought their holy religion into disrepute?

The offending monk listened patiently to the never-ending sermon. Finally he broke in and said, "Brother, I dropped that woman at the river. Are you still carrying her?"

—Anonymous

Like the monk, most of us are still carrying a burden we too could have "dropped at the river" long ago. Our own experiences and those of thousands of other people we have counseled, taught, or encountered at the forgiveness seminars we conduct across America and Europe have convinced us that most of us have *not* yet healed our old wounds or made peace with our pasts. We have not forgiven the people who hurt us, but more important *we have not let go of the pain*. And it has not let go of us.

Indeed, many of us wake up each morning and fill an enormous suitcase with pain from our pasts. We stuff it with grudges, bitterness, resentment, and self-righteous anger. We toss in some self-pity, envy, jealousy, and regret. We load that suitcase with every injury and injustice that was ever done to us; with every memory of how others failed us and how we ourselves have failed; and with all the reminders of what we have missed out on and what we can never hope to have. Then we shut that suitcase and drag it with us wherever we go.

To comprehend the impact of carrying pain from the past into the present, you need only observe the behavior of someone who drags real baggage through a train station. Take a moment to imagine such a scene. Think of a man with a bulging suitcase in each hand and an overstuffed shoulder bag making him lean to one side. Sweating and struggling, he grumbles at the travelers who move too slowly and envies the ones who glide by unencumbered by excess baggage. He worries that he will miss his train and wonders if the trip is even worth his time or trouble. He stops to rest and glares at his luggage, kicks it, curses at it, and then gets angry at himself. "Why do I always pack so much stuff?" he mumbles, and sighs, "I don't really need it."

Like the tired, irritable, downtrodden traveler, our excess emotional baggage weighs us down, saps our energy, slows our progress, and sometimes even convinces us to cancel the trip—giving up on our goals and aspirations or settling for far less than we planned originally. Up until now, *you simply did not know there was any other way to travel*.

Time and time again we have witnessed the debilitating impact of carrying pain from the past into the present. It not only prevents us from doing and becoming all that we could, but it also saddles us with new and often more debilitating problems, including:

- physical ailments and illnesses
- addictions and compulsive behaviors
- relationship problems

- job burnout
- negativity
- child abuse and domestic violence
- ineffective parenting
- lethargy, depression, and suicide

These are the impasses you reach when unhealed wounds and unfinished business influence the choices you make. These are the dead-end streets you turned onto, even though you *did the best you could* to cope with the pain and live your life, both at the time you were hurt and every minute of every day since.

Doing Your Best to Survive

It is our unshakable conviction that all people do the best they can with the insight, tangible resources, and emotional support they have available to them. You are doing the best you can right now, and at the time you were hurt, you did the best you could to cope with your pain. Because you were young, vulnerable, and probably confused by what you were feeling, you may not have fully understood what was happening to you or how you were reacting to it. If the circumstances had been different, if you had more experience, time, money, skills, or alternatives, perhaps you could have done things differently. But you did not have those things. Perhaps you had no one to turn to for guidance, few role models to show you the productive, healing things to do when you were hurting.

So please, as you read this chapter and especially if you recognize yourself in these pages, remind yourself that you did not consciously choose to get stuck hating or hurting or holding grudges. No matter how badly you were hurt, you never said, "I think I'll nurse this wound for the rest of my life and let it use up my energy and take away my peace of mind." You are not bad or weak or sinful because you are still weighed down by old pain and unfinished business. We all have trouble letting go of these things.

Haunted by the Past

- A bitter child custody battle is waged by former spouses who have not recovered from the pain of their divorce.
- A teenage girl, sexually abused by her father, hires a gunman to kill him.
- A spurned lover's heartbreak turns to hatred, and he terrorizes the woman he once adored.
- Forty years after two brothers vied for their parents' affection, they remain sworn enemies, taking their lifelong rivalry to court, where they each sue for control of their parents' estate.

Stories like these make newspaper headlines. And if we were writing the headlines, we would give all four stories the same one—PAINFUL, UNFORGIVEN INCIDENTS FROM THE PAST CAUSE NEW PAIN, NEW PROBLEMS.

Although your life experiences may never appear in the newspaper or on the evening news, many of the stories you could tell would probably fit under that same heading. The decidedly unpleasant memories that linger in the cobwebbed recesses of your minds, the wounds you have not healed, the injuries and injustices you have not forgiven, do indeed come back to haunt you. The bitterness and resentment you feel and the grudges you hold are the most obvious examples of this phenomenon.

Holding a Grudge

Are you one of the millions of men and women who harbor bitter, angry, or resentful feelings toward their parents or siblings, refusing to speak to them at all? Are your family relationships so strained and stressful that any family get-together is preceded by three days of anxiety and followed by three weeks of guilt, disappointment, or depression? Reeling from the aftershock of a divorce, have you felt or given in to an overwhelming urge to make sure your children, parents, friends, and neighbors know that the dissolution of your marriage was entirely your former spouse's fault?

Have you attempted to induce guilt or ''even the score'' with your mate or lover by bombarding that person with a running account of all the hurt he or she caused in the past? Or wished that harm would come to the co-worker who spread rumors about you, maliciously gossiped about a boss who criticized you, or "slacked off" at work because you did not get a promotion or pay raise or because you felt unappreciated?

If you have ever done any of these things, then you know what it is to hold a grudge.

Indeed, a grudge is like an emotional scab that we poke and rub and pick at until it becomes infected and poisons every corner of our lives. For one thing, holding a grudge consumes an enormous amount of energy. We use up our energy on vindictiveness, keeping score, and conjuring up ways to get even; we land a few punches and inflict a few wounds, lashing out at both the people who hurt us and those who just happen to be in the line of fire when we let loose. With so much of our time and emotional energy going into this seemingly endless cycle of pain, smoldering rage, and subtle or not-so-subtle paybacks, we have little left for the good things in life and none at all to make ourselves and our circumstances any better than they are.

What's more, collecting injustices, holding grudges, and walking around with unresolved and unexpressed anger boiling inside us takes its toll on our physical health and emotional well-being. It creates stress, elevates blood pressure, and increases stomach acidity, contributing to such physical ailments as ulcers, colitis, and arthritis. Our grievances hang around our neck like invisible albatrosses, and we get backaches, chest pains, anxiety attacks, and migraine headaches. With our heart racing and adrenaline pumping, our head spinning and our ears ringing, holding a grudge just plain does not feel good.

And neither does the emotional fallout that accompanies it. Nursing our wounds, we withdraw, have difficulty maintaining friendships, are generally intolerant, and are unable to look at events from other people's perspectives. We become suspicious and hypersensitive, more likely to be hurt again, always ready to start an argument, forgetful, subtly uncooperative. Our negativity and bitterness alienates everyone around us, and we are left alone, lonely, high up in our tower of righteous indignation with only our pain and fantasies of revenge for company. This is not where we wanted to go, but it is *always* where holding a grudge takes us.

Dead-End Streets

Holding a grudge is the most obvious example of what we do because we have been hurt. However, unhealed wounds, unforgiven acts, and unfinished business also get played out in much more subtle and ultimately more devastating ways.

Painkillers and Emptiness Fillers

Bruce, a thirty-six-year-old customer service supervisor for a national hotel chain, attended a two-day forgiveness seminar we conducted in Phoenix, Arizona. When we met him he had already been through a drug and alcohol rehabilitation program. Clean and sober for nearly a year, he recognized that his recovery depended on more than simply not drinking or taking drugs. "I spent twenty years numbing the pain," he said. "Now I have to start healing the wounds." His story illustrates a chain of events that occurs with alarming frequency—first other people hurt you, then, because of what you do to cope with the pain, you end up hurting yourself.

The youngest son of well-educated, achievement-oriented parents, Bruce, like his brothers who entered school before him, was expected to excel academically. But unfortunately he had a serious learning disability that was not diagnosed until he had endured seven years of hearing teachers tell him that he was stupid, lazy, hopeless, and incorrigible, of listening to his classmates ridicule him, and of losing countless privileges—from watching TV to playing Little League baseball—because his parents believed he was willfully refusing to improve his schoolwork.

By the time he reached the third grade, Bruce had stopped trying to learn and instead devoted himself to avoiding additional ridicule and humiliation. He cheated on tests, paid smarter students to do his homework for him, and each day during reading class intentionally misbehaved so that he would be sent to the principal's office before it was his turn to read aloud. He slid by until a perceptive student teacher recognized what he was doing and arranged for him to be tested. Once his learning problem was identified and he was taught how to compensate for it, the criticism from teachers and the ridicule from his peers stopped, but Bruce's feelings of inadequacy, self-doubt, and humiliation remained.

At fourteen he discovered alcohol. "The first time I got drunk was the first time I felt okay," Bruce explains. "Ever since I was a little kid, I'd always had this sinking feeling in my stomach, this buzzing in my head. I was very jumpy and withdrawn. But when I drank I felt like nothing could hurt me. I loosened up, and people actually seemed to like me." And drinking proved to be something Bruce was good at. His peers actually praised him for being able to "hold his liquor." Drinking contests—to see how much or how fast alcohol could be consumed—were competitions that enabled Bruce to be a winner for the first time in his life.

Bruce went to college, where he maintained his reputation as a "party animal," and began using drugs as well as alcohol. "I'd try anything," he admits. "I wanted to have fun. And I did have fun, but the truth was that I needed drugs and booze to bring me up and to slow me down. I needed them to help me relax and to give me more energy. I didn't *want* to see things clearly, because I didn't like what I saw. So I kept myself at least a little buzzed all of the time."

Bruce graduated from college, married, and worked his way up the corporate ladder to a well-paying, responsible position with a national hotel chain. But despite his success, the only time he felt confident or came close to liking himself was when he was drunk or high on cocaine. "I didn't think I was addicted," he explains. "I felt together and on top of things." Of course, he was neither. In fact, he was deeply in debt, and his wife was threatening to leave him. Eventually, someone caught him getting high at work, and he was given a choice—check into a rehab program or be fired.

"It was a tougher choice than you'd think," he says. "In fact, I went into rehab figuring I'd go through the motions, get out, and go back to doing whatever I damn well pleased. Of course, the staff picked up on that right away, and they didn't let me get away with it." As he began to recover from his addiction, Bruce was appalled by his past behavior. He had been willing to risk everything he had and everything he could become for the sake of warding off the pain and filling the empty spaces left by the failures, ridicule, and humiliation he had experienced so long ago.

Most of us—as children and as adults—have longed for some magic potion that could keep us from thinking about the things that bothered us. No matter when or how we were hurt, our first instinctive reaction was to *stop the pain*. Once we found a way to do that, we tended to continue doing it, using any and every means available to bury and block unpleasant emotions; to anesthetize and swallow whatever we were feeling.

For instance, countless men and women bury their pain under mountains of work—and you may be one of them. Or maybe you distract yourself with various thrills, from sex to gambling to shopping sprees. Perhaps you numb your pain with tranquilizers or boost your confidence with "uppers." You certainly are not alone if you stuff down your fear, anxiety, and loneliness by stuffing yourself with food; if you feel empty and fill yourself up with whatever you can find in your liquor cabinet, medicine chest, or refrigerator.

And when the pain or emptiness returns—as it always seems to—you simply take another dose of your preferred "painkiller" or "emptiness filler," traveling the same escape route again and again and again. Then one day you look up and realize that the pain is still there, that you have not gotten away from it but have spent years of your life running in circles and accumulating problems that are even more painful than the ones you had originally. All you wanted to do was stop hurting—an understandable and universal motivation if ever there was one—but unfortunately the path you chose was a dead-end street that left you in the middle of nowhere saddled with unhealthy habits and even self-destructive addictions.

On the fateful day that you "hit bottom," no matter where bottom is for you, you are liable to despise and doubt yourself more than you ever have before. You do not know if you can find the strength to improve your situation or if you even deserve to be better off than you are. You see, because you were hurt, you may have never believed in yourself or liked yourself much at all.

Low Self-Esteem

Perhaps one of the most harmful side effects of being hurt is how we learn to view ourselves because we were rejected, disappointed, ridiculed, betrayed, or abused. The wounds inflicted by others invariably damage our self-esteem. As Melinda, whom you met in chapter 1, did when her lover rejected her, we come to believe that we are not "good enough somehow," that we were hurt because we were in some way deficient in the first place. We are convinced this is a universal response to being hurt, no matter what form that hurt takes. It happens to us all.

For instance, if, like Bruce, you were criticized, humiliated, or ridiculed for the mistakes you made or the tasks you failed to accomplish, there is a good chance that you too learned to view yourself as an incompetent or inadequate person in general, a failure altogether. If you were abused, you may have come to believe that you were "inherently bad" and thus brought the pain and unfair treatment upon yourself. Or because of the abuse you may see yourself as "damaged goods," someone who is scarred and defiled and different from "normal" people. If you were told you were ugly or stupid or lazy or not likely to amount to much, those opinions not only hurt you at the time, but were taken to heart, becoming an integral part of your identity. They still determine how lovable and capable you think you are. And if you were rejected by a lover, the real or imagined flaw that you thought might explain the rejection— your sexual performance, for instance, or your physical appearance, your preoccupation with your career, or your deficiencies as a homemaker—was incorporated into your self-image. You were told that you did not *do* something well enough, and you took that to mean that *who you were* was not good enough—a perception that stayed with you and may still be with you today.

We can hear our own low self-esteem in statements like "I can't do anything right," "I'm such a klutz," "Of course, I was too dumb to figure out what was happening," and "It won't work out. I'm not what they're looking for. I'm not creative enough"—or pretty enough, or smart enough, or funny enough, or strong enough.

Besides holding low opinions of our abilities, we almost always act out our beliefs about who we are. For instance, because her mother abandoned her as an infant, Sandy, whom we introduced in the previous chapter, saw herself as a misfit, someone with no roots, no real place in the world, and so worthless that not even her own mother could love her. During her teens, a misfit is precisely what Sandy became. From the way she dressed to her refusal to communicate with her parents or therapist, Sandy alienated herself from other people—dramatizing what she already believed herself to be—alone and unwanted.

Although not always seen so graphically, your self-esteem influences your behavior constantly. Most notably and tragically, when you do not like yourself, you tend to hurt yourself. You neglect yourself and abuse yourself and commit what we call systematic suicide. You don't exercise. You eat foods that are not good for you. You don't get physical or dental check-ups or wear your seat belts or protect yourself from sexually transmitted diseases. You isolate yourself from the people who care about you, come home from work, plop down on the couch, and watch television shows you don't even enjoy. Very often you become dependent on the painkillers and emptiness fillers we described earlier. In general, you plod through life wrapped in cotton gauze, never seeing the beauty around you, never really feeling joyful or excited or challenged. What you do and don't do as a result of low self-esteem kills you a little bit at a time, shortening your life and making each day much less fruitful or satisfying than it could be.

In addition, because low self-esteem breeds low expectations, when your sense of self-worth has been damaged, your outlook tends to be pessimistic. You are likely to approach both new situations and ongoing problems thinking, "I can't do this," or "I can't change that." And what powerful words those are. When your first and most common reaction is "I can't," you are bound to get stuck in a dead-end job, continue a harmful habit, convince yourself to stay in an unfulfilling or abusive relationship, or find endless excuses not to in any way change yourself or your circumstances. Low self-esteem is summing up your life with the following words, uttered by a woman who once sat next to us on an airplane: "The way I figure it," she said, "you can only play the cards you were dealt when you were born. I can't help it if I was dealt a losing hand." She believed—and if your self-esteem has been damaged, you too may believe—that the most you can expect out of life is the bare minimum to survive, that the most you can hope to do is get by.

Self-esteem, damaged by painful past experiences, convinces you that *you do not deserve* more than that; that *you must settle for* the way things are; that *you are incapable* of being or doing anything more or better. And this perception, combined with unhealed wounds and unfinished business from the past, steers you down one dead-end street after another, beginning with one that promises smooth sailing and no disappointments whatsoever. It is the path taken by those of us who are bound and determined not to risk being hurt again.

Playing It Safe

"During my entire childhood," Mark, a twenty-eight-year-old physical therapist, says bitterly, "there was not one holiday, one birthday, or any other day that was important to me in any way that my father didn't manage to ruin. Anything I looked forward to, he kept me from having, and anything I got he took away from me.''

Mark's father is a great big bear of a man with an enormous chip on his shoulder. "My dad thought everyone was out to get him," Mark explains, "and he dealt with that by always making sure he got the other guy first." We do not know what made Mark's father such a bitter, jealous, suspicious man, but that is the man he had become long before Mark was born, and his almost paranoid perspective on life colored nearly every moment of Mark's childhood.

Mark grew up feeling isolated, cut off from the rest of the world, and alienated from other people because his father neither trusted nor approved of anyone. Mark and his sisters were even prevented from developing close ties with their relatives, especially with their uncle Dan and his family.

"My father hated his brother," Mark says. "All we ever heard was what a horrible person he was. What a fake his wife was. How bad his kids were. How they all looked down on us." These constant tirades against his uncle confused Mark because his relatives "went out of their way to be nice to us. We always looked forward to spending time with them, but we hardly ever got the chance to."

Each year at Thanksgiving, Christmas, and Easter, Mark's family was invited to their uncle's home. On each occasion Mark's father accepted the invitation but then backed out at the last minute. "I can't tell you how many holidays we spent all dressed up eating leftovers around the kitchen table because my dad decided that Uncle Dan's invitation was part of some conspiracy to make him look bad and that he wasn't going to give his brother the satisfaction."

To make matters worse, even though he was a highly skilled electrician, Mark's father had trouble holding down a job. When Mark's father *was* working, he made all kinds of extravagant purchases—buying furniture, new cars, stereo equipment, toys, clothes, and even televisions for his children. "Then when he lost his job he took it all back," Mark sighs. Anything purchased on a payment plan was repossessed. Mark and his sisters had to give up what was given to them. Their toys, clothes, and other items were sold at a yard sale.

Expressing feelings of disappointment or unhappiness was not an option for Mark and his sisters. "One time, when I was about eight, I made the mistake of saying what I was thinking, and my dad threw me out of the house." Mark shudders as the scene replays in his mind. "Literally tossed me out the door and told me that if I liked Uncle Dan so much, I could go be his son because he didn't want me." His father locked the doors and windows and left Mark outside for several hours. "I didn't think he was ever going to let me back into the house or back into the family."

At some point during his childhood Mark decided he could not take any more pain and disappointment. In the midst of the chaos and confusion created by his father, with a mother who suffered as much and as silently as her children and no friends or relatives he could turn to, Mark came to the conclusion that must certainly have seemed logical to a wounded and vulnerable young boy—if he did not expect good things to happen, he could not be hurt when they did not occur. He learned not to look forward to happy holidays, social occasions, or being able to keep any possession he treasured.

It is important to note that Mark's decision was more of an instinctive reaction than a carefully thought out choice. Somewhere deep inside his subconscious mind he had come to believe that expecting good things to happen was a dangerous thing to do.

When we first met Mark, we couldn't help but notice that he expected the worst from any situation. He wasn't just prepared to be disappointed by his father anymore. He anticipated disaster and braced himself against disappointment every day and in every imaginable circumstance. For example, he filled out applications to graduate school but did not submit them, explaining, "I wasn't going to get into the program I really wanted anyway." Each year as the time for his vacation approached, he visited a travel agent and brought home brochures describing various exotic places he'd always wanted to see. He would never actually take any of those trips, however. "It's all hype," he convinced himself. "Those places would never be as good as they looked in the brochures." He is even on the verge of losing his job with a rehabilitation center that has a well-earned reputation for helping people regain their mobility after injuries and illnesses. "Everybody here is gung ho about everything," Mark explains, "but I think they build people's hopes up too high." He finds it difficult to set "lofty" goals for his patients or even to encourage them to reach for the goals he does set. "My supervisor calls that a negative attitude," Mark says. "I call it being realistic."

Expecting little and constantly guarding against disappointment *was* realistic when Mark was growing up in the shadow of an explosive and unpredictable father. It once helped him survive, but it no longer serves him. Today Mark's determination not to be hurt again and his "never expect anything but the worst" attitude do not protect him. Indeed, they ensure that he gets less out of life than he could.

Many of us who approach life in this way are well aware of what we are missing. We look back on the opportunities we missed by playing it safe or the life we might have led if we had only chosen a path other than the one of least resistance, and we feel the very pain and disappointment we had hoped to avoid.

Building Walls

The decision to play it safe and not risk being hurt again is most often seen in the way we relate to other people, specifically in the ways we push people away from us and build walls to keep them from getting close enough to do us harm. That we would want to keep a safe distance from other people certainly makes sense. After all, *people* perpetrated the injuries and injustices that first hurt us, and sadly those people were often the ones who were closest to us. As a result, we may have come to the conclusion that if we had not allowed those people to get close, if we had not entrusted them with intimate knowledge of who we were and what made us tick, if we had not allowed them to ''get under our skin,'' they never would have been able to hurt us as badly as they did. Quite frequently, and often without knowing we were doing it, we found ways to make sure no one got that close to us again.

For instance, you may have decided that the ''best defense is a good offense,'' and like Patricia, who still feels the sting from ridicule she received as a child, you become cold, cynical, and even cruel at times. Perhaps you are prone to sarcasm, compelled to criticize, or are a whiz at coming up with a put-down for every occasion, cutting others down to size or using a certain look that tells them to back off and stay away. And they do. As a business colleague of Patricia's puts it, ''She sends out a message that says 'Don't cross me,' and I'd be a fool to try. I've seen her in action. She goes right for the jugular and doesn't let up. I sure don't want to be on the receiving end of one of her tongue-lashings, so I keep my distance.''

Some of you, on the other hand, do not actively push people away. Instead you may retreat, withdrawing from human contact physically or emotionally or both. Perhaps you keep a safe distance from others by keeping to yourself and maintaining short, impersonal conversations. You may avoid socializing in any setting or go to work and get your job done, interacting with your co-workers as little as possible. Sometimes when people try to get to know you or start conversations with you, you feel irritated, other times merely surprised. Why is this person trying to be friendly? you wonder, and although you will be more polite about discouraging friendliness than Patricia might be, you will discourage it nonetheless—by not responding or giving one-word answers or making an excuse to get away from the person.

Those of you who retreat from closeness do not necessarily isolate yourselves entirely, yet you find it difficult, if not impossible, to share certain aspects of yourself with others. Indeed, the times you need people the most are precisely the times you withdraw further into your shell. When you are hurting, you cannot let them know. You cannot ask for their support, and if they offer it, you assure them that nothing is wrong or that something is wrong but you do not want to talk about it. This hurts them. They accuse you of not trusting them, and they are usually right.

In other instances, you may *unintentionally* alienate people with your negativity. The pessimism and self-pity born of unhealed wounds and holding grudges can make you lousy company. Friends and colleagues eventually run out of sympathy and grow tired of hearing you whine and complain.

Conversely, some of you get along wonderfully with everyone. However, you do this without ever actually getting close to anyone. You interact constantly, but you reveal very little about who you really are. "If they really knew me, they wouldn't like me," was the lesson your painful past experiences taught you, so you create an impression. You play a role that you believe is more acceptable than "being yourself." You are cute, funny, and adorable or the life of the party. Or you might be the ultimate caretaker—listening to everyone's problems but never talking about your own—or the fixer-upper who loans money, offers rides, baby-sits on short notice, or otherwise manages to be there to save the day. You become a trivia expert or a joke teller or the great debater who makes sure everyone respects your intelligence and pays no attention to the less impressive aspects of who you are. Maintaining this facade takes a lot of energy and creates a lot of anxiety. Something from your past, some unhealed wound, has convinced you that devastating consequences will occur if your mask should slip for even an instant, if other people should accidentally discover that you feel pain, have doubts, or are flawed in any way.

Then again some of you may create visible barriers to closeness. You may be loud and boisterous and use crude language. You neglect certain areas of personal hygiene. And most commonly you hide behind a wall of fat. Research on obesity shows that women in particular use their bodies to speak for them, to say, ''No. Go away. Don't get close to me,'' and this is especially true for women who have been sexually abused, raped, or hurt in other ways.

Finally, some of you settle for pseudocloseness, seeking sex when what you want is love, turning every interaction into a seduction, and indulging in countless one-night stands with partners who are virtually interchangeable and largely meaningless to you.

Regardless of the approach any of us take or the type of wall we build, the result is the same. We end up feeling lonely, isolated, trapped in a holding cell of our own creation. We wanted to keep people from getting close enough to hurt us. We believed that was what we had to do to survive. But when all is said and done, when all the barriers to closeness have been constructed and cemented into place, we realize we have also kept people from getting close enough to love us, to care about us, comfort us, encourage us, and provide us with the sort of emotional support we need to lead a full and fulfilling life. Once again, we experience pain when pain is precisely what we were hoping to avoid.

Damaging the Relationships We Do Have

Since we have been hurt in different ways and adopted different attitudes and behaviors to cope with the pain, not all of us end up lonely and isolated. Many of us do have friends and lovers or are married and have been for any number of years. We do not cut people out of our life completely, yet our unhealed wounds can have an enormous impact on the quality of our relationships, how long they last, and what we are willing to endure in order to keep them. In fact, our most intimate relationships often offer us a setting in which to reenact old scenes with new actors in the leading roles.

For instance, although less than a year has passed since Stan and Amy exchanged their wedding vows, they are already convinced that getting married was a mistake. ''This marriage is looking more and more like a replay of my last one,'' Stan sighs. And Amy agrees, ''Sometimes when we fight, it's like déjà vu. I think, 'Haven't I had this argument before?' And I have—with my ex-husband.''

Stan and Amy met soon after their first marriages officially ended. In fact, their initial conversations were built around commiserating about divorce proceedings, which were marked by painful, knock-down-drag-out fights over infidelities, mental cruelty, and the division of community property. Even so, neither one was aware that they were bringing a dangerous hidden agenda into their new relationship, and essentially the same one—to get out before they got hurt again. Although they did not set out consciously to compare each other with their former mates or their present relationship with their first marriages, they couldn't help drawing those comparisons. And as soon as they began feeling as if they were reenacting their pasts, both were ready to run as far and fast as they could.

Like Stan and Amy, you may bring your old pain and unfinished business into your present-day relationships and helplessly watch as your fears of being hurt again prevent you from trusting or maintaining intimacy. Indeed, intimacy itself may scare you half to death.

Rejection, betrayal, deception, abuse, infidelity, and especially abandonment severely damage our ability to trust. As a result, we may find it difficult if not impossible to wholeheartedly believe that another person will not hurt us, that we can depend on people to be there when we need them, that they will continue to accept us once they discover we are not perfect, or that they will not use the information we share with them to harm us. Since trust, interdependence, acceptance, and honest communication are all prerequisites for intimacy, our past history can most definitely bar us from having or feeling comfortable in intimate relationships.

If you grew up in a chaotic household or a family that kept secrets, or if your parents were overbearing or overprotective, you bring attitudes and behaviors into intimate relationships that create the same effect as the inability to trust. For you, closeness stirs up old fears of losing control, of being smothered, of losing your sense of who you are, and of being asked for more than you are willing or believe you are able to give.

Regardless of the reason, when our need to maintain distance outweighs our desire for closeness, our relationships suffer. We balk at the idea of making a commitment or are unable to let down our guard in front of someone we love. We have countless arguments over intimacy itself, unresolvable conflicts about who isn't giving enough and who is asking for too much. Our sex life may deteriorate. We devote the lion's share of our time and emotional energy to our children or our work, pulling farther and farther away from our partner until the two of us are leading completely separate lives while living under the same roof.

On the other hand, your unhealed wounds may take you to the opposite end of the spectrum. Past rejection, abandonment, or other injuries and injustices may have left you desperate for closeness and willing to go to any extreme in order to find and keep it. For example, Wendy, a twenty-six-year-old dental assistant whose father abandoned her family when she was eighteen months old and made no effort to contact or support his children for the next fifteen years, grew up feeling insecure and damaged. "Other kids had divorced parents," she says. "But they saw their fathers. I didn't even know mine. He thought so little of me that he could just walk away and never look back. It's only been in the last year that I stopped thinking there was something about me that made him leave."

Like so many other people who have been abandoned by a parent, spouse, or lover, Wendy was never sure that some inherent aspect of herself had not led to the abandonment, and she was petrified that other people she cared about would abandon her as well. "I went through a half dozen boyfriends during high school," she says, and then laughs. "I drove all of them crazy. I wanted to be with them all the time. After a date, I'd count the minutes it took them to get home and then I'd call them and think of a million things to say so I wouldn't have to hang up the phone. And if they were five minutes late to pick me up, I just fell apart."

Surprisingly, Wendy handled the end of each relationship remarkably well. "I went right out and found a new boyfriend," and was even more possessive the next time around. "How I ever found a man to marry me is anyone's guess," she sighs. She did marry, but before long that relationship was falling apart, too.

"I really was impossible. I called Jack at work ten times a day. I stopped at his office during my lunch hour, and if he couldn't see me because he had a meeting or something, I assumed he didn't want to see me and we'd fight about it when he got home. I freaked out every time he worked late, every time he even glanced at another woman. Once we even had a fight over his reading the travel section of the newspaper. I accused him of checking out places to run away to when he left me."

No matter how many times Jack reassured Wendy that he loved her and had no intention of leaving her, it was not enough. Finally, and fortunately for them both, when he reached the end of his rope, Jack convinced Wendy to come with him to see a counselor. They have been in individual and couples therapy for almost a year now, and although Wendy would be the first to admit that she and Jack are not out of the woods yet, it looks like her story will have a happier ending than the one pain from her past would have written for her.

Others among you may not have been so lucky. The things you did because of your debilitating fear of rejection and abandonment drove away your spouses and lovers and friends. You clung too tightly and were left with no one to hold. As so often happens when pain from the past dictates how you live your life in the present, your worst fears are realized.

For some of you, it would have been better off if your relationship *had* ended. But it didn't. Fear of rejection and abandonment may have led you to put up with a damaging relationship or stay in a physically and emotionally abusive one. The message you received from your unhealed wounds told you that being beaten, degraded, and diminished was still better than being alone. So you stood paralyzed at the end of yet another dead-end street with that old demon low self-esteem telling you that such treatment was more or less what you deserved and that you didn't have what it took to get out of a situation that was hurting you.

The Ultimate Dead-End Street—Repeating the Past and Perpetuating the Cycle of Abuse

Thirty-one-year-old Marcy, whom we introduced in chapter 1, is a medical researcher, married, and the mother of a two-year-old daughter. Most of the time she manages to juggle a home life that she expects to be neat, orderly, and organized in every imaginable way and a career that requires the utmost vigilance and precision. But every once in a while some unforeseeable and uncontrollable event disrupts her carefully orchestrated routine. Whether confronted with a traffic jam or a slow-moving supermarket checkout line, Marcy comes completely unglued. Even more intolerable are the mistakes she makes herself. The slightest error, no matter how insignificant it may seem to someone else, leaves her fighting tears, sends her into a depression that can last for days, and may even lead to thoughts of suicide.

Why is Marcy's reaction to disrupted routines and her own errors so extreme? Because delays, interruptions, and her own mistakes trigger feelings she knew all too well as a child of alcoholic parents who went on drinking binges that disrupted the lives of every family member. Early in her life, Marcy came to believe that the slightest mistake on her part could destroy the delicate balance in her household; that her own sanity and survival depended upon her ability to anticipate and preferably control any aspect of family life that might upset her parents and give them an excuse to drink. Of course, Marcy's parents drank no matter what she did, but she kept trying to be perfect enough to make them stop. She still strives for perfection and still reacts to imperfections as if they will lead to the same chaos and devastation she lived through as a child.

Although her circumstances today are decidedly different from what they were when she was a child, although she no longer lives with her parents, and even though her father is dead and her mother has not taken a drink in the past four years, Marcy still lives in precisely the state of pain, fear, and anxiety she experienced during childhood. She has set herself up in a situation and adopted an approach to life that continues to inflict the same *kind* of pain she felt when she was a young girl. Her perfectionism and drive to control every aspect of daily living reopens old wounds and prevents them from healing. Although she never intended to, Marcy has arranged her life in such a way that she is destined to repeat her past over and over again.

If you look closely and fearlessly at your own life, we believe you will also see that much of what hurts you today is a repetition of how you were hurt in the past. Unwittingly and for the most part unconsciously, you, like Marcy, set yourself up to be hurt in the same way again and again and again.

Like damaged self-esteem, this appears to be a universal reaction to painful past experiences. It seems that each time we enter a new relationship or approach a new situation, at a subconscious level, we tell ourselves that *this time* we will ''do it right'' or *this time* we will ''get what we need'' (in other words, what we did not get in the past). Unfortunately, because we do not fully comprehend and have not worked through what happened when we were hurt in the past, instead of doing it right or getting what we need, we get the exact opposite. Things go wrong again, we get little or none of what we need again, and of course, we get hurt again.

Thus Melinda, still aching from being rejected by Steve, got involved with men who were ''on the rebound'' from broken relationships of their own. Steve had said that Melinda was not there for him when he needed her, so she made sure to ''be there'' for these new men. Indeed, she nursed them through their pain. But since it was her caretaking that attracted them to her, when they no longer needed care, they found little common ground on which to maintain a relationship, and ultimately they left her. Today Melinda realizes that those relationships had "rejection written all over them," but at the time she was drawn to those men, drawn down a road that would lead to rejection time and time again.

Similarly, Darlene, who learned from a father who repeatedly disappointed her by missing visits that "you couldn't count on people to do what they said they would," still assumes this to be true. In every imaginable situation she takes on other people's responsibilities as well as her own. When she delegates tasks at work, she winds up doing them herself before other people can get to them. When she asks her husband to stop at the grocery store on his way home, she ends up buying those groceries herself and telling him not to bother. Helping her kids do school projects generally means doing the whole project for them. The list of extra tasks she takes on because she cannot trust other people to "do things right or quickly enough" is endless. Understandably, Darlene is overwhelmed, and at least once a day she realizes that she is. She boils over with bitterness and resentment. Once again, she is "in a lousy place because other people are irresponsible and unreliable. How come I can get all these things done and they can't?" The simple answer is that Darlene does not let them, and by not letting them she keeps the pain from her past alive.

As it did for Darlene, each repetition of a past injury or injustice reinforces our original perception, whatever it may have been. It can take years and countless painful experiences before we stop setting ourselves up for new pain and start to examine and work through the old.

Unquestionably, the most devastating example of repeating the past is found in the thoroughly documented facts about child abuse. There is ample evidence that a mind-boggling number of parents who abuse their children today were themselves abused as children. Their own experience showed them how frustration, confusion, and rage could be unleashed on the nearest and most defenseless target; that when a parent's pain becomes too much to bear, they inflict pain on their children. The same sort of lesson was learned by many spouse batterers, some sex offenders, and almost anyone prone to violent, explosive behavior. It can be seen in parents who criticize and demean their children as they were once criticized and demeaned or who smother and overprotect their children as their parents once smothered and overprotected them.

Tragically, time and time again we do unto others that which was done unto us, unwittingly perpetrating a cycle that began when we were injured or treated unfairly or when our parents were or their parents before them.

Fortunately, it is possible to *break the cycle,* the cycle of abuse as well as any other cycle or repetitive pattern you find yourself in today.

You *Can* Change the Road You Are On

At the time you were hurt and ever since that time, with the insight, resources, and emotional support you had, you did the best you could. You did the best you could to stop the pain, to anticipate danger, and to avoid being hurt again. Yes, some of what you did ended up hurting you, and some of what you did hurt other people. And most important, what you *did not do* made a tremendous difference in your life. You did not heal your wounds or complete your unfinished business, but you *can* do that now.

Because you were hurt, you made certain choices. Those choices served you at some time in your life, but they may not serve you now. You cannot travel back in time and use what you know now to make different decisions, but you *can* make new choices today.

The attitudes and behaviors you adopted did indeed help you survive. However, as you matured and your life circumstances changed, they stopped working for you. In fact, they became handicaps, insuring that you got less out of life than you wanted or deserved. You cannot take back the things you have already done, but you *can* change your attitudes and behaviors to improve the present and create a brighter future.

Abuse, rejection, betrayal, deception, ridicule, and humiliation may be leading you down a dead-end street. Unhealed wounds and unfinished business may have led you down a dead-end street right now, but you can turn around and get back on the main road, the one that will take you to the life *you* want and deserve.

There *is* an alternative to painkillers and emptiness fillers, to playing it safe, building walls, damaging relationships, repeating the past, and perpetrating a cycle of pain and resentment. That alternative is the healing process that we will describe in the remainder of this book. We begin in the next chapter to offer some helpful hints for traveling the road to *forgiveness*.

CHAPTER FOUR

THE HEALING PROCESS: A JOURNEY TO WHOLENESS

You now have a better understanding of how you've been hurt. Disappointment, rejection, abandonment, betrayal, deception, ridicule, humiliation, and abuse occurred even though you did not want them to. But did you know that you may also have been hurt by what you did want *but did not get* from parents, spouses, lovers, friends, and anyone else who mattered in your life?

You wanted:

- love
- closeness
- safety
- affection
- attention
- guidance
- encouragement
- commitments
- validation of your self-worth

But one or more of these essential types of emotional support and nourishment were taken from you when you were hurt. You lost them when the bond of trust or love or friendship between you and the person who hurt you was severed. And you grieved for these unmet needs, for what was lacking in your life, for what you lost when you were hurt.

Like someone who loses a loved one, you needed to mourn. You could not help but feel the sadness and the pain. Nor could you escape the instinctive desire to in some way control these emotions so that they would not consume or overwhelm you. *You went through an internal process in response to an external event.* The death of a loved one is the external event for someone who is grieving. For you, it was the injury or injustice you experienced. You began your healing process as soon as the painful incident occurred, but more often than not you got stuck. People who grieve sometimes get stuck, too, but you were more likely to because your loss was neither as tangible nor as final as the death of someone you loved.

What you lost was the ability to have a vital need met *by the person you thought should meet it.* However, even though your parents, spouse, lover, or whomever else you relied on to furnish emotional support and nourishment did not provide what you needed, you did not stop needing those things. So you looked for other ways to meet your needs, frequently heading off in hot pursuit of the painkillers and emptiness fillers we described in chapter 3. As we also pointed out in that chapter, much of what you did to compensate for what you lost did not heal you. Indeed, some of what you did caused you harm. At the very least, it got you stuck.

Getting What You Need Without Hurting Yourself or Anyone Else

The most significant difference between the grieving process and the healing process is that in the latter, the people we loved and whom we expected to love us in return did not cease to exist. Although some of the people who hurt us may be dead now, they did not die immediately after they hurt us or failed to meet our needs. And neither did the hope that one day they would give us the love, attention, encouragement, praise, or unconditional acceptance they were unable to provide in the past. Ten, fifteen, even thirty years after we experienced the loss of emotional support and nourishment, we may still be trying to "win it back." And one of the reasons we have not yet healed ourselves is that we still expect the people who hurt us to heal us—by making up for what *they* did and what *we* lost.

When this does not happen—and it never does—we feel disappointed and disillusioned, as wounded by our unmet expectations as we were by the original injury or injustice. The pain lives on and on and on. We will not be able to let go of it until we accept the fact that we cannot get our needs met *now* by the people who did not meet them in the past.

So, you needed love and you did not get it. You needed closeness and safety and affection and the kind words and encouragement that would have strengthened your self-esteem, but they did not come your way, they were not given to you by the people from whom you wanted them, the very people who were "supposed to" provide them for you.

You still have those needs, and you must find *new* ways to fill them. The old ways do not work. They never worked. All the alcohol, drugs, food, work, sex, or spending sprees you could indulge in over a lifetime would never actually give you what you did not get from your parents, spouses, lovers, friends, or anyone else who hurt you. You may have to give up the notion that those people can undo what they already did or make everything "all right" for you again. You are no longer a child. Your parents cannot make your hurts "all better" the way they once kissed your bruised knees and bandaged fingers and pronounced you cured. Healing does not work that way.

Your life may be falling apart at the seams right now. Or it may simply be less productive, satisfying, or peaceful than you want it to be. Whether your life needs a major overhaul or just some fine-tuning, chances are that you have gotten stuck in one of the early stages of the healing process. No matter where you are, it is time to accept that the past is past. It is gone, and you can't get it back. To move on in your healing process, you must turn your attention to the needs you have *now* and how you will fill them *now*. As an adult, it is *your* responsibility to take charge of your own life and do what is best for your own physical health and emotional well-being, to make the choices that will enable you to heal the old wounds and create a new, more productive, and fulfilling adult life.

That is what the people you will read about in this book did. They chose to heal. It was not an easy choice for them to make, and it was not an easy course to stick with once they made that choice. It will not be easy for you, either, and that is why, in this chapter, we would like to offer a few guidelines, words of caution, and encouragement for traveling the road to forgiveness.

Choosing to Heal

Throughout your healing process, you will have choices to make. In fact, since you were faced with decisions as soon as you were hurt, you have already made many choices. At that point, you may have chosen to block out and bury unpleasant thoughts and feelings, perhaps opting to numb your pain with alcohol, drugs, food, or work. Later you may have chosen to believe that old wounds no longer affected you or influenced your life. And because of that belief, you may have decided not to get help at all. You organized your life in a way that would ensure that you did not have to face the past and could avoid similar problems in the future.

Nine times out of ten, such choices hurt you. But you did not willfully or knowingly make choices that would cause you pain or prevent you from healing. You made the best possible decisions based on the information and resources you had at a time when you were vulnerable and reeling from the pain.

Many of us were quite young when we made decisions that would continue affecting our lives for years to come, and most of the truly debilitating choices were made with little conscious thought or awareness. In fact, we may not have known we were choosing at all!

When we begin to make *conscious,* conscientious choices that enable us to fulfill our needs and enhance our self-esteem, our healing process turns in a new direction, one that leads us toward forgiveness and a better life. For instance, we may choose to enter therapy, to join a support group and participate fully, to end an abusive relationship or leave an unfulfilling job, to attend personal growth workshops and absorb as much learning as we possibly can, to give up a self-destructive habit, to begin recovering from an addiction, or even to contact someone who hurt us and attempt to rebuild that relationship. Each choice is made after thoughtfully considering the available alternatives and the possible consequences—including the possibility of pain, humiliation, and distress. Because we know we are choosing, and we know what and why we are choosing, each choice advances our healing process, *even when what we decide to do does not bring the exact results we hope for.*

As you continue on your healing journey and at every crossroad and turning point along the way, the choices you make will reflect your answers to the following questions:

Where am I now?
Where would I rather be?
And what is the next bold step I must take in order to get there?

Where Are You Now?

Throughout this book, when you read about people who have chosen to heal and forgive, you will identify with some but not all of what you read. At certain points in each person's account, you will find yourself thinking, "That sounds like me. I've felt that way. Yeah, I do that, too." On the other hand, certain ideas may seem completely foreign to you. You may wonder why on earth Suzanne or Sandy or Bruce or Melinda chose to do what they did and feel fear, anger, or resentment well up inside you. You may even think, "No one's ever going to get me to believe that the S.O.B.'s who hurt me were doing the best they could!"

Your reactions—no matter what they may be—will most likely reflect where you are in your healing process right now. You can relate to the thoughts, feelings, and behaviors that are similar to those you have already experienced or are experiencing now, but not to the ones that come at points in the healing process you have not yet reached. But what point have you reached? Where has the pain from the past taken you? These are difficult questions to answer. Indeed, they are difficult questions even to consider. To acknowledge that those old injuries and injustices have taken you anywhere forces you to face the fact that something that may have happened a long, long time ago has altered the course of your life and is still affecting you. Such an admission is likely to dredge up feelings of shame, remorse, or outrage. Tears may even well up in your eyes as you realize that your life today is a mess or at the very least different from what you hoped it would be because pain from the past has taken you down various dead-end streets. Difficult as it may be, we urge you to take a close look at where you have been and where you are now because you were hurt.

You can answer that question by reviewing the dead-end streets we described in chapter 3 and fearlessly asking yourself what you have done or are still doing to numb the pain and fill the void in your life, to play it safe and keep your distance. You can discover exactly where pain from the past has taken you by taking a reading on your self-esteem, examining your relationships, identifying the ways in which you repeat the past, and determining if your attitudes and behaviors unwittingly hurt other people. However, if you are willing to take an even closer look, you can gain insights about *why* you do what you do and make some choices about what you could do differently.

Throughout this book, we will encourage you to develop a *clearer* understanding of your own behaviors, attitudes, and feelings about certain issues. To achieve this end we have included a number of *clarification strategies*—thought-provoking questions or paper-and-pencil exercises like the one that follows. Although for one reason or another you may feel reluctant to stop reading and actually complete the exercises, we encourage you to take a stab at all of them. They will help you apply what you read to your own life and reveal things about yourself that you may not have been aware of before.

Clarification Strategy Number 1: Dead-End Streets

On a sheet of lined paper, draw a vertical line down the middle of the page, creating two columns. Then further divide the right-hand column with two more vertical lines, creating four columns in all—one wide and three narrow.

In the wide left-hand column list the "dead-end streets" you have traveled down during your lifetime, any "painkillers and emptiness fillers" you have ever used, and anything you have done that has detracted from your physical or emotional well-being. Here are some possibilities:

Alcohol	Prescription drugs
Sugar	Nicotine
Caffeine	Workaholism
Isolation	Binge eating
Over-/undereating	Promiscuity
Frenetic activity	Perfectionism
Gambling	Illicit drugs
Excessive spending	Chocolate

Too much/too little sleep   Not taking risks
Foods   High cholesterol
Stuffing your feelings   Lack of exercise
Becoming dependent on a   Too much TV watching
  relationship   Overachieving
Hitting and belittling children   Self-pity
Physically/emotionally abusing   Negativity
  spouse   Slacking off at work
Picking verbal/physical fights

No doubt you can think of others. When you have listed the ones you have used, in the first column, check the ones you are still doing.

In the second column, mark with an asterisk (*) those that you seem to do more or only do when you think about or want to squelch feelings about past injuries and injustices. If you find it difficult to make that connection, think about times when you felt angry, resentful, frustrated, hurt, or as if you had been treated unfairly. To which of the items did you turn?

Now, in the third column give *the items you have checked* an A, B, or C rating. Choose one-third of those items to give an A rating—indicating that you want to get to work on changing them right away. A B rating should go to another third—which represent your second-highest priorities to change for the better—and a C should be given to the last third, which you'd like to change someday but are not pressing at the moment.

Finally, in the fourth column rank order your A-rated items, assigning the number one (1) to the item that you consider the most important to change, a two (2) to the next most important, and so on until all A items have been given a different numerical ranking.

This clarification strategy enables you to courageously face what you are still doing because you were hurt, but it also gives you an opportunity to pat yourself on the back for having already abandoned certain self-destructive behaviors. Most important, however, it gives you a starting point for deciding what bold steps you can take to improve yourself and your life.

Be Gentle with Yourself

Identifying where you are now may leave you feeling discouraged and depressed. None of us derive pleasure from examining our pain. None of us are comforted by reviewing the bumpy, downhill course we have traveled in our effort to cope with that pain. The Little Judge inside you may let loose a barrage of criticism: "Look at what you've done to yourself," he says. "Look at this mess you call a life. What a weak, stupid, incompetent, thoroughly unlovable person you are. Obviously you got what you deserve."

And the Perennial Victim that also lives inside you may reply, "But I was hurt. Look at what they did to me. Who could expect more of me then or now? This is my lot in life. I'll never change it." Either line of thinking is self-defeating.

We did not ask you to think about where you are now so that you could beat yourself over the head with the information you gathered. That won't help you heal or move on. Indeed, it is one of the reasons you have become stuck.

So please treat yourself gently. Yes, you made mistakes. We all have. But you have punished yourself enough. You have spent enough time comparing yourself with other people and reminding yourself that you do not measure up. We won't deny that some of the things people do because they were hurt are more destructive than others or that some circumstances are more dire and difficult to remedy than others. But we will state emphatically that *comparing old wounds, present circumstances, and healing processes does not serve you in any way whatsoever.*

You were hurt the way you were hurt. You did what you did. You are where you are, and indeed, there is nowhere else you *can* be at this particular moment in time. Your unique circumstances and life experiences have brought you to this point, and no matter where that is—or how it compares with where anyone else is—it is the one and only starting point for *your* personal journey to forgiveness.

Where Would You Rather Be?

To answer that question, you must first ask yourself another, even tougher one: How does *not forgiving* serve me? What do I get from it, and what am I afraid I will lose if I give up my grudges and resentments?

As we pointed out in chapter 1, hanging on to the pain and doing what you have done because you were hurt *has* served you at various times in your life. It has temporarily stopped the pain, kept fear and anxiety at bay, protected you from being disappointed, rejected, betrayed, or otherwise hurt again. But it has also hurt you. It has created new, equally painful problems, often placing you in the exact situations you were hoping to avoid.

At this juncture in your life and your healing process, you must determine if what you get from not forgiving is truly worth what you give up. Do you want to keep what you have or reach out for more? Will you, out of fear or anger or pride, hold on to your grudges and resentments, or will you choose to heal?

Perhaps you think that, given the choice between hurting or healing, anyone would choose healing. And perhaps anyone would— *if* they could push past their fears quickly and easily. When you face the prospect of change, and healing is most definitely a form of change, two fears emerge immediately—fear of being hurt again and fear of the unknown. The fear of being hurt again is one you have been working on since you were hurt and will work on throughout your healing process. Fear of the unknown—not knowing what your life will become as a result of the healing process and a sometimes overwhelming urge to stick with what you have, which is familiar even if it is not particularly satisfying—can be conquered by creating a vision of the destination you hope to reach.

This vision of the life you hope to lead and an image of the person you hope to become are prerequisites for healing. The desire to be somewhere other than where you are now is the motivating force that gets you moving in a new direction, and your vision of the destination you hope to reach is what guides you every step of the way. It is what convinces you to keep trying, even on those days when peace of mind seems further from your grasp than ever before.

Having determined where you are, you must now ask yourself, "Where would I rather be?" And your answer must go beyond wishing to stop, escape, or no longer feel the pain. Perhaps that is what you have been wishing for and trying to do for years now—and it has not worked. In addition, the image of punishing the people who hurt you, having them beg your forgiveness or hearing them apologize and dedicate the rest of their days to making up for what they did to you, is definitely a vision. But it is not a healing vision. A healing vision is one that describes the positive attributes you want to develop, how you hope to feel, and what you want to be able to have and do as a result of healing old wounds and completing unfinished business. Everyone you will read about in this book developed a healing vision long before they actually forgave anyone. So we urge you to take some time to design a healing vision of your own. Think about:

- habits you have that you hope to abandon;
- ways your present relationships will change for the better, as well as new relationships you would like to develop;
- changes and/or advances you hope to make in your career, your home life, your physical condition, or your state of mind;
- problems you hope to resolve, adventures you'd like to have, risks you want to take;
- how you would like to feel as you move through your days;
- what you would like to be able to say to yourself before you fall asleep at night (or upon awakening in the morning).

At this point, you may have trouble coming up with a specific description of your future or picturing a better future at all. That's okay. If you are at one end of a long, dark tunnel, it is hard enough to spot the light at the other end, much less visualize what lies beyond that. The vision will become clearer as your healing progresses. As you continue to move through the stages, the fog that has surrounded you for so long will begin to lift—or lift farther than it has—and you will be able to paint a detailed picture of where you want to go. For now a general idea will do.

One of the more enjoyable, imaginative ways to create your healing vision is to pretend that it is already two or three or five years into the future and that you want to describe your life circumstances to a friend whom you haven't been in contact with for a while. You simply write that "friend" a letter updating them about how well your life is going, a letter like this one, written by a participant in one of our forgiveness seminars:

Dear Grace,

    I can't believe two years have flown by already! So much has changed. I was such a sad sack back then, but now I'm proud to announce that I'm better than I've ever been. I used to walk around in a daze, but now I'm aware of what is going on around me. I'm much more attentive and understanding as a parent. (My kids are still in a state of shock!) I don't take my frustration out on them anymore. I don't yell as much or hit them at all. I'm certainly not the best parent in the world, but I'm not the worst, either, and even though I used to think so, I never was that bad to begin with. As you can see I've learned to like myself, and it shows in everything I do.

I'm a more creative teacher, and I really get involved with my students. I've even gone back to school myself, and in another year or two I'll be a school guidance counselor. I finally stopped bitching about there being no decent men around who want to get involved with a woman with kids. I started going to "Parents Without Partners" and yes, I've met someone. I've got a long way to go before I really trust and am open to loving and being loved again, but I'm making progress. I still think Joe's a bastard, but at least I talk civilly to him when he comes to pick up the kids for visits. Oh, yeah, I quit smoking and joined a health club. It must have helped because I've only gotten sick once this year instead of catching every "bug" I come in contact with.

Two years ago I decided that I wanted to feel whole, well, happy, healthy, excited, and fully alive; to get in bed at night thinking, "Today was a good day, a day I lived in the very best way I could, not abusing myself or anyone else." Then, before I shut my eyes, I wanted to say, "And tomorrow will be even better!" I don't always do that, but I'm getting there.

With love,
Beverly

This letter, in which Beverly fantasizes her future progress, gives you a clear idea of the goals she set for herself when she chose to heal her old wounds, including those she suffered as a result of her divorce. We urge you to write this sort of foresighted letter as well.

Realize that your vision will change from time to time. For example, you may have noticed that Beverly did not make any reference to actually forgiving her ex-husband, Joe, or even wanting to forgive him. Later in her healing process, the desire to sever her emotional ties to Joe by giving up the grudges she held against him would become a priority for Beverly. But at the time she wrote that letter, she could not even imagine doing that, much less set it as a goal for herself. The important point is that Beverly did have an image of her destination, and you need one, too. It must be positive and meaningful to you, one that you want enough to be willing to do the work you need to do in order to get to it.

Getting There

Each of us has our own timetable for healing, and none of us knows in advance how much time we will need to move through the process.

IT TAKES AS LONG AS IT TAKES

Healing is an internal process. It happens inside you and therefore cannot be measured or controlled by arbitrary external factors, including calendars. You simply cannot decide that by this time next year you will have healed all your wounds and forgiven everyone who ever hurt you; that on a certain date in the near future you will have straightened out every mess you ever got yourself into, changed your entire outlook on life, and be well on your way to living happily ever after.

Healing takes as long as it takes. Patience is most definitely required, but when we say this, we do not mean that you sit around and wait patiently for healing to happen. There is always work for you to do.

What we *are* urging is that you respect your own process and internal time clock; to visualize the healing process as a river flowing through you. If you want to reach your destination, you still have to steer and paddle your boat, but you will waste less energy and feel less frustrated if you paddle *with* the current rather than against it.

THE PATH TO FORGIVENESS IS NOT A STRAIGHT LINE

When we first summarized the six stages of forgiveness, we mentioned that no stage is clear cut and that you do not move from one step to another in a linear fashion. It would be nice if the healing process (or any process) worked that way. But it does not. As you continue working to complete your unfinished business, there will be moments when you will feel as if the clouds have finally lifted; joyful moments when the progress you have made is so real you can taste it; hours, days, and even weeks at a time when you feel peaceful, and pain from the past does not cross your mind at all. On the other hand, some of the territory through which you will travel may feel more painful and self-defeating than anything you've ever experienced.

There will even be times when you wonder if you aren't moving farther away from peace of mind instead of closer to it. The ups and the downs, the peaceful moments, the triumphant ones and the trying ones, are all part of the process.

In addition, you may stay in certain stages for what seems like an eternity. While this certainly will be discouraging and may stir up feelings of sadness, anxiety, and frustration, it does not mean you have stopped healing or that you will never move on to the next stage. Even when you seem to be standing still, you are in the process of healing.

When you reach an impasse—whether it's finding you are not ready to let go of your anger or having difficulty pushing through your fears about letting people get to know you—*allow yourself to be where you are*. Try not to view temporary setbacks as total failures. Instead, try to see them as areas of yourself that you are still working on. We are all incomplete and working on something. And if you truly want to be better off than you are, you will have to keep working even when you can find no visible signs of progress. Progress will come. When you grow tired of being where you are, you will find a way to move on. We know this because we have been stuck ourselves and because we have witnessed so many other people maneuver themselves out of deep, dark holes into the light of day.

In addition to getting stuck in a stage, from time to time and for various reasons, you may find yourself slipping back into a stage that you thought you'd completed. For instance, regardless of how far we've come, most of us will slip back into the victim stage periodically, especially if we are experiencing stress or are faced with some sort of crisis. Under such circumstances, we may feel that we have earned the right to indulge ourselves or feel sorry for ourselves and for a time act like the victim we used to be. But slipping back like that does not erase the work we've already done. Indeed, the progress we've made enables us to be aware of the slip, tire of the stage rather quickly, and sooner or later pick up again where we left off.

YOU DO NOT HAVE TO HEAL ALONE

Any burden becomes lighter when you share it. You do not have to heal yourself all by yourself. You can get counseling, join a support group, or participate in a self-help group or twelve-step recovery program like Alcoholics Anonymous, Al-Anon, or Overeaters

Anonymous. You can take advantage of the supportive people already in your life—relatives, friends, and co-workers who can provide all sorts of nourishment and encouragement. You may not think anyone you know now actually has what it takes to help you. But if you merely consider the possibility and look around you, you may be pleasantly surprised by what the people who have been there all along can offer you.

In addition, you can increase your insight and learn new skills by reading books, taking courses, attending lectures, workshops, and seminars, listening to audio tapes, or keeping a journal.

We suggest these measures because although we sincerely believe that you have always done the best you could with the *insight, resources,* and *emotional support* you had, we also believe that by increasing any or all of these three things, you naturally begin to do better and automatically enhance your healing process.

What Is the Next Bold Step You Must Take?

To help you answer that question for yourself, in the next six chapters—which explain the six stages of the healing process—we offer you general guidelines, suggestions, and the benefit of our own and many other people's experiences, encouraging words, and strategies. The description of each stage can help you as you continue on your own journey to forgiveness and a better life.

CHAPTER FIVE

DENIAL

Remember that suitcase full of hurts we talked about earlier, the one we drag around behind us? Well, it's time to open it up and look inside. Yes, painful memories will emerge, and they will be difficult to think about. In general, the ones that cause the most discomfort and the ones that you most want to push down again as soon as you start thinking about them are the ones that really matter—and the ones *you have probably been denying for a long, long time*.

So it's time to ask yourself, Who has hurt you? When? and most important, Whom haven't you forgiven? Sometimes the answer to these questions is obvious, but we urge you to look below the surface as well and identify the people you keep imprisoned in more subtle ways. Look at how you relate to the people who once hurt you. Are those relationships strained, argumentative, stressful, depressing? Are you holding a grudge, harboring resentments, giving them the silent treatment? Are you waiting for them to make up for what they did, to apologize and beg your forgiveness, to suffer as much as you have?

And don't overlook the people who are no longer a part of your life, people who are no longer living, or old lovers, friends, or playmates whom you have not seen or heard from in years. If thinking about them still hurts or makes you feel angry or anxious, chances are that they are a source of unfinished business for you.

Clarification Strategy Number 2:
Naming Names

After you have taken some time to think about the questions we just posed, take out a sheet of paper and, looking back as far as you can remember, list *everyone* who has ever hurt you in any way. Name names, if you can remember them, or make identifying notes if you cannot remember names. Include the people who inflicted small scratches and, of course, those who opened gaping wounds. Include the people you believe you have forgiven as well as those you know you have not. And do not forget the "institutions" that have caused you pain—schools, courts, the media, and so on. The list does not *have* to be terribly long, but it will probably be longer than you thought it would be when you started to make it.

Go back over your list and mark with an asterisk (*) each person or institution you have not forgiven. Then choose three whose wounds you most want to or need to heal, with at least one representing a painful past experience you have tried valiantly to forget. Identify those wounds by writing one or two sentences explaining exactly how you were hurt. For instance, Warren, whom we introduced in chapter 1, wrote, "My father hurt me by treating me like the invisible kid, never showing that he loved me or noticing anything I did and then throwing salt in the wound by remarrying, having more kids, and being the kind of father to them that he never was to me." And Harriet, a thirty-eight-year-old artist who is currently engaged in a seemingly endless custody battle with her ex-husband, identified him as a source of pain and wrote, "Larry hurt me by having an affair and not even having the decency to cover his tracks. He made me look like a fool in front of our mutual friends and then tried to turn our kids against me by bribing them with expensive gifts and trips and telling them we would still be together if I wasn't so cold-hearted."

When anger and resentment are still fresh in our minds, describing how we were hurt is fairly easy, although not painless, to do. However, if we have been blocking and ignoring our hurt feelings for years, we may find that words are hard to come by or that we resist writing them down because we feel as if we are betraying someone we love in spite of how he or she hurt us. Marcy certainly felt this way. The tears she had refused to shed for so long rolled down her face as she wrote, "I love my mother, but she did hurt me. She hurt me because she was an alcoholic, and when she was drunk, which was most of the time, she could not really be a mother to me or my brothers and sisters. I had to handle everything, and that wasn't fair.''

You too may find any number of frightening emotions rising to the surface as you try to complete this clarification strategy. If those emotions seem too overwhelming, take a break. Put aside your list and come back to it another day. But do come back to it.

When You Name It, You Claim It—and You May Not Want To

Acknowledging that you were hurt, describing the hurt, and telling its full story is a vital element of the healing process. However, naming and therefore claiming your painful past experiences is an extremely difficult thing to do. At this point in your healing process, you may not be ready to do it. Indeed, you may have a number of powerful reasons *not* to acknowledge and examine your old wounds and unfinished business.

First of all, you probably do not *want* to believe that certain things really happened to you. If you were watching TV and witnessed someone experiencing such horrifying or humiliating treatment, you would switch channels. And when you think about admitting that acts that repel you actually happened to you, you switch channels, too—turning off your thoughts and feelings about that painful past experience.

Then there is the notion that certain experiences brand you as unlovable, inadequate, and deficient. To acknowledge that you were once damaged by abuse, rejection, abandonment, betrayal, or any other painful past experience would also acknowledge that perhaps you are "damaged goods" today, still flawed in some fundamental way. You do not *want* to see yourself in that light. You desperately want to believe that you are okay. And since acknowledging how you were hurt and what you have done because you were hurt threatens that belief, you do not acknowledge it.

What's more, other people might find out the "horrible truth" about you and think less of you because of it. Unfortunately, you may have already had experiences that reinforced this perception. You revealed your painful past experience to a parent or sibling, a friend, a co-worker, or your spouse, and, perhaps because they felt uncomfortable hearing about what happened to you or felt helpless to relieve your suffering, their reactions were far from encouraging.

"You mean that still *bothers* you?" they gasp incredulously. "It happened years ago. You should just forget about it."

"You're making mountains out of molehills," they insist. "How bad could it have been? You've done pretty well for yourself, haven't you?"

"Worse things have happened to other people," they remind you. "Why don't you count your blessings instead of bellyaching about the past?"

Chances are that you came away from those conversations feeling more determined than ever to keep your old hurts hidden— hidden from other people, but also from yourself. You begin to doubt that you even have the "right" to feel as you do.

Most of all, though, you may be *afraid* to face your painful past experiences. You may be afraid that the pain would be more than you could bear, that you would drown in your own tears or become so upset that you would be unable to function. You may be afraid because once you admit how you were hurt and, even more so, what you have done because you were hurt, you will have to change. You will have to act and react differently from the way you have in the past, and you do not know how to do that. You do not know whether or not you could survive if you did that.

If, while working on the clarification strategy or while reading the chapters that preceded this one, you were tempted to ignore, overlook, or otherwise dismiss certain past experiences, or if you found yourself thinking that your old injuries and injustices were:

- unimportant,
- water under the bridge,
- irrelevant to your life today,
- not worth dredging up again,
- over and done with,
- or better off forgotten,

then you may be in the denial stage of the forgiveness process. And even if you are not in this stage now, you *have* been in it at some time in the past. Everyone, without exception, spends some time in the denial stage, entering it at the moment they were hurt, returning to it periodically, and sometimes getting stuck in it for years on end.

In Self-Defense:
Entering Denial at the Moment You Were Hurt

My father never actually told me not to talk about the incest. He did not tell me that revealing the secret would destroy my mother. He made no overt threats. However, he did inform me that he could read my mind, that he knew when I was thinking about "it."

To be safe from this telepathic invasion of privacy, I was very careful not to think about what was happening. I blocked incest from my mind, along with a great many other thoughts and feelings and, indeed, most of my childhood. It was all lumped together and filed away under the heading "Too Dangerous to Dwell On." If a painful memory or unpleasant emotion slipped through to my consciousness, I simply pushed it back down again. I did not want to think about the past, not any of it.

This enabled me to convince myself that incest had not hurt me. Although I never denied that the abuse happened and could remember it when I allowed myself to, I did deny that it affected me or my life. I acted as if it didn't matter, as if it weren't important.

Suzanne's healing journey began the moment she was hurt—and so did yours. At that moment, your top priority was to stop the pain, or at least to ward it off until you could think clearly again. To do that, you, like Suzanne, used some form of *denial,* a psychological defense activated by your subconscious mind and employed for what starts out as a positive reason—to help you cope with circumstances that you are not prepared to handle and to protect you from feelings that you fear will overwhelm or destroy you.

"I can't remember most of it," says Amy, a twenty-four-year-old graduate student. When she was a nineteen-year-old college sophomore, Amy was raped by an acquaintance, another student whom she had been tutoring for several months. "I do remember that we were working in his dorm room instead of the lounge, and that he was paying more attention to me than to his physics assignment," she continues. "But I told him to cut that out, and things seemed to be under control." When the tutoring session ended and Amy got up to leave, however, the young man grabbed her and threw her down onto his bed. "The last thing I remember is thinking, 'This can't be happening,' " she says, shuddering. "And then, I guess I must have switched off my brain or something because it's just a blank after that. I don't even know how I got back to my dorm." Although five years have passed, Amy still draws a blank when she attempts to recall what happened to her. "I'll get these flashes once in a while," she explains. "But since I'm not sure if those things actually happened or if they're just things I think *might* have happened, I don't let them upset me. I just push them out of my mind."

At the moment you were hurt, you were too young, too shocked, or too wounded to cope with or fully comprehend the events and emotions you were experiencing. You needed to protect yourself, to step back and put a safe distance between yourself and that unsettling experience. So, like Amy, you negated reality, wholeheartedly believing that something did not exist when, in fact, it actually did, or you blocked out unsettling experiences, pushing unpleasant thoughts and unwelcome emotions to the back of your mind, sometimes to the point of forgetting about them completely.

"I pretended that it didn't really matter, that it was a one-time thing that would never happen again," Darlene sighs, explaining how she initially coped with her father's missed visits by viewing each as an isolated incident. "I couldn't accept the idea that my father had let me down," she continues. "So each time he did, I sort of wiped the slate clean, tried to forget the last time, and told myself there wouldn't be a next time." With all thoughts of previous disappointments tucked safely in the back of her mind, young Darlene, hopeful and excited, would take up her post on the front steps and wait for her father to arrive. When he did, it proved that she was right to "forget about the other times." When he didn't, Darlene kept her disappointment from overwhelming her by immediately "explaining away" her father's behavior, once more convincing herself that it would never happen again.

At the moment you were hurt, you could not cope with or fully comprehend the fact that you had been hurt by someone you loved or trusted or depended upon to meet your needs. The injury or injustice raised the possibility that the person who hurt you might not love you or care about you at all, and that thought caused unbearable pain or extreme confusion. You needed to find a way to understand what was happening, a way to keep yourself from drowning in a tidal wave of emotions. So you minimized the impact and importance of your experiences and your feelings; kept your emotions at bay by generalizing, analyzing, or theorizing about your experiences; or, like Darlene, excused, justified, and "explained away" the injury or injustice so that you would not have a reason to feel upset about it.

"I just tuned them out," says Bruce, recalling how he protected himself from the barrage of criticism fired at him by teachers who believed he was not performing up to his potential, the nagging and threats he heard from his parents, who believed he was intentionally "slacking off" at school, and the taunts of his peers, who called him "dummy" and "retard."

"As soon as they started in on me, this shield went up," he says. "It was automatic. They'd be talking, but I'd be thinking about something else, song lyrics, or a scene from a Three Stooges movie, or the Little League game I'd pitched, anything that kept their words from getting through." As you may recall, for many years afterward Bruce continued the habit he'd developed during childhood, ultimately discovering that alcohol and drugs were even more effective than his own imagination at keeping unpleasant realities from "getting through" to him.

At the moment you were hurt, if you had been hurt before in the same or similar ways, you realized that you simply could not leave yourself open and vulnerable to each and every blow. You needed to make sure that the next time you encountered abuse, disappointment, rejection, ridicule, or humiliation, it would not hurt as much as the last time. So, like Bruce, you created diversions—changing the subject or keeping yourself too busy, too high, or too preoccupied with other matters to think about unpleasant situations or feel anything at all—or covered up your true feelings with false cheerfulness, an impenetrable suit of armor, or an "attitude" that kept other people at a distance.

At the moment you were hurt, like Amy, Darlene, and Bruce, you instinctively defended yourself against threats to your safety, security, and sanity. You did this automatically, unconsciously, and for positive, practical reasons. You simply were not equipped to acknowledge, understand, or do anything constructive about the painful experience.

Maintaining Denial:
Pushing Down Pain Over and Over Again

Once you switch it on, denial is exceedingly difficult to switch off. Like a computer programmed to perform a certain function when certain information is entered, your subconscious mind reactivates denial whenever you reexperience something similar to the original injury or injustice—by remembering it or feeling the emotions associated with it. What's more, as time passes you discover the previously described, equally powerful reasons *not* to acknowledge pain from the past.

Unfortunately, by automatically covering up the very things you need to see in order to heal old wounds and complete unfinished business, denial—which originally helped you survive trying and painful circumstances—ends up hurting you, preventing you from truly making peace with the past or making the most of your present and future.

While shielded from reality by denial, sometimes for decades after you were hurt, you will not see the connections between your past experiences and your present circumstances. You will consider old injuries and injustices to be "ancient history" and sincerely believe that they did not affect you then or do not affect you now. You may think that you do not have a care in the world, ignoring the fact that you find yourself in the same undesirable situations over and over again or that you react to certain situations or people in certain ways without knowing why. Other people may notice that your life is not the bed of roses that you believe it is, but you do not want to hear what they have to say. You just put on a happy face and tell anyone who asks that you are "fine, fine, fine."

However, you are not trying to "put one over" on people by smiling all of the time or shutting your eyes to the unpleasant realities in your life. You may not even know that is what you are doing. You are not pretending that painful past experiences did not affect you or no longer affect you. You sincerely believe it. Nor are you willfully misrepresenting reality or stubbornly refusing to "see the light." You are simply presenting the "facts" of your life as you see them. Unfortunately, there is very little you can see while enveloped in a cloud of denial.

I married quite young, and by the time I reached my late twenties my marriage was failing. I was plagued by mysterious aches and pains and beginning to show signs of job burnout. I always felt alone. I felt different and estranged from every other human being on the planet. And I not only felt isolated, I also approached life in a way that would insure that I continued to feel that way. I wouldn't let myself get too close to people for fear that they might find out my secret. I literally pushed them away, although I was not aware of doing it. I saw myself as meek and bland, a sorry sort of pushover, but I came across to others as angry and ready for a fight. As a former co-worker put it, "Suzanne, you greeted the world with a stance that said, 'Don't mess with me, don't cross me. I've been crossed before, and I'm not about to be crossed again.'" No wonder people kept their distance and I remained isolated.

I did not like myself. I believed treading water to keep from drowning was all that anyone should expect of me and all that I could expect out of life. And sometimes even that seemed like too much to handle, and I thought about suicide on more than one occasion.

But I did not make the connection between the dire straits I was in then and the abuse that had occurred so many years earlier. I continued to deny its impact on my life and continued to view it as insignificant—so much so that when I took a friend's advice and went to see a counselor, I talked about my marriage, my job, my health, and my life in general, but never once mentioned incest. And although I resolved a few of my immediate problems, I did not heal the real wounds. I ignored those wounds and went through the motions of getting on with my life. But I couldn't get very far. Although I did not know it at the time, I was stuck in the denial stage of the healing process.

Getting Stuck in the Denial Stage

Denial is as comfortable as an old pair of sneakers, as sticky as flypaper, as automatic as breathing and habit-forming to boot—which is why, in spite of the dead-end streets it leads us down, we can get stuck in denial for a long, long time.

"It wasn't that bad," Marcy says of the chaos, confusion, and emotional devastation that occurred while she was growing up in a family turned upside down by her parents' alcoholism.

"It could have been worse," Sandy insists, pointing out that she could have been bounced from foster home to foster home or mistreated by her adoptive parents instead of *just* being abandoned by her biological mother.

"I got over that years ago," Mark asserts, in spite of the fact that he still expects the worst of any situation and was so haunted by memories of the special occasions his father ruined that he seriously considered canceling his wedding and running off to be married by a justice of the peace.

"It doesn't bother me anymore," says Melinda, claiming that she never even thinks about Steve—except when she is reminding herself that she is a fool to expect the men she finds attractive to be attracted to her.

Marcy, Sandy, Mark, and Melinda are stuck in the denial stage of the forgiveness process. Like Suzanne, they were hurt years, even decades, ago, but they have yet to acknowledge the impact of their painful past experiences or examine—let alone heal—their old wounds. If you too are stuck in denial, chances are that you view your painful past experiences in one of the four ways we are about to describe and use that point of view to convince yourself that you do not really *need* to heal and forgive.

It Never Happened

The first of four approaches to denying painful past experiences, believing that you were not hurt in the first place, is usually reserved for extremely traumatic experiences like rape, incest, or physical abuse or incomprehensible ones like learning that your spouse had an affair or overhearing your best friend spread a vicious rumor about you. Occasionally what happened to you—especially if it happened when you were a young child—was so painful or terrifying that the only way you could cope with it was to completely block it from your conscious awareness. As a result, you have what psychologists call an occluded memory. You can recall certain incidents up to a point but then draw a complete blank—the way Amy, who was raped, does—or you have only vague memories of whole stretches of time. There is something you so desperately need to forget that you simply cannot retrieve any information about that event or that period of your life—for example, not remembering "anything" about your kindergarten or first-grade experiences.

Much more common than completely blocking a painful past experience, you may focus your attention on the possibility, no matter how remote, that the incident might not have happened at all. For instance, having overheard your friend's malicious gossip about you, you might tell yourself that she might not have been saying what you thought she was saying, that you misunderstood what you heard or didn't hear the part where she defended you and said the rumor wasn't true. Maybe that wasn't the distinct scent of perfume all over your husband's shirt, you think, maybe it wasn't him, but someone who looked like him, strolling in the park with his arm around a woman who looked like—but might not have been—his secretary. Maybe you imagined those hurtful things your mother said to you, and maybe you dreamed that your father came into your bedroom and molested you.

The *hope* is that you dreamed or imagined or really did not see or hear the things you are not yet ready to face. Although at some level you know that the injury or injustice did indeed happen, you hold on to the thread of hope that it might not have—dismissing, denying, and running away from your pain, humiliation, guilt, sadness, and self-doubt. This perspective can lead to getting stuck in the denial stage indefinitely, because as time passes and life goes on, the memories you do have grow dimmer and it becomes easier and easier to persuade yourself that the incident was just a bad dream after all.

It Happened, but It Didn't Affect Me

The second approach to denying painful past experiences involves negating, not the events themselves, but the impact they had on you at the time they occurred. As Suzanne did for so many years, you may maintain that injuries and injustices that could reasonably be expected to cause pain, anxiety, guilt, humiliation, or other distressing reactions did not have that effect on you.

"Because I knew it was the best thing for everyone involved, it didn't bother me," you say, intellectualizing experiences like your parents' divorce or your own, giving up a child for adoption or giving up your college education to support a family your unemployed, alcoholic father could not. These are experiences that by their very nature *had* to have an effect on you. Recalling events that you openly admit would hurt anyone else, you insist that they did not hurt you, explaining away the loss of a loved one ("His death was a blessing; at least he wasn't suffering anymore") or excusing emotional and physical abuse ("She didn't know what she was doing"). No matter how you do it and whether or not you realize you are doing it, you are still deceiving yourself, still finding reasons not to examine how you were hurt or what you have done because you were hurt.

It Affected Me, but It Wasn't That Bad

Those of you who use this approach to deny painful past experiences may acknowledge that you were hurt but believe that you do not have to deal with unfinished business because it was not "a big deal" to begin with. You may cope with unpleasant realities by telling yourself that your experiences were less painful than they actually were or are insignificant because they were not as painful as they could have been under other circumstances.

For instance, as a child growing up under the influence of her parents' alcoholism, Marcy could not accept the idea that her parents— who were supposed to be good and help her feel safe and secure— could do things that were bad or irresponsible. Unable to make her parents' erratic, irrational, and frightening behavior fit her image of them, and unable to alter that image without threatening her own sense of safety and security, Marcy blocked her awareness of the bad and irresponsible things her parents did. As a result, until recently, when she looked back upon her childhood, she remembered very little of it beyond a few isolated "good times" that took place when one or both of her parents were temporarily on the wagon. Maintaining the denial that began so many years earlier, Marcy insisted that her youth really was not "that bad" and therefore not worth "getting all worked up about" today.

What's more, no matter how bad your past was, you can always come up with examples of how much worse it could have been or point to people who had more devastating experiences than yours. Sandy did this by reminding herself that her life *after* being abandoned by her mother could have been more damaging than it actually was. She negated not only the pain and inadequacy she felt about being "dumped on a doorstep," but also the years of depression, alienation, and substance abuse she went through because of the original injury to her self-esteem.

You may minimize or cover up your pain by reassuring yourself that even though your parents got divorced, for instance, they did not fight over custody or did not abuse you or were not alcoholics. Or, if your spouse had numerous extramarital affairs, you might console yourself with the fact that he or she did not drink or did not beat you or abandon you or gamble away all your money and force you to go on welfare.

Perceiving your experiences as "not so bad" or not as bad as they could have been keeps you from getting off the denial merry-go-round and getting on with your life.

It Used to Affect Me, but I'm Over It Now

Far and away the most common approach to denying the impact of painful past experiences, believing you have "gotten over" those old injuries and injustices and completed your unfinished business not only blinds you to the damage done when you were hurt, but also keeps you from acknowledging your present-day problems—the things you have done and continue to do because you were hurt.

This approach is so appealing because you really *want* to believe you are no longer affected by your past painful experiences. Indeed, you will refute all evidence to the contrary. Everything is "fine, fine, fine," you tell yourself and everyone else. And even if it isn't, you are convinced that your addictions, failed relationships, indiscriminate sexual activity, inability to hold down jobs, depression, ulcers, and other present-day problems have absolutely nothing to do with what happened to you in the past.

In fact, whenever you so much as think about those old injuries and injustices, you may feel silly, oversensitive, or as if you are making a big deal over nothing. Buying into the prevalent societal attitude that we should get over things quickly, move on, and never look back, you tell yourself, "I really *should* be over this by now," and more often than not you go right on *pretending* that you are over it. You declare yourself "healed" even though you have never actually examined your old wounds; faced, felt, and worked through your pain; or gained insight into and changed your automatic response to various people and situations. In spite of your protests to the contrary, you have not completed your unfinished business. You have just, more ingeniously, hidden it behind your wall of denial.

The High Price of Denying Pain from the Past

By now you may be wondering what is really wrong with denying painful past experiences. If you want to believe that you were not hurt or that you have gotten over the hurt, why shouldn't you? If you can get away with it, why not maintain the illusion that life is a bed of roses? Because you can't get away with it for long. Eventually denial will turn on you and leave you stranded at the end of a dead-end street.

The first thing we noticed about Terry, thirty-six and the director of an alcoholism treatment program, was her smile. It dominated her heart-shaped face, scrunching her emerald-green eyes into narrow slivers. It lit up any room she entered, and not once since we met her at an addictions conference have we seen her without it. Indeed, with her ever-present grin, her throaty laughter, and the way she jauntily tossed back her head of thick, silky blond hair, Terry appeared to be a remarkably cheerful, optimistic, and carefree woman.

Like Suzanne, Terry was sexually abused during childhood. "But that's ancient history," she assured us, widening the Cheshire-cat grin that would remain on her face throughout our conversation. "It doesn't affect my life today. In fact, in some ways I'm a better person because of it." Considering her general demeanor and the confidence she exudes while making this assertion, it was easy to assume that Terry had indeed worked through her experience, made peace with her past, and forgiven the molester, her grandfather. But had she really?

"There was nothing to forgive," she insisted, looking at us as if we were crazy to think otherwise. Indeed, she sounded almost indignant as she explained, "I was my grandpa's little princess. He adored me. He'd *never* do anything to hurt me."

Although you may be doing a double take, just as we did at the time, Terry believed every word she said. Denial had created that point of view and maintained it for more than two decades. She had not—as we thought originally—healed her old wounds. Indeed, she could not, because she was completely convinced that she had no wounds to heal, that being sexually molested by her grandfather had not adversely affected her in any way.

As a young child, Terry was left alone with her grandfather on Saturday afternoons while her mother and grandmother did volunteer work at a local hospital. Each and every Saturday for almost two years, her grandfather sexually molested her. Only seven years old when the abuse began, Terry was too young to fully understand what was happening or why. Seeing everything as black or white, as most young children do, when she tried to cope with and comprehend the situation, she ran into a brick wall. She felt hurt, frightened, and confused by the things her grandfather did and made her do when they were alone together. Yet she was also convinced that if the grandfather she adored loved her as much as she believed he did, he could not do anything to hurt her in any way. Since he could not love her and hurt her at the same time, and since she needed him to love her in order to feel good about herself, she concluded that he must not be hurting her. Indeed, she reinterpreted the experience so that sexual abuse not only did no damage, it actually helped her feel special and secure. Automatically and within the confines of her subconscious mind, the idea was formed and adopted as truth. And for the next twenty-six years, Terry operated as if it were true, smiling and laughing and waltzing through life as if she hadn't a care in the world.

Unfortunately, having convinced herself that being sexual with her grandfather allowed her to feel like his lovable little princess, Terry missed that feeling after the incest ended—two years after it began. And by unconsciously "reinventing" reality and turning sexual abuse into proof that she was special and worthwhile, Terry inadvertently set the stage for twenty-six years of seeking out sex to reaffirm her self-worth. Even though she completely denied that she had been hurt, the hurt was still there, and what she did because of it made a difference in her life.

Sexually active by age thirteen, Terry's first "promiscuous phase," as she calls it, lasted seven years until, at age twenty, she settled into a "real" relationship with one of her college professors. It lasted two years and was followed by a year of frenetic sexual activity, including numerous brief affairs and countless one-night stands. Then there was another relationship. It too lasted two years and was followed by another promiscuous phase.

At age twenty-six Terry went into therapy but declared herself cured after just three sessions. "After all, enjoying sex and being good in bed isn't exactly a problem," she says, laughing heartily.

So Terry blithely continued down her dead-end street. Two abortions, several cases of venereal disease, the risk of contracting AIDS, and threats against her life made by one lover, who did not take kindly to being dumped, did not deter her. She even risked her professional reputation by sleeping with patients at the alcohol treatment program she ran. The obvious dangers that accompanied her promiscuous phases were ignored completely. And the pain she felt when she realized yet another relationship was failing was minimized, added to the collection of "pleasant memories" she had begun accumulating when she first decided that childhood sexual abuse had been a positive rather than a painful or frightening experience.

Terry was repeating her past—right down to having relationships that lasted exactly as long as her incest experience. She was negating the risks she took just as she negated the idea that her grandfather would do anything to hurt her. She smiled all the time, but she also smoked two packs of cigarettes a day and had an ulcer. Life was not the bed of roses she insisted that it was. She was paying the price for denying pain from the past.

Like Terry, when we minimize, justify, rationalize, reinterpret, make more palatable, and flat-out deny painful past experiences, the only direction we can go is downhill. While we talk ourselves out of pain, drown our sorrows, numb our fear, bury our feelings, distract ourselves, put on a happy face, and tell anyone who asks that we are "fine, fine, fine," our life circumstances do not improve. Our problems do not get solved. Our old wounds do not heal.

Although you may believe that "ignorance is bliss," it is not. Denial is a general anesthetic. When you numb one emotion, you numb them all. When you flush away your bad feelings, the good ones go down the drain, too. Consequently, it is impossible to *genuinely* feel bliss or any other positive emotion while pushing down pain from the past. Lost joy, excitement, and peace of mind are part of the price you pay for your one-way ticket away from unpleasant realities.

You also pay in energy and enthusiasm, because denial leaves you drained and exhausted. Take a moment to recall or imagine what it is like to get through the day when you are in physical pain. Think about having a strained back or a sprained ankle or a monstrous headache but refusing to "give in" to the pain. No matter how hard you try to ignore it, the pain nags at you, keeps you from concentrating on paperwork or telephone conversations, makes you grouchy and irritable. Your pain calls the shots all day long. You cannot move about freely or engage in certain activities, because you might reinjure yourself and feel more pain. You cannot and indeed do not feel like doing more than the bare minimum to get by. And by the time the sun sets, you are too exhausted to do anything but "zone out" in front of the television or crawl into bed and fall asleep. That zombielike existence is identical with the life many of you lead while denying psychological pain. And with each passing day it gets more difficult to anesthetize the pain with denial alone.

Even though denial is so easily activated and even though you have so many convincing reasons to maintain it, your denial defense system eventually stops working. The feelings you buried periodically rise up from their graves. Memories of old injuries and injustices come back to haunt you, and when they do, your internal defense mechanisms alone can no longer protect you. Maintaining denial over an extended period of time requires outside assistance, and you get that assistance from alcohol, drugs, food, indiscriminate sex, codependent relationships, workaholism, gambling, shopping, endless TV watching, and any other compulsive or distracting behavior imaginable. When rationalizing, minimizing, blocking, and intellectualizing can no longer ''switch off'' your brain or stop the onslaught of frightening emotions, you reach for the painkillers and emptiness fillers we described in chapter 3 and then become saddled with new problems.

These new problems become yet another way to avoid facing the ''big'' problem. You blame your unhappiness on your weight, your job, your rotten marriage, your financial difficulties, or your addiction, never looking below the surface at the unfinished business that led you down that dead-end street in the first place. What's more, because the problems you do recognize are protecting you from the painful past experiences you are not yet ready to face, you can never truly solve them. You go on diets but give up five pounds short of your goal. You end one abusive relationship only to find yourself in another. You get sober, but after a few weeks or months in recovery, you relapse, going on a binge that makes your old habits look like child's play.

When you bought your one-way ticket away from pain, all you really wanted to do was get on with your life. But as you can see, you got stuck on the denial merry-go-round instead.

Getting Off the Denial Merry-Go-Round

At age thirty-three, there was very little about my life that could be described as loving or peaceful. Not only couldn't I soar above the turmoil, but I felt like I was trapped right in the middle of it.

To make matters worse, I was finding it difficult to go on denying that incest had left its mark on my life. As John Powell, author of *Why Am I Afraid to Tell You Who I Am?*, put it, ''When you bury feelings, you bury them alive,'' and it was becoming increasingly apparent that my feelings were very much alive. In fact, while I was trying ever more desperately to push them down, my memories of and feelings about being sexually abused were pushing me toward a turning point. Sooner than I realized I would have to choose whether to go on living in pain from the past or take my first steps toward healing.

During this period of inner turmoil and confusion, my sister and her family came to my home for a visit, and during that visit, my sister and I had an argument. I honestly do not remember why we argued, but in an attempt to settle our disagreement we left the house and went for a walk. This did not seem like the wisest of decisions at first, for the petty argument escalated into a full-blown fight. Furiously, I accused her of expecting too much of me. "I can't be perfect for you," I declared. "I've got other things on my mind, things that have happened to me that you don't even know about."

Suddenly, inexplicably, she began to cry—sobbing uncontrollably just as I had done so often in the preceding months and years.

"What things?" she asked, but I could not tell her. She asked again, this time adding a second question: "Does it have to do with Dad?" When I nodded, she gasped, "Oh, God, not you, too!"

And that is how I learned that it was not just I who had been sexually abused by our father and not just I who had suffered silently and kept the secret for all these years. For the first time in my life I had an ally, someone who could understand my feelings because she had felt them herself. She had already acknowledged that incest had hurt her, and that served to make her a model as well. She advised me to get back into counseling and this time to talk about the abuse.

Although finding out that her sister was also a victim of their father's sexual abuse did indeed lead to a turning point in Suzanne's healing process, she would have reached that point eventually anyway. It may have taken longer. She might have missed out on having her sister as an ally. The remainder of her healing process might have proceeded differently, but ultimately she would have moved on. We are pointing this out because we do not want to leave you with the impression that some external event—over which you have no control—must occur before you can change. Your internal healing process may be influenced by what is going on around you, but it is not controlled by those outside forces. You can leave the denial stage whenever you choose to.

It is also significant that Suzanne's conversation with her sister would not have been a turning point for her if she had chosen not to take advantage of it, if she had refused to tell her sister what was bothering her or lied when she was asked if what happened to her involved their dad. During the twenty years that passed since the abuse had ended, Suzanne had many other opportunities to stop denying pain from the past, most notably when she had been seeing a counselor. Because she was not yet ready to get off the denial merry-go-round, she did not take advantage of the opportunities that presented themselves. By the time she spoke with her sister, however, she was ready. Being ready made facing her painful past experience possible—but not necessarily easy or painless.

> My sister nudged me in the direction of healing, but I must be honest and tell you that I took my first steps reluctantly at best. I stood on the threshold of change, but from my perspective it looked like the edge of a cliff. I was sure that moving an inch in any direction would send me plummeting into a bottomless pit of pain. What I really wanted to do was escape the pain, to not feel it anymore. I had suffered enough, I thought.
>
> I walked into the counselor's office and without taking off my coat asked, "Do you hypnotize people?" She asked me to take a seat, but I merely repeated my question. More than anything, I wanted to be hypnotized, told that the sexual abuse never happened, cured instantly, and sent on my way. You can imagine my dismay when this counselor informed me that "the only way out of pain is through it." I most definitely did not want to go through any more pain.

The fact of the matter is that once you stop denying, the pain gets worse and you will be tempted to deny it once more. We can only remind you that denying your feelings did not really make them go away. Indeed, no matter what you did, they kept coming back, creating new problems for you each time you had to push them back down again. As Suzanne's counselor put it, "You can't brush feelings under the carpet. They just come up and make ripples that you will trip on."

You do not have to continue tripping over your feelings. You can get them out into the open, realizing that feeling, even feeling pain, is a step toward healing.

Moving On

You may or may not be ready to tackle the "big" hurts, the ones you've been hiding from yourself ever since you first felt them. If you are, then the following strategies will help you move out of the denial stage of the healing process.

However, if you are *not* ready to do that, if there are certain issues that are still too painful to face, that's okay. You will face them when you *are* ready, in the time frame that feels right for you. You can use the following strategies to gain more insight into the injuries and injustices that you feel more comfortable thinking about.

If you did not complete the Naming Names Clarification Strategy on page 78 of this chapter, return to it now. Think about how you were hurt, list the people and institutions that caused you pain, identify those you have not forgiven, and describe in writing exactly how three of these people or institutions hurt you. If you can, make one of the hurts you describe a "big" one.

Clarification Strategy Number 3: Nondenial Statements

"I was hurt."
"What happened to me still hurts."
"That was no way to treat me."
"It was wrong."
"I've suffered because of what I went through."
"I haven't gotten over it yet."
"It *was* that bad."

These are nondenial statements. They affirm the fact that you were hurt and that the injuries and injustices you experienced did have an impact on your life. You may be able to think of others, and we encourage you to jot them down.

Then, one at a time, read the descriptions of how you were hurt that you composed as part of the Naming Names strategy. As soon as you have finished a description, read the nondenial statements. Read them out loud. Shout them if you want to. Acknowledge at last that the abuse, betrayal, rejection, ridicule, or humiliation really happened and really hurt, strengthening your resolve not to deny them anymore.

Clarification Strategy Number 4:
The Apology Letter

Now we would like you to write a letter, a letter addressed to yourself *from* someone who hurt you. It will be a letter of apology, a letter written from the point of view of a person who hurt you, apologizing for how he or she hurt you.

First identify the person whose letter this will be. It can be one of the three people who inflicted the injury or injustice you described in the Naming Names strategy. Or it can be someone else. The person does not have to be alive. It does not matter that you may never receive a real apology from that person. What does matter is that he or she hurt you and *owes* you an apology.

Once you have identified whom your letter will be from, write your letter from that person's point of view. Write the apology you now know you deserve, the letter that is long overdue, the words that say what *you* need to hear. The following letters, contributed by some people who attended our forgiveness seminars, may give you a few ideas for your own.

dear vincent,

i want to tell you how sorry i am for not getting to know you, for letting you go.

you were with me nine months, and how wonderful a period that was. i cannot expect you to understand that i could not keep you because of the shame i felt as an unwed mother. i cannot expect you to understand that i could not keep you because of the shame my parents felt as outstanding community citizens. i cannot expect you to understand that i could not hold you, bond with you, that it was best for the nurse to take you immediately away. no, that can never be understood.

i wish that i could see you. i wish that i could hug you just once. i wish we could have grown old together. please know that i love you and miss you. please know I never meant to hurt you. i am well and happy and my life has been a good one. i trust that you are happy and that you will continue to grow and to love. i am glad i wrote, i am glad that i shared my love with you at last.

mother

Dear Jeffrey,

This is a letter that partially explains why I rejected you as a son.

It seems that your mother doted on you—you were her pride and joy—you actually came between her and me. I really was very proud of you as a son, but I always looked for faults and tried to criticize you. I was hurting! She preferred you to me.

I really should've understood you were powerless—you were just a kid—you happened to be bright, so I mocked your schoolwork. I should have worked with you in athletics, but you didn't need me as much as I hoped you did. You were a natural—so what I did was ignore you and your accomplishments—I was jealous!

I wish I could go back and really appreciate what a great son I had—but I hurt too much at the time. I'm sorry I hurt you.

Love,
Dad

Dear Laura,

I never knew I was hurting you like I was. I always wanted what was best for you, and I thought that protecting you from life by making you scared of everything and everyone was the way. I also thought telling you everything you did could be better would just get you to reach higher—I guess I wanted everything for you that I never had myself.

I never meant to talk about you as if you weren't there and I never meant to be so selfish, but it was scary being a parent, and I didn't want to make any mistakes—I guess that's why I could never say I was sorry about anything. Instead I just got angry at you as if every mistake I made as a parent must have been your fault.

I guess I still do that, and that couldn't be very nice for you. I might be too old to change. But I'd really like to try.

I love you,
Mom

Writing the letter of apology is a foolproof way to break through the wall of denial you have built around that particular painful past experience. Merely acknowledging that such a letter could be written automatically acknowledges that the injury or injustice did occur. By actually writing it, however, you go one step further. Your letter of apology confirms—in writing—that you were hurt and that you are aware of that fact. You are not denying it anymore.

Whether it takes days or decades, you will eventually leave the denial stage of the forgiveness process. The day will arrive when you acknowledge that:

- you have been hurt;
- you still feel the pain;
- you can talk about your experiences without self-destructing;
- you do not have to
    shut down your feelings;
    push unpleasant thoughts to the back of your mind;
    ignore, minimize, or dismiss the connection between your
    present circumstances and your painful past experiences.

You can expect to return to this stage from time to time, especially when you feel overwhelmed by new events or old emotions, when the demands of daily living take precedence over tackling certain issues and at various points throughout your healing process.

If, however, you find yourself unable to move from this stage for long periods of time, you might want to ask yourself, "What's going on in my life *right now*?" Chances are you are experiencing other stresses and you know intuitively that *right now* is *not* the time to look at and deal with this other "big hurt." Perhaps you are going through a divorce, or are in the process of changing jobs or moving, or one of your children is seriously ill. These situations would put you in a vulnerable state and leave very little energy for dealing with past issues. It would make sense, then, for you to keep up your defenses about the past and put everything on hold while you devote your time and energy to dealing with all that is going on right now in your present life.

On the other hand, now that you know what denial is and what you say and do while in the denial stage, you are less likely to get stuck in it for extended periods of time. Indeed, because you know that denial will ultimately lead you down another dead-end street, you can choose to move back onto the main road as quickly as possible.

After you leave the denial stage, you will enter one of three stages—self-blame, victim, or indignation. As you move closer to healing and forgiveness, you can expect to spend some time in all three of those stages. Although not necessarily the first you will enter, the first we will next describe is self-blame.

CHAPTER SIX

SELF-BLAME

"This can't be happening to me," Harriet thought when she first learned about her husband Larry's affair. But she did not deny the situation for long. Indeed, her pain and confusion would not stay buried for more than a few hours at a time, and she was soon less interested in denying what happened than in figuring out *why* it had happened. She phrased her soul-searching question in terms that are all too familiar to anyone who has ever been hurt. Over and over again, she asked herself, "What did I do to deserve this?"

Because her marriage had been floundering ever since she left a part-time job to open her own interior decorating firm, Harriet was able to come up with plenty of answers to that question. And when she finally confronted Larry, his accusations confirmed her conclusions.

Perhaps assuming that the best defense was a good offense, Larry made it quite clear that he considered his infidelity to pale in comparison with Harriet's wrongdoing. She was more interested in her career than her marriage, he told her. "And I could see how he thought that," Harriet explains. "I *had* been spending a lot of time and energy getting my business off the ground. And I did think my work outside the home was a lot more exciting than cleaning and cooking and carpooling and making nice to his colleagues at company parties. I really had been neglecting him."

What's more, Larry, whose own career in banking was stagnating, accused Harriet of "rubbing his nose" in her success. From his point of view, her enthusiasm about her work and her accounts of the recognition she was receiving were attacks on his manhood. In addition, because she was often too tired or preoccupied to muster interest in lovemaking, their sex life "stunk," he said. Maybe he was wrong to have an affair, he admitted, but she drove him to it.

Although hearing your spouse blame you for his or her extra-marital affair might make you angry, Harriet took Larry's criticisms to heart, and because there was an element of truth in them, she assumed full responsibility for his infidelity. When their gut-wrenching conversation ended, Larry promised to end his affair and Harriet promised to be a better wife and lover.

For months she stretched herself paper thin, striving to be the perfect mate while continuing to run her demanding business. She canceled her own plans in order to attend business functions with Larry and maintained a frantic pace at the office so that she would not have to bring work home with her at night. She arranged for romantic candlelit dinners, paraded around in sexy lingerie, and made love whenever Larry was in the mood—even when she was not.

"I literally drove myself crazy trying to be what he said he wanted me to be," Harriet sighs. "I ran myself ragged trying to make up for not being a good wife in the past. I guess it was too late to repair the damage I'd done, or maybe I just couldn't cut it. All I know is that I failed."

Harriet came to that conclusion when she learned that Larry had resumed his affair. "Then I made the biggest mistake of my life." She shudders, recalling how she stuffed Larry's things into two garbage bags, went to the bank, marched into his lover's office, and dumped Larry's things on her desk.

"I told her, 'If you want him, you can have him,'" Harriet continues. "Then Larry showed up and I started screaming at him, causing this horrible scene that everyone in the building couldn't help hearing."

As tears begin to flow, Harriet says, "So you see this whole damn thing really is my fault. If I had been a good wife to begin with, he would never have had an affair. If I had just put my business on the back burner and paid more attention to him, I could have won him back. And I should never have flipped out the way I did.

"Because of my stupidity, at the custody hearing, he'll have an office full of witnesses to swear I'm crazy, incompetent to raise my own kids. And maybe he's right. Maybe I'm as self-centered and cold-hearted as he says I am. I just don't know anymore."

Having moved out of denial soon after she was hurt, Harriet proceeded directly to the *self-blame stage* of the forgiveness process. Focusing on what *she* might have done to cause the problem helped her explain *why* she had been hurt and showed her what she could do to remedy the problem and avoid being hurt again. However, as is always the case when we blame ourselves for the injuries and injustices that other people perpetrated, the conclusions Harriet drew were inaccurate, and therefore the actions she took were ineffective. She got hurt again, and again she blamed herself. Indeed, she got trapped in a vicious cycle of self-blame and self-punishment, so that she now spends most of her time thinking about the painful, unexpected turn her life has taken and berating herself for what she believes she did to bring about her own pain and confusion.

Self-Blame

When we leave the denial stage, we take a giant step forward toward healing and forgiveness, but we also come face to face with realities that are not only painful but incomprehensible as well. Indeed, our painful past experiences may threaten some of our most fundamental beliefs about how we, other people, and our lives are supposed to be.

"Never in my worst nightmares did I imagine something like this happening to me," Harriet says. "Husbands may have cheated on their wives for centuries, but I never believed mine would cheat on me. Two out of three marriages may end in divorce, but mine was supposed to last forever. And fighting over custody, trying to compete with Larry for our children's love? It's just mind-boggling. It doesn't make sense."

No, it does not make sense. It never does when the people you love, trust, or depend upon hurt you, betray your trust, or let you down. In fact, the state of confusion that you find yourself in after being hurt is as difficult to cope with as the pain. That is why, in the self-blame stage of the forgiveness process, you attempt to comprehend the incomprehensible and find reasons for the unreasonable by assuming full responsibility for the hurtful things other people did to you.

"Why Is This Happening to Me?"

While in the self-blame stage, you decide that bad things happened to you because:

- you did something to make them happen;
- you were not good enough in some way;
- you did not do what you could have done to prevent them from happening;
- you set yourself up to be hurt by expecting too much or ignoring the signs of impending disaster.

You hold yourself accountable for other people's actions, absolving them of all responsibility for extramarital affairs, sexual or physical abuse, ridicule, lies, or, in the case of Marcy's parents, getting drunk.

According to Marcy, when her parents were sober, they were "the most normal, loving parents in the world, and everything was great." While under the influence of alcohol, however, nothing Marcy's parents did made sense. "They'd laugh at things that weren't funny," Marcy recalls. "Like a dinner that was burned to a crisp or smashing up the car or one of them falling down the steps. Or they would suddenly lose their tempers, shouting, cursing, and throwing things at each other and us. They would 'forget' to pick us up from school or to buy groceries or to come home at all. They would show up at school functions drunk or pass out on the bathroom floor or leave us sitting in the car for hours while they stopped in at a bar for a 'quick one.'"

By the time she was ten, Marcy had lived through an infinite number of these Jekyll and Hyde transitions. She had seen her mother reach for the liquor bottle whenever anything upset her in any way. She had heard her father's tirades about the "upsetting" circumstances that drove him to drink. She had figured out that her parents could not be trusted to act like normal parents when they were drunk and that they drank when they were upset. Therefore, she concluded, "If I made sure that nothing upset them, my parents wouldn't drink, and all of us could live a normal life."

In addition to holding yourself accountable for other people's actions, when you think about old injuries and injustices from a self-blaming point of view, you focus exclusively on what *you* did to deserve them or did not do to prevent them. And even when you cannot find a specific thing that you said or did to prompt the person who hurt you to act the way he or she did, you may still believe that you were at fault. You may be convinced that something about you drew that painful experience to you, as Suzanne was.

> During those six years when my father was sexually molesting me, I never thought that I had actually done anything to make the abuse happen. But I did believe there was something about me that attracted his unwanted attention to me.
>
> At six years of age, all I really knew about myself was what my parents and other adults told me, and the only thing I heard them say about me was "Oh, what a pretty little girl you are." No one ever mentioned that I might be smart or good or creative or anything else except pretty, so I figured that maybe incest was what happened to pretty little kids. "If only I was not pretty," I thought, "then my father would not be sexually abusing me."
>
> Understandably, I spent a good deal of my childhood wishing that I looked different, that I could wake up one morning and not be pretty anymore. Once the abuse itself stopped, I stopped worrying so much about my appearance. Yet for years to come I remained convinced that there was something inherently wrong with me, that I was the proverbial "bad seed" and would perpetually find myself in some kind of trouble. Whenever anything unsettling or unexpected happened to me, I thought that I had once again drawn that experience to me, that by virtue of some flaw I couldn't even name, I had deserved to be hurt or disappointed or betrayed again.

Unable to believe, among other things, that bad things do sometimes happen to good people, we *blame ourselves*—and only ourselves—for what happened, even when it could not have been caused by us.

"This Wouldn't Have Happened If..."

The urge to blame ourselves for getting hurt is so powerful that victims of violent crimes—selected at random by criminals who were intent on raping, robbing, or mugging any available target—frequently feel responsible for being victimized. "If only I hadn't walked down that street, then this would not have happened to me," they say. "If only I had left the office earlier or parked closer or worn different clothes. If only I had fought or screamed, or had not tried to fight and kept my mouth shut." Of course, victims of violent crimes are not the only ones who use this sort of logic.

Trapped by an unplanned pregnancy, drained by the demands of medical school, having to be supported by his parents and in-laws and even then barely making ends meet, Warren's father was less than thrilled with his life, and it showed. Warren saw it. He saw a man who was cold and distant, who constantly criticized and argued with his wife, who was rarely home and, when he was, paid little attention to his son. Warren saw all of this and thought it was his fault. "If only I had never been born," he thought, "then my mom and dad would be happy." What's more, when he was treated like the "invisible kid" or "shooed away like a mosquito," Warren was hurt and believed he deserved to be. "If only I was a better son," he thought, "then my father would love me."

"If only I had not made that scene," Harriet said, "then Larry wouldn't be trying to turn our kids against me."

"If only I had told my mother," Suzanne said years after her father's sexual abuse had ended, "then she would have made my father stop molesting me."

"If only I had been more on top of things," Marcy said, "then I could have kept my parents from drinking."

As you can see from these examples, "if only" is the calling card of the self-blame stage.

If only you had . . .

said no;
kept your mouth shut;
trusted your instincts;
been a better son, daughter, spouse, lover, parent, or person.

If only you had *not* . . .

expected so much;
been so naive or trusting or needy;
kept your mouth shut;
married so young;
been so fat, thin, poor, dumb, pretty, or sensitive.

Then bad things would not have happened to *you*.

These statements—and we are sure you can think of many more—represent what you believe you *could* have done to avoid being hurt. Some contain an element of truth. Suzanne, for instance, could have told her mother about the abuse, just as Harriet could have chosen not to create a scene at the bank where Larry worked, or you could have said ''no'' when the circumstances warranted it. Other ''if only'' statements do not have so much as a grain of truth to them. Nothing Marcy could have done would have controlled her parents' drinking, for instance, and being poor or pretty or marrying young may actually have nothing whatsoever to do with why you were hurt.

What's more, only in retrospect do you see what you could have done. Although you may often wish that you knew then what you know now, you did not. You knew what you knew and did what you did. But that idea will not console you while you are in this stage of the healing process. Self-blame convinces you not only that you *could* have conducted yourself differently, but that you *should have*.

''I Should Have Seen It Coming.''

Self-blame is almost as automatic as denial because we were programmed from early childhood to anticipate danger and circumvent it. Well-meaning adults offered us the benefit of their experiences. They told us, ''Don't touch that or you'll get burned,'' ''Don't climb that tree, you'll fall and break your arm,'' ''Don't run in the house, you'll trip and hurt yourself.'' Trying to protect us from harm, the grown-ups in our lives always seemed to be two steps ahead of us, warning us about the ways we could get hurt and leaving the indelible impression that by being vigilant and behaving in certain ways, we could control external events—from getting burned to catching colds.

And when adults said things like ''Don't make noise or you'll upset your father,'' ''Don't dress like that, people will think you're cheap,'' or ''Don't wear your heart on your sleeve or people will take advantage of you,'' they convinced you that you could anticipate and control other people's reactions to you as well.

''Every time my father pulled one of his stunts,'' Mark says, ''I felt like I had been dunked in ice-cold water. Everything would be going great. We'd be getting along, getting all of these presents from him or getting ready to go someplace or do something we'd been looking forward to for weeks, and then whammo! it was all over.'' Mark's father would lose another job, go on another tirade about Mark's uncle Dan, or find another way that someone was slighting him or his family—and his children would suffer because of it.

"I always felt like I should have seen it coming," Mark recalls. "That I should have known he would find a way to ruin things again. I turned it all around so that it wasn't his fault for being the way he was, by *my* fault for expecting him to be any other way."

As a result of your programming, when you are hurt—regardless of how you are hurt or by whom—like Mark, you automatically tell yourself that you *should have seen it coming and done something to prevent it.*

How Self-Blame Serves You

When you look back on painful past experiences from the vantage point of the self-blame stage, the things you could have done (but did not do) jump out at you, while other aspects of the experience fade into the background. Indeed, while in this stage all you can see is that you were too foolish, too stupid, too naive, or too trusting to avoid being hurt or that something inherently "bad" about you led to the mistreatment and unwanted attention you received.

Although this is obviously a painful point of view, it did serve you at one time. It gave you something that you needed—an explanation for what happened to you. Although that explanation was at best inaccurate and in some cases patently untrue, it was *less* threatening and *less* painful than other explanations you might have considered.

"It Couldn't Be Their *Fault."*

Self-blame served you because, at certain times in your life, it was *safer and more comfortable* to believe that you brought pain upon yourself than to hold the person who hurt you accountable for his or her actions, especially if you loved the person who hurt you and were young or felt dependent on that person at the time you were hurt.

For instance, although Marcy made a valiant effort to keep her parents from attending a countywide science fair in which her fourth-grade science project was entered, Marcy's mother insisted upon being present when her "genius daughter won first prize." So drunk that she staggered when she walked, Marcy's mother drove Marcy to the fair, stopped to drag her father out of a bar so that he could be there, too, and then interrupted Marcy's presentation to the judges. Attempting to present a more persuasive sales pitch, she rambled incoherently and then stumbled, crashing into the card table that held Marcy's project. Her project—and her pride—destroyed, Marcy ran to the nearest ladies' room, where she cried until there were no tears left in her.

Under those circumstances, you might assume that Marcy's anger was directed toward her mother, but it was not. In order to be angry at her mother, Marcy had to hold her mother accountable for her own actions, and Marcy could not do that. If she did, she would also have to acknowledge that her mother was a drunk who could not be trusted to provide the safety, security, and love that Marcy needed—that all children need and expect from their parents.

So Marcy reminded herself that her mother had been proud of her, that she had only been trying to help. Her mother loved her, Marcy told herself, and would never knowingly do anything to hurt her—which meant that the humiliating scene could not have been her mother's fault.

"I blamed myself," Marcy explains. "I should have handled things differently from the start. I should have realized that trying to keep her away from the science fair would end up upsetting her. If I hadn't been so selfish, so caught up in wanting to win that stupid prize, I wouldn't have entered the competition and had no reason to keep her away. She wouldn't have gotten upset or gotten drunk or done what she did."

Using logic that was undeniably convoluted, Marcy found a way to blame herself for what happened to her at the science fair and, by doing so, maintained the illusion that her mother was trustworthy, loving, and "normal." Her image of the person she loved remained intact, and everything in her world was the way it was supposed to be—except for Marcy herself. But that was okay. Marcy believed that if she tried hard enough, she could "fix" herself, and that once she did, everything would be "fine" again.

Although you may not have gone to the extreme lengths Marcy did, chances are that self-blame once served you in this way, too.

"It Won't Happen Again."

Self-blame also served you by restoring your sense of control and showing you how you might be able to save yourself from additional pain and heartache.

Mark still shivers when he recalls the time he was eight years old and made the mistake of "mouthing off" to his dad. When in a rage, Mark's father slapped him, then picked him up and tossed him out of the house. "If you like Uncle Dan so much, go live with him, because I don't want an ungrateful spoiled brat like you in my family," Mark's father shouted before slamming the door and locking it.

Mark remembers how he pounded on the door, begging for someone to let him in; how his sisters watched him through their bedroom window until his father's huge hands grabbed their collars and pulled them away; how he sat on the stoop for as long as he could and then huddled in the car until nightfall when his mother came to get him.

"The whole time I was out there," he says, "I prayed. I begged God to make my father take me back. I promised to be good, to never say mean things to my father again. I swore I would never be ungrateful, that I would be thankful for whatever I got and not feel disappointed—ever. If someone would just come get me and let me back in the house, I swore I would never let anything like what happened happen again."

Although at the time you were hurt your top priority was to stop the pain, running a close second was your desire not to be hurt like that again. Like Mark, you struck a bargain with God or vowed to yourself that you would do anything it took to prevent bad things from happening to you again. And once you did that, you regained something all of us lose when we are broadsided by incomprehensible injuries and injustices—our sense of control.

At the time you were hurt and for years afterward, you believed that putting even part of the blame where it belonged—on the person who hurt you—meant that you were at that person's mercy. He or she could hurt you again, and again there would be nothing you could do about it. On the other hand, if *you* were to blame, you were also in control. You could also more easily control your own thoughts, feelings, and behavior; *your* expectations and *your* temper; or the amount and kind of information *you* revealed—thus controlling the ammunition other people could use against you.

In addition, the idea that you somehow made the painful experience happen counteracts the powerlessness you felt while it was happening. Because you were young or caught off guard, because the person who hurt you was physically stronger than you were or had a psychological advantage over you or simply did something you did not expect him or her to do, you were indeed powerless to stop the hurt from happening. And powerlessness is terrifying. In fact, it is often the most terrifying aspect of painful past experiences. If you allowed yourself to dwell on your own powerlessness, you would no doubt live your life in a constant state of terror, anxiously expecting to be victimized again and again. On the other hand, by concluding that "I made it happen," and believing that "I can keep it from happening again," you stopped feeling like a helpless victim of circumstances, at least temporarily.

And the truth of the matter is that self-blame *is* only a temporary, stopgap measure for coping with pain and confusion. You must move beyond it in order to truly heal your wounds and get on with your life. Unfortunately, for many of you this is far more easily said than done. Like Harriet, because of the choices you made and the opinion of yourself that you developed, you may find yourself trapped in a vicious cycle of guilt, shame, and self-punishment.

Getting Stuck in Self-Blame

Think about the bad things that have happened to you, the old wounds you would like to heal and the unfinished business you would like to complete. What do *you* believe you did to deserve those injuries or injustices? What do you think you could have done to prevent them? What do you believe you should have known at the time you were hurt?

Clarification Strategy Number 5:
Getting Unstuck

After you think about the above questions, take a few minutes to write a list of statements that *you* used or still use to blame yourself for what happened to you, statements that begin with:

If only I had . . .
If only I had not . . .
I should have . . .

Although you wholeheartedly believe those statements, and even though they did serve you temporarily, they were *never* the real reasons for your painful past experiences. As a result, the things, based on these beliefs, that you did to avoid being hurt again rarely, if ever, worked. Whether you chose to change some aspect of yourself, attempted to control every imaginable element of your environment, or negated your own needs and became a martyr, your efforts to prevent bad things from happening were doomed to fail. Each time they did, each time you were hurt again, lost control again, or felt powerless again, you had an opportunity to explain your circumstances differently, to recognize that you did not bear the sole responsibility for what happened to you.

If you did not do that, if instead you became more convinced of your own shortcomings and tried even harder to be "good enough," then you got stuck in the self-blame stage.

Tunnel Vision

People who get stuck in self-blame develop tunnel vision. They pursue, sometimes obsessively, a single goal—to fix the flaw they believe originally caused their unhappiness. For instance, Patricia, in addition to adopting her distorted version of the Golden Rule, blamed her unhappy childhood on being overweight. This was certainly a logical conclusion, for no one could call her "Fatty Patty" if she were not fat. However, her obsession with losing weight, which began in her teens, went beyond wanting to make sure that she was not ridiculed anymore. Today she is at least ten pounds *under*weight but still tells herself that she could meet the right man, be taken more seriously at work, have more energy to get things done, and remedy all other ills if she could just lose another five pounds. Having developed bulimia while in college, Patricia still binges and then purges by using laxatives and vomiting several times each day. She also exercises compulsively. She is stuck in self-blame.

You may be, too, if you are still trying to "fix" the part of yourself you believe drew pain to you; telling yourself that you could be happy today if only you were thinner, more muscular, kinder, quieter, or had more money in the bank; thinking about those flaws at least several times a day and any time you are under stress; or if your efforts to be good enough in those areas interfere with other aspects of your life.

Perfectionism

People who hang on to the idea that they should have seen injuries or injustices coming and done something to avoid them frequently become perfectionists. For instance, Marcy, who is no longer living under the influence of her parents' alcoholism, still operates from the belief that nothing bad will happen to her as long as she does everything right and as long as everything in her world conforms to her expectations. What's more, whenever things do not go according to plan or she makes the slightest mistake, Marcy still feels guilty, ashamed, and as if she and the world are completely out of control. Sometimes she gets so upset with herself that she wishes she could "lock herself in a dark room and never come out." She is stuck in self-blame.

You may be too if you:

- panic or feel extremely anxious in response to situations that are beyond your control or to your own mistakes;
- replay certain scenes over and over again in your mind to figure out what went wrong;
- frequently get depressed, remind yourself of your previous failures, and find that you cannot concentrate on anything but what you did wrong; or
- feel stressed out and suffer from headaches, ulcers, colitis, or other stress-related illnesses.

Feeling Responsible for Everyone and Everything

People stuck in self-blame often go from blaming themselves for a specific situation to blaming themselves for everything, from believing they could have prevented their own pain to believing that they should prevent anyone from ever experiencing pain.

For instance, when Alison, the only child of doting parents, was very young, she came to believe that she was responsible for her parents' happiness. "I was the center of their universe," she recalls. "Every time I turned around they were saying, 'You're so wonderful. You make me so happy. Nothing makes me as happy as my little angel does.'" Obviously, hearing such things was not what hurt Alison, although it did set the stage for how she reacted when she got hurt.

Alison's father, an exceptionally talented musician, was a manic-depressive, and when he was depressed Alison suffered with him, because no matter how hard she tried she could not make him happy. Consequently, when her father committed suicide, Alison, who was twelve at the time, believed that he took his own life because she had failed him.

"My mother did all the right things," Alison explains. "She even took me to a therapist. But I never told the therapist or anyone else that I felt responsible. I was too ashamed to say it."

As a result, Alison got stuck in self-blame. Believing that her father killed himself because she failed to make him happy, Alison even now becomes extremely anxious whenever she encounters people who are unhappy or circumstances that might make someone unhappy. At work, at home, or while socializing, she cannot relax until she is absolutely certain that everyone around her is comfortable and satisfied. She suffers terribly when her co-workers argue or her husband has a bad day. She cannot even enjoy a meal unless everyone who is dining with her enjoys theirs.

Like Alison, you too may be stuck in self-blame, especially if you feel responsible for everyone and everything; feel unhappy when your spouse, parents, or children feel unhappy; feel compelled to do something to make them happy; constantly try to "fix" things, gloss over unpleasant realities, or apologize for things you couldn't possibly have caused—like the weather, power failures, the flu bug, and of course, other people's words and actions.

Martyrdom

Caroline's day begins at 5:00 A.M. when she helps her son with his paper route and keeps on helping for the rest of the day. She helps her daughter and four foster children get ready for school. She helps her husband relax when he gets home from working the graveyard shift at a nearby factory. She helps other foster parents with their problems, helps her siblings and neighbors by baby-sitting on a moment's notice. She carpools, cleans house for her aging mother, and from dawn until dusk takes care of anyone and everyone—except herself. She makes lovely clothes for the kids but wears the same shapeless smocks she has been wearing for years. She has time to listen to everyone's troubles but no time to see a doctor about her arthritis. She simply does not believe that she deserves attention or has a right to have anything for herself at all.

Why does Caroline bend over backward to meet everyone else's needs while negating and neglecting her own? Because she is still atoning for a sin she believes she committed almost thirty years ago—when she called the police because her father was beating her mother. Her father packed up and moved out the next morning. His wife and five children never saw him again. From that moment on, Caroline felt responsible for every hardship her family suffered, and to make up for what her mother and siblings lost when her father left, she became the glue that held her family together. There was nothing she would not do for them, nothing she would not sacrifice, and there still isn't. Stuck in self-blame, Caroline became a martyr.

You may have too if you neglect yourself, make countless sacrifices, and put everyone else's needs before your own; are everyone's earth mother, their sounding board, or the superperson who tries to do it all; or if you say "yes" to every request you receive, no matter how it inconveniences or overburdens you.

Internalized Oppression

Warren, who believed that his father would love him and that his parents would not argue if he were just a better son, devoted himself to making his father proud of him. He studied hard and excelled academically, went out for sports, starred in school plays, won citizenship awards, and gave his father impressive handmade gifts—none of which made his father show more interest in him. And as a result Warren never felt satisfied with or proud of his own accomplishments. Indeed, because they did not earn him his father's love, achievements that would have boosted anyone else's self-esteem diminished his. He saw only that he had not been good enough—again.

Although Warren left the self-blame stage long ago, the "not good enough" label stayed with him for the rest of his life, just as your negative opinions of yourself will stay with you if you let them.

Self-blame destroys self-esteem. Each day spent blaming yourself for pain from the past is a day spent despising yourself and reminding yourself that you do not measure up. You cannot appreciate your own uniqueness. Indeed, like Sandy, who saw herself as worthless and unlovable because her mother abandoned her soon after she was born, you may wish that you were someone else entirely or could have someone else's life. You do not take risks, for you are convinced that you would only fail or be disappointed. You rarely if ever feel a sense of accomplishment. You isolate yourself and underestimate yourself and neglect yourself. All of this further diminishes your sense of self-worth, perpetuating the pain you felt that first time when someone hurt you and you convinced yourself that it was entirely your fault.

The person who once hurt you is not hurting you now. He or she may not be in your life any longer and may not even be alive today. But the hurt is very much alive, because *you* are keeping it alive and *you* are hurting yourself with the things you tell yourself about yourself. You tell yourself that you are fat, stupid, ugly, lazy, incompetent, unlovable, worthless, and more. You punish yourself by repeating the messages that the people who hurt you conveyed to you through their actions as well as their words. You internalized those messages and incorporated them into your identity. As Ann Neitlich puts it in her book, *Building Bridges: Women's and Men's Liberation,* you became your own oppressor.

Thus, Marcy does not need her parents to create a chaotic or humiliating scene in order to feel panicky and out of control. She creates her own pain and anxiety each time she makes a mistake and tells herself, "You can't do anything right," or encounters unexpected delays or interruptions and tells herself, "You blew it. You should have known this would happen."

And Mark does not need his father to "ruin things" for him. He ruins them himself each time he tells himself, "Don't get your hopes up. You'll only be disappointed."

And Alison does not have to see her depressed father in order to feel like a failure. She reminds herself of it whenever anyone in her world is unhappy or dissatisfied.

Having picked up where the people who hurt you left off, you too will wear your "not good enough" label, damage your self-esteem, and perpetuate your pain—until you extract yourself from the self-blame stage.

Moving Out of Self-Blame

To move closer to healing and forgiveness, you simply must stop blaming—and punishing—yourself for the hurtful things other people did to you. Of course, this does not mean that you should deny any responsibility you *did* have. If you did play a part—by not telling anyone that you were being abused, for instance, or cheating on a spouse who found out and left you or if you never said an encouraging word to your son, who, as an adult, refuses to speak to you—then you can regret *that part* if you want to. But before you waste another moment of your life regretting anything, you must sort through the self-blame. Yes, you may find some truth in it, but rarely will you be as guilty as you think you are.

Clarification Strategy Number 6:
Moving Out

Get out the list of "if only" and "I should have" statements you prepared earlier in the getting unstuck strategy on page 110 and take an objective look at them. Really try to detach yourself. In fact, you might want to imagine that the hurt happened to someone else and that "other" person is telling you about that experience and using those self-blaming statements.

From this objective observer point of view, ask yourself, "Which statements are simply *not* true?" For instance, Suzanne's belief, "If only I hadn't been such a pretty little girl, my father would not have molested me," falls into this category. Her father did not molest her because of any one reason. Not because she was pretty and not because there was something about her that drew bad things to her, as she had also feared. In fact, her father's actions were no reflection on her whatsoever. *Strike the patently untrue statements from your list.*

Then ask yourself, "Which statements reveal that I have assumed responsibility for other people's actions, actions that were, in reality, beyond my control?" Marcy, for instance, felt responsible for her parents' drinking—but that was their responsibility, not hers. And Caroline held herself accountable for the fact that her father abandoned his family—but he was an adult and *chose* to leave. She did not *make* him make that choice. Likewise, you did not make your father beat your mother or cause your parents' divorce or force pills down your son's throat and turn him into a drug addict. *Strike these statements from your list, too.*

"Which statements reflect circumstances or aspects of myself that I couldn't possibly change or influence, especially at the time I was hurt?" Strike any statements that refer to things like poverty, your race, religion, or gender, your size at the time you were hurt, not trusting, not falling in love, being older when you got married, and so on. They were existing conditions that you did not create.

Any items that remain on your list probably have an element of truth to them. Yet you must sort through those statements, too. Which have you *distorted* by assigning yourself a larger role than you actually played? Which have you turned into *general indictments* of yourself—for instance, taking "I did something that I now realize was stupid" and turning it into "I am a stupid person"? Which are *reasonable today,* making sense to you in retrospect, but which required insights you did not have—and in all likelihood could not have had—at the time you were hurt?

To answer that question, Suzanne recently visited the town where she grew up.

> I suppose I wanted to see, as an adult, the place where *it* happened. I knocked on the door of my old house, explained to the new owners that I had once lived there, and they let me look around.
>
> Then I crossed the street and went to see Estelle, who still lived where she had lived when I was a child. Though I wanted to tell her why I was visiting and what had happened to me so many years ago, I did not. But I suddenly realized then that being a lifelong child advocate who had been aware of child abuse long before it was publicized in the media, Estelle would have understood what was happening while it was happening. I realized too that if I had told her, she would have helped me and I would have avoided decades of guilt, shame, and heartache.
>
> But I had not told her, and as we drove away from her house, I couldn't help reminding myself of what I could have done but did not do. Tears welled up in my eyes, and I once again felt stupid and ashamed.

Suzanne had temporarily returned to the self-blame stage. But she did not linger there or get stuck, because she had learned that *it simply is not useful to blame herself now for what she could have or should have done in the past*. And you must learn this as well, finally accepting that you cannot do anything about those things now— except use them to stop repeating the past. You can change the behaviors or attitudes that actually contributed to the problem by not keeping secrets anymore or persistently talking about your feelings instead of bottling them up inside you or not trying so hard to make other people do things your way. Even more important, you can become aware of how self-blame operates in your life today, how old guilt and shame overflow into the present, and what you do or do not do today because of it.

Think about that now. What have you done and what do you continue to do to change or control the aspects of yourself that you blame for old injuries and injustices? Under what circumstances and in what ways do you assume responsibility for and try to control other people's actions? What are you sacrificing because you believe that you are not good enough to deserve more? What do you tell yourself about the kind of person you are, and how do you punish yourself?

Does any of this serve you any longer? Is it really helping you in any way? We suspect that it is not. We suspect that blaming, berating, and belittling yourself is only perpetuating your pain. Fortunately, anything you have done because of self-blame you can stop doing. You can take some time and make an effort to *forgive yourself* for your mistakes and your humanness. You can bid farewell to the self-blame stage in much the same way that you exited the denial stage—with a letter. Moving through this stage is a process, just as it is part of the process to move from the denial stage. Perhaps this letter will advance the process by giving you some insight into how you've been blaming yourself.

Clarification Strategy Number 7:
The Self-Blame Letter

Take out a sheet of paper, date it as you would a letter, and open the letter with the following salutation:

Dear Self-Blaming Part of Me,

Then, addressing the voice inside you that berates and criticizes you, apologize briefly for the actions or inactions that were truly your fault, the things that you did or did not do that could have changed the circumstances that wound up hurting you. Only refer to the "if only" and "I should have" statements that you did *not* eliminate while completing the earlier strategy. Do not apologize for anything that really was not your fault in the first place.

Next, in bold, capital letters, write, BUT I HAVE PUNISHED MYSELF ENOUGH, followed by what you have done to punish yourself or atone for your "sins." If you would like to, you can fill this section of your letter with sentences beginning with "I have spent enough time..."

When you have said all that you want to say, end your letter with one or more of the following affirmations:

- I used to believe that I deserved to be hurt, but now I know that I did not deserve it.
- I used to believe that I made the hurt happen, but now I know that it was not entirely my fault, that some of what happened to me I was not responsible for at all.
- I used to believe that I had to carry this load of guilt and shame for the rest of my life, but now I know that I have punished myself long enough, and now I can leave the self-blame stage.

Although this letter, like your efforts to sort out what was and was not your responsibility, moves you closer to the exit door of the self-blame stage, there is still one more step you must take. You must begin to treat yourself differently than you did while punishing yourself for the pain other people caused you.

Taking Care of Your Inner Child

[People have] to learn to heal themselves, to take that damaged little child inside of them and make it better. Most people are walking around with a damaged child inside of them. Sometimes, when my husband and I have an argument, I get a flash of what he was like when he was five years old; I can see that this isn't about what is happening now. It's some old memory tape he's got going in his mind with his mother or his father or his sisters. A lot of people go through life beating themselves up the same way they were beaten up.

—actress/producer Marlo Thomas

The vulnerable, frightened child you were (or felt like) when you were hurt lives on inside of you. This inner child represents both the little kid you used to be and the part of you that can still be playful, stubborn, silly, and incredibly wise. Your inner child knows what you need to feel safe, secure, and loved. It knows and suffers when those needs are not being met. If you listen to your inner child, you know when it is time to take care of yourself instead of sacrificing yourself to take care of others; when you need to slow down instead of running around like a chicken with its head cut off; when you need to cry or be comforted or cut loose and have some fun.

While in the self-blame stage, however, you do not listen to the child inside you. Indeed, you go out of your way *not* to hear what it has to say. You negate your inner child, just as you were negated— when you were a child or when you were hurt as an adult. As Marlo Thomas put it, you beat yourself up in the same way you were beaten up by others. Like parents who respond to their crying children by hitting them and saying, "Now you have something to cry about," you give your inner child guilt, shame, and punishment when it needs love, attention, and nurturing.

As you work toward leaving the self-blame stage, you must begin to take care of your inner child instead of neglecting or abusing it. You must listen to the part of yourself that tells you that you feel sad, scared, or abandoned and comfort that vulnerable child inside of you.

How do you do that? Well, how would you comfort a real child who was hurting? To start with, you could listen and pay attention to what he had to say, trying to understand what he was feeling and why. Then you might:

- make motherly, nurturing statements like "It's okay. It will be all right. I'll help you through this";
- give him a little gift;
- take him to a place he finds fun, peaceful, or relaxing;
- give him time to himself;
- let him cry;
- let his household chores wait while he took a nap or went for a walk or drew a picture;
- assure him that he was loved by you and remind him of the qualities that make him a unique, lovable, capable, worthwhile human being;
- make sure that he knows that the hurtful thing that happened to him was not "all his fault."

To finally let yourself "off the hook" and stop perpetuating your pain, you must do these very things *for yourself,* right down to allowing yourself to experience the joy, playfulness, and spontaneity that you may have missed during your real childhood. You finally leave self-blame by taking care of the hurt and vulnerable inner child that you have been punishing for so long.

As you did when you left denial, when you leave the self-blame stage, you move another step closer to healing and forgiveness. You have made progress because you are no longer:

- blaming yourself for what happened to you;
- assuming responsibility for other people's actions or circumstances that were or are beyond your control;
- berating yourself for what you did wrong or failed to do;
- punishing yourself for not being good enough.

As Virginia Satir put it, you realize that "you are not responsible for the rain that falls, but only for your reaction to it," and that reaction no longer needs to be a self-punishing one.

Once you let go of self-blame, however, you also relinquish the illusion of power and control it gave you. For years and years, self-blame has masked your feelings of helplessness. Once you remove that mask, you begin to recognize that, whether or not you should have been able to, you *were not* able to prevent the hurt from happening. You were powerless to stop it and were at the mercy of the people who hurt you. Acknowledging this invariably helps to catapult you into the next, decidedly uncomfortable, frequently self-destructive stage of the healing process—the victim stage.

CHAPTER SEVEN

THE VICTIM STAGE

I reached a point where I no longer believed that being pretty or anything else about me drew my painful past experiences to me. Nothing I did made my father molest me. He did not have to do what he did. But he did do it—and because of him, my life was a mess. I was as powerless to change my life as I had been to prevent the abuse, I now thought. The situation was hopeless, I believed. I was not responsible for what he had done—or anything else. I had been victimized, and that was reason enough not to do anything more than just get by.

Suzanne had left the self-blame stage and arrived at the *victim stage* of the forgiveness process. She reached it after her counselor convinced her that she could get rid of pain only by going through it, after she sat down and began the most difficult but ultimately most rewarding work she had ever done, and after she had joined an incest survivors group. First intending to sit with her mouth shut and be helped through osmosis, she soon began participating fully and was even able to admit to them that she too had survived incest. Yes, Suzanne had begun to heal. But, as everyone does, once Suzanne hit the victim stage, she frequently felt that she was moving farther away from inner peace, instead of closer to it:

When I finally got in touch with my pain, I wallowed in it,

feeling more justified than ever about doing the bare minimum necessary to exist. Who could blame me for not being successful or completely on top of situations, or for coming home from work, plopping down on the sofa, and falling asleep in front of the television? Having had such a terrible childhood, it was a miracle that I could even hold down a job and keep my head above water, I thought.

I went from denying my experience to paying attention to it twenty-four hours a day and from keeping my thoughts and feelings bottled up inside me to talking about them over and over again to anyone who would listen. Incest became my identity. The most important aspect of my self-image was what had happened to me between the ages of five and twelve. That was all there was to me. If I tried to acknowledge any other facet of myself, I reminded myself that I was not very good at being a mother or a teacher or a friend. And how could I be? I had been scarred and damaged. No one should expect much from me, I believed, and I certainly expected very little from myself. In a near constant state of depression and despair, I was all but convinced that my lot in life was to be miserable.

The Victim Stage

As it was for Suzanne, the time that you spend in the victim stage is likely to be the most painful and self-destructive part of your journey to healing and forgiveness. No matter how you look at it, the victim stage is not a pretty sight. And while you are in it, you will definitely *feel* stuck, stymied, trapped, and as if nothing about you or your life will ever improve.

Like Harriet, Craig was hurt by his spouse's infidelities. Toward the end of their eight-year marriage, Craig's wife had numerous affairs and made no effort to hide them. "She had flings with guys I considered my friends," he explains. "Guys I did business with, guys who went to the same health club I did. For a while there, it seemed like everywhere I went, I ran into someone who had slept with my wife." The couple separated and reconciled several times before Craig discovered his wife in their bed with another man and left for good.

After several days of "intense pain," Craig went into denial. Thinking that he had to put the past behind him and "just get on with it," he made several drastic changes simultaneously—giving up a lucrative business, moving from the Midwest to New York City, into an apartment that he shared with four other men, and enrolling in law school. "I guess I thought that if I changed everything about me and started over as a completely new man, I would forget about my marriage and also make sure I never went through anything like that again," Craig explains.

As you might expect, the drastic changes Craig made did not heal his wounds. Halfway through his first semester at school, he plunged into the victim stage. "I couldn't stop thinking about what my wife did to me and how messed up everything was because of her," he recalls. "I couldn't stop thinking about how messed up things were, period. I was thirty-two years old and worse off financially than I had ever been. I went to school every day, where I was treated like a lamebrained eighteen-year-old, went back to my tiny room in an overcrowded apartment, studied until I couldn't stand it anymore, and then drank until I was sedated enough to go to sleep. While I was drinking I'd go over everything again and again, and every day something else would happen to remind me of how bad off I was. I was stuck in school, with a six-year commitment to the navy, with no lover and no hope. There was no way out."

Like Suzanne, Craig was plagued by two of the most devastating of all feelings—helplessness and hopelessness—and at some point in your healing process, you probably will be, too. All you will want to do is lick your wounds and feel sorry for yourself. You will retreat from the world and the demands of daily living, give in, give up, and have a good old-fashioned pity party. The victim stage of the forgiveness process is where you go to do that. Everyone, without exception, visits this stage at least once, because anyone who has ever been hurt has been *victimized*.

From Victimization to "Victimhood"

Victimization describes what happened *to* you. A specific event or series of events—happenings that were beyond your control at the time they occurred—may have hurt you, terrified you, or took something that you needed away from you. Whether you were sexually molested by a baby-sitter, neglected or humiliated by alcoholic parents, lied to or betrayed by a friend, or hurt in any other way, because you suffered and were powerless to prevent your own suffering, you were by definition victimized.

Once we have been victimized, we never forget it. The sense of helplessness and hopelessness that we felt at that time is filed away in our subconscious mind. And as a result, we are likely to *feel like* a victim whenever we encounter situations that seem to be forced upon us or require us to do things that we do not want to do—even though those situations may bear little or no resemblance to the events that first elicited those feelings. When we encounter situations that we perceive as being beyond our control, the victim part of us takes over and we pay a visit to the victim stage.

In the past you have probably acted like a victim without knowing that was what you were doing. However, the signs are impossible to miss once you know what they are. In the victim stage, almost everything you *say* can be negative or self-defeating. You may *feel* lonely, sad, tired, wired, guilt-ridden, powerless, out of control, suspicious, or downtrodden. You may *think* that you are a weak, helpless, needy, frightened person whom no one could possibly love or appreciate; you may *believe* that people have ulterior motives and will hurt you if you let your guard down for an instant; you may *expect* very little of yourself; or you may *brood* about how you were hurt in the past and about the problems you have in the present.

Your actions may reflect your victim point of view. You may complain about the situation but do nothing to change it; not assert yourself; become wishy-washy, hypersensitive, or belligerent—lashing out at everyone and everything *but* the real source of your anger. You may become a world-class excuse maker, justifying your inaction *and* your self-destructive pursuits. You may even look the part, huddling and cowering or walking with your head down and your shoulders slumped.

More often than not, you want to make the situations in which you feel powerless more palatable or reward yourself for getting through them by partaking in the countless consolations modern society offers to people who feel like victims. You may run to the liquor cabinet, the refrigerator, or the shopping mall. You may stop off at the automatic teller, get some cash, and head for the nearest racetrack or gambling casino. You may curl up in front of the television with a box of chocolates or make a beeline for the nearest nightclub and find someone with whom to have a one-night stand. From manufacturing junk food to pandering to the latest form of instant enlightenment or inner peace, there are enormous profits to be made by catering to the victimized, and as far as we can tell no one who provides goods and services to people in the victim stage is likely to be forced out of business any time soon.

Feeling and acting like a victim is an automatic response and can become a habit—a dangerous one because each time the victim part of you is given free rein, it gets stronger. And before you know it, you are trapped in a downward spiral of helplessness and hopelessness that turns the fact that *you have been victimized* into the belief that *you are a victim*—and nothing more.

"I felt like the letter *I* for incest was emblazoned on my chest," says Suzanne. "I was not in touch with any other aspect of myself," she explains. And you may not be, either. You may have branded yourself with an *A* for abuse or a *D* for divorce or identify yourself solely as an adult child of alcoholic parents or someone who was given up for adoption. Regardless of the specific label you wear, you probably see yourself first and foremost as a victim and live your life accordingly. When this occurs, you have achieved *victimhood*—if such a thing could actually be considered an achievement.

Victimhood is an attitude, a stance, a way of relating in the world, and a reflection of the prevailing feelings we have about ourselves. The victim part of ourselves becomes the largest, most important portion of our identity, and "victim" becomes a label that describes not just what happened to us, but *who we think we are*. Based on this belief, we write the scenario for the soap opera of our lives, cast ourselves in the victim role, and play our part day in and day out.

Three Victim Scripts

There are three basic roles that people play to act out their victimhood. Although you are capable of playing any of the three starring roles and may, in fact, switch back and forth between them, you usually favor one and will no doubt recognize which role that is—the Wallower, the Self-Indulger, or the Meaner.

The Wallower

"Dear Victim Part of Me," wrote one participant in a recent forgiveness seminar, "I have had many pity parties and pity banquets with old pictures and records and tapes of her voice and even videotapes to make me feel even more miserable. I have felt sorry for myself and felt sorry for myself and felt sorry for myself. When I have been empty, I have brought on the pain rather than feel empty or seek out something more worthwhile to do—or feel."

If you follow the wallower script, chances are that you have had a few "pity banquets" of your own, spending hours, days, weeks, or longer bingeing not on food or drink, but on self-pity. Wallowers have probably found a million different ways to say, "Oh, poor me," and have milked their pain to the limit. They may feel sorry for themselves and loudly proclaim their victimhood by whining, complaining, and rejecting any and all suggestions that might help them feel better. They are unlikely to be at the top of anyone's "fun to be around" list and in fact spend vast amounts of time alone and lonely.

"The victim part of me pushes people away," another workshop participant wrote. "I try to do everything myself—not because I can, but because I feel I can't count on people to be there for me when I need them. If I asked for their help, they would end up deserting me, too, and that would hurt worse than not having them in my life in the first place."

Wallowers are likely to be depressed, passive, or manipulative. "That's okay. I'll be all right. You go ahead without me," moans the wallower, whose portrayal of the long-suffering martyr may be worthy of an Academy Award. They are in a rut, and their low energy, low aspirations, low achievement, and barren human relationships make sure that they do not get out of it.

The Self-Indulger

Another rotten day, Darlene thinks at 2:00 A.M. as she gets out of bed and heads toward the kitchen. Her secretary did not send out a batch of memos immediately after Darlene asked her to, so Darlene had to send them out herself. Because she was sure that her husband wouldn't remember to pick up the dry cleaning as she had asked him to, she drove ten miles out of her way to do it herself—only to discover that he *had* remembered and gotten there before her.

"You should have called to tell me you were going to do that," she expressed her outrage when she got home.

"But I told you I would when you asked me," he protested, and they got into another argument about how irresponsible he was and how she drove him crazy by asking him to do things but doing them herself before he had a chance to.

As a result, Darlene was already aggravated when it came time to bake cupcakes for her daughter's birthday party. Actually she was only supposed to supervise while her daughter baked, but it seemed easier to do it herself. "I really don't understand why she got so upset about that," Darlene sighs as she roots through the refrigerator. "And she had no right to yell at me for using pink icing on them, even if she *did* ask for blue. Pink is for girls, isn't it? Why couldn't she see that I was only trying to help?"

By now Darlene is standing at the kitchen counter eating the cupcakes in question. "What did I do to deserve such an ungrateful child?" she wonders, peeling the paper off another cupcake and taking a big bite. "I bend over backward to make life easier for people, handle all of the details for them so that they don't have to. And do they appreciate it? Do they show the slightest sign of gratitude? Of course not."

She hesitates briefly before reaching for another cupcake. If she eats it, there will not be enough left for the birthday party. But her daughter won't care, Darlene decides. After all, she said she hated them. "Besides, I baked the darn things, I can eat them if I want to," she says, and eats not one but three more cupcakes. On her way back to bed Darlene realizes that she'll have some explaining to do when she weighs in at her diet club meeting. "Oh, who cares," she declares as she crawls into bed. "I had a rotten day. I deserve a break from that stupid diet."

Darlene's late night raid on the cupcakes intended for her daughter's birthday party is a classic scene from the script of the self-indulgent victim. If you, too, play the self-indulger role, you probably live your life according to a simple credo: "I have been hurt, therefore I have earned the right to do whatever I want to do—without worrying about the consequences to myself or other people."

Self-indulgers act out their victimhood in all of the obvious ways—by drinking, using drugs, bingeing, gambling, engaging in indiscriminate sexual activity, or going on shopping sprees. As one forgiveness seminar participant put it, "The victim part of me buys things. Lots of things. Things I can't afford. It thinks those things will make me feel better, that giving myself gifts will make up for everything else that's missing. If my closet is full, maybe I won't feel so empty. But that really doesn't work, because I always feel empty anyway.''

Unfortunately, like this letter writer, while acting out your self-indulger script you may simply indulge yourself again each and every time you feel empty. ''I have been hurt,'' you remind yourself. ''I've earned this. I've paid for it with my pain. . . . Nobody understands me.''

Because you use your pain, helplessness, and hopelessness to justify anything that you choose to do or not do, you can be maddeningly irresponsible, indulging yourself in more subtle ways—for example, by:

- driving the family car but never bothering to put gas in it;
- using all of the hot water even though you know other people are waiting to take showers;
- drinking the last of the milk without buying more or adding ''milk'' to the grocery list;
- taking twenty items into the express lane at the supermarket;
- tying up the telephone for hours even when you know some-one else is waiting for an important call;
- putting pink icing on cupcakes when you were asked to make blue icing.

You might act with complete disregard for how your actions might affect the people around you, and when they comment on your irresponsible, self-indulgent, often downright adolescent behavior, you might bristle. ''I don't owe anybody anything,'' you think. ''The people who hurt me didn't give a second thought to how *their* behavior affected *me,* so why should I go out of my way to take other people's feelings into consideration?'' And you probably don't. In fact, you probably continue to indulge yourself in spite of the risks to your health, happiness, relationships, and peace of mind.

The Meaner

At first glance, those who play the leading role in the third victim script do not *look* like victims. They do not seem the least bit downtrodden or depressed and would sooner pick a fight than cry or cower in a corner. They are the meaners, belligerent, intolerant victims with very short fuses. They can be seen in all their glory, loudly grumbling in slow-moving checkout lines at the grocery store, pounding on the elevator buttons in the lobbies of high-rise buildings, and stopped at traffic lights on crowded city streets. When the traffic signal turns green and the driver in front of them does not accelerate instantly, they press down on the horn and keep honking for what seems like an eternity to the other driver, whom they have scared out of his wits.

Meaners are put-down artists, known (and avoided) far and wide for their barbed comments, sarcasm, ridicule, and one-upsmanship. They are extremely critical, and nothing—from their theater seats to the service in a restaurant—is ever good enough for them. Mark's father, with his suspicious nature and chip on his shoulder, was a meaner. Many racists, sexists, homophobics, child abusers, and spouse batterers are meaners—victims whose pain gets transformed into sidewinding anger directed at generally defenseless targets, who sadly join the burgeoning ranks of the walking wounded.

Craig's stay in the victim stage cast him as a meaner. Angry at his wife and at himself, but not yet ready to focus his anger on the source of his pain, Craig lashed out in all directions. Under his breath, but loud enough to be heard, he made biting comments about his professors. He engaged them in arguments that he called "debates" which were really outlets for his endless fury. He labeled his female classmates "air-brained bimbos" and took perverse pleasure in discussing subjects that he knew would go over some of their heads. It was not unusual for him to reduce waitresses to tears with his scathing criticism of their service. And it was only after he was arrested for starting a fistfight outside a bar that he stopped and asked himself, "What the hell am I doing?"

Sadly, most meaners and in fact most victims in general do not ask themselves that question. Instead they keep repeating the same behaviors and reinforcing their belief that they are hopeless victims of pain both from the past and from their present circumstances.

Of course, if you are a meaner, you do not *want* to feel and think and act the way you do while in the victim stage. You do not get up in the morning and tell yourself, "I think I'll feel miserable and wallow, indulge myself, or be mean today." No, you resort to acting out your victim script because that is *all you can do* when the realization that you were victimized catches up with you—and it always does. Like it or not, the victim stage is part of the process. And believe it or not, for a time this stage, like all of the others, does serve you.

Dealing with the Pain: How the Victim Stage Serves You

As painful, emotionally draining, and physically debilitating as the victim stage can be, *you are still healing*. In fact, it is in this stage that you are able to meet several important, previously neglected needs.

First of all, *you need to blame someone for the bad things that happened to you,* and in the victim stage your perspective on who was responsible for the injuries and injustices you experienced is more realistic than it was in either the denial or self-blame stages. You put the blame where it belongs—on the people who hurt you.

"My father really screwed me up," Mark said, reversing his earlier belief that he was "screwed up" because he had always expected too much and set himself up for disappointment. While in the victim stage, Mark finally accepted that what his father did— breaking promises, backing out of things at the last minute, taking back gifts he had given to his children and selling them to strangers, demanding total loyalty and complete agreement with his paranoid point of view, and leaving his son outside in the cold for hours—was no way to treat a little kid.

"I hate him for what he did to me," Terry asserted once she finally stopped denying that her past experiences had done anything but make her a better person. In the victim stage, she could see clearly that her grandfather's sexual molestations had been inappropriate and uninvited, that he had used her and involved her in activities she was too young to cope with or comprehend, that he had left her a legacy of pain and confusion.

"They were more interested in their booze than us," Marcy admits tearfully. "My parents and their drinking destroyed my childhood and messed up my life."

"He didn't have to do what he did," Harriet sighs. "Maybe I wasn't the best wife in the world, maybe I did put more energy into my career than my marriage. But that didn't give him the right to have an affair. And nothing justifies trying to take my kids away from me. I don't know why he's doing this to me, but he is, and it's wrong."

No matter how you say it, in the victim stage you take the burden of guilt off your own shoulders and place it squarely on the people who hurt you. This serves you because in order to let go of pain from the past and forgive the people who hurt you, you must first acknowledge that they hurt you and were responsible for the actions that caused your pain. Consequently, while in the victim stage you pave the way to work through your painful past experiences later in the healing process.

You need to know and say that you are a victim of something. "I used to think I was crazy," Marcy says. "The way I overreacted to everything and thought that really devastating things would happen to me if I made a mistake. The way I tried to control things that nobody can really control and could never relax and enjoy myself because I was always watching, trying to anticipate what could go wrong. Now I know that a lot of adult children of alcoholics do those things. I can't say that makes me feel good. In fact, knowing how messed up I am because of the way my parents were and looking at how much I have to do to get my life together makes me very depressed and exhausted. But at least it all makes some sense to me now."

When you transform your "if only" statements from "If only I had done things differently, I would not have been hurt" to "If only he [she/it] had not hurt me, I would not have suffered the way I have for so long," you finally have a reasonable explanation for your reactions to various situations and for some of the problems that have plagued you for years. It isn't a terrific explanation, of course. It does not restore your sense of power or motivate you to change. In fact, while in the victim stage, you tend to use it to justify your inaction and absolve you of responsibility for improving your present circumstances. But still, you are comforted as Marcy was by the knowledge that you are not crazy, that you are instead a victim of something, and that anyone who had gone through what you went through could realistically expect to lead a less than perfect life.

You need to grieve for what you lost because you were hurt. Although less obvious than the death of a loved one, divorce, getting fired from your job, or other losses traditionally associated with the grieving process, all of you lost something when you were hurt. You may have lost your innocence, the sense of trust, safety, and security that you needed to be a child during your childhood, the love and acceptance you hoped to receive from your parents, friends, spouses, lovers, or children, or the encouragement and emotional support you needed to feel worthwhile. You need to mourn those losses that were real to you and painful—and which you could not grieve for while denying your pain or punishing yourself for what had happened to you.

In the victim stage, you finally take the time to feel sorry about what you wanted but did not get, to ache inside and cry an ocean of tears, to recognize how bad you felt and how unfair it was to be hurt by someone to whom you turned for love, acceptance, and encouragement. You need to do this. Like a widow or widower, you need to mourn before you move on.

You also need to give yourself the attention and comfort that you did not receive when you were hurt, as Suzanne learned to do.

> No one was there for me while the abuse was happening. There was no one to pay attention to the pain I was going through at that time. No one could comfort me because no one knew what was happening. They could not see that I was hurting, and to tell you the truth, I didn't think they could see me at all. I felt invisible.
>
> When I reached the victim stage, I vowed that I and my pain would not be invisible anymore. We would get the attention we had deserved all along. I gave myself and my pain my full attention. I thought about the incest constantly. I cried over it regularly. In fact, with the exception of getting up and going to work each day, I paid attention to nothing else. And when I could, I got other people to pay attention, too, telling them my tale of woe and crying on their shoulders. I know now that I needed to do that—even if I did not need to do it as much or for as long as I did.

By focusing on your pain and brooding about the past as well as the circumstances of your life today, you give yourself the attention that you once longed for but did not get from other people. You are able to console and comfort the frightened and damaged child inside of you. And at least until they get sick of your wallowing, whining, and complaining, you get other people's sympathy and attention, too. "Oh, you poor thing," they say. "What an awful thing to go through. It must have hurt you terribly." Better late than never, you think, and you feel consoled by the kind and comforting words you so needed to hear when you were hurt.

As you can see, the victim stage may not be pretty, but it does serve you—temporarily. Unfortunately, getting your needs met in the victim stage is a dangerous double-edged sword. Blaming your problems on the people who hurt you, identifying yourself as a victim, mourning your losses and paying attention to your pain work to your advantage only in small doses, taken for short periods of time.

And the truth of the matter is that most of us overdose on

self-pity while in the victim stage. We cross the line between
mourning our losses and making excuses for binges and excesses and
not changing the things we *can* change.

Paying the Price for Playing the Victim Role

Regardless of the script you choose to follow, when you play the
role of a victim, it takes a toll on both you and the people around
you.

Low, Low, Low Self-Esteem

The victim stage does even more damage to self-esteem than the
self-blame stage did. Not only do you see yourself as not good
enough in various ways, but you also believe that there is absolutely
nothing you can do to change that. Convinced that you were permanently
and irreversibly damaged by your painful past experiences, you may
very well see yourself as so weak, worthless, and ill fated that you do
not *deserve* to be more or better than you are. As a result, your
self-esteem is diminished further by your inability or refusal to take
risks, by your resistance to trying anything new because you are
afraid that you will lose what little you have. And that fear is
paralyzing. Even more than your hopelessness, your fear motivates
you to push away the people who could help you, reject all advice
that might actually move you out of the victim stage, and cut yourself
off from the rest of the world. This, of course, keeps the cycle going.

Systematic Suicide

If you do not like yourself, you do not take care of yourself. If you
believe that pain, heartache, and little else are all you can expect
from life, you are not particularly invested in prolonging your life.
While in the victim stage, you do nothing to improve the quality of
your life. In fact, you often make matters worse. What you do—from
abusing substances and overeating to driving away the supportive
people in your life—and what you do not do—from not exercising to
not bothering to get regular medical check-ups—shortens your life.

You kill yourself a little bit every day, committing what we call systematic suicide.

We have often heard experts in the field of suicide prevention say that suicide is "a permanent solution to a temporary problem," and systematic suicide fits this description as well. The damage we do to our physical and emotional health can last long after we have left the victim stage. What's more, because so much of what we do or do not do keeps our energy level low, leads to feelings of guilt and shame on the morning after, or saddles us with new, seemingly insurmountable problems, we feel all the more helpless and hopeless— and stay stuck in the victim stage.

Getting Exactly What You Try to Avoid

When Harriet hit the victim stage, she became severely depressed. She felt sad, had little energy, and used what she had to keep her business from failing the way her marriage had. "I didn't have anything left over for the little things," she says. "I wasn't motivated to do anything. I turned down invitations, refused to date, hardly left the house except to go to work. I cried myself to sleep at night, when I could get to sleep at all."

During this time, Harriet's relationship with her children suffered. She could not be there for them. She had nothing to give to them physically or emotionally, and they were affected by it. "They kept saying, 'You're no fun anymore,'" Harriet recalls. "But how could they expect me to be? Their father destroyed me. He destroyed my life. That's not something you laugh and sing about." But Harriet's children weren't really asking her to laugh and sing. They wanted— and needed—her to parent them, to show interest in them, to encourage and validate them, to set limits for them, and to help them understand and cope with the divorce and custody battle that was hurting them, too. Meeting or at least attempting to meet those needs was, in fact, Harriet's responsibility as a parent, but she could not live up to it while in a state of depression and despair.

One evening during dinner, when Harriet's mind was, as usual, focused on her problems and not on her daughter's attempt to convey something that was of great importance to her, Harriet's daughter got angry and said, "Maybe we *should* go live with Dad. At least he pays attention to us." And the situation came to a head.

"Suddenly I realized that I was on the brink of getting exactly what I was most afraid of,'' Harriet recalls. ''I was scared to death of losing my kids, but by feeling sorry for myself and being too wrapped up in my own problems, I was being the lousy parent my ex-husband said I was, the sort of parent who really didn't deserve her kids' love and loyalty. *I was the one who was making happen what I didn't want to happen.*''

And that is precisely what you do while you are trapped in the victim stage. Whether you fear rejection, abandonment, or being lied to, criticized, or pushed around, your worst fears are realized. The negative consequences you hoped to avoid become the new realities you have to cope with *in addition to* coping with the old wounds and unfinished business from your past.

Victims Beget Victims

The most devastating aspect of the victim stage and the reason it is absolutely essential that we extract ourselves from it is that victims beget victims. Perpetuating the cycle of pain and misery is never our intention, but it is what *always* happens when we get stuck in the victim stage.

> Although it did not excuse his behavior or change the fact that I had been hurt by what he did to me in the past, not long before my father died, I learned that he had been sexually abused himself as a young boy. This did not give him the right to abuse his children, of course, but it did shed some light on the reasons incest happened in our family.
>
> Victims beget victims, and my father was indeed a victim. He was wounded as a child and robbed of his dignity as an adult when he injured his back and could not work to support his family. He did not have the insight, support, or resources to work through his pain, so instead he passed it on to his children, leaving us to deal with it for decades afterward.
>
> Although I did not abuse anyone physically or sexually, for a time I too perpetuated the cycle. While obsessed with my own healing process and my own pain, like Harriet, I was unable to live up to my responsibilities as a parent. My daughter and our relationship suffered because I was too busy being a victim to be a mom. Fortunately we have repaired most of the damage and rebuilt our relationship, but it took years of hard work and pain that could have been avoided.

Whether you wallow and neglect the people you love, indulge yourself and, as a result, hurt others, or inflict wounds with your sidewinding anger, you too perpetuate the cycle of victimization. Each day that you remain in the victim stage is a day that you may do damage to someone, and in addition to hurting them, you hurt yourself—accumulating guilt and shame that will block your own healing process and your own efforts to forgive the people who once victimized you.

Breaking the Cycle: Moving Out of the Victim Stage

You were victimized. That is a fact. At that time, you were helpless and unable to control the people or events that hurt you. That too is a fact. Today your life is less than it could be as a result of being hurt and what you did because you were hurt. Yes, that is a fact, too. However, everything else is *a choice*. Continuing to feel helpless is your choice, as is wallowing, self-indulging, and being a meaner. Doing very little and expecting even less is your choice. Repeating old patterns and begetting new victims are the outcomes of your choice to remain in the victim stage. But now it is time to make different choices, smart choices that restore your power and your hope—without hurting you or anyone else.

This will not be easy. Moving yourself out of the victim stage is a lot like trying to move a huge boulder that has landed in the middle of the road. You cannot accomplish either task with your bare hands, merely by pushing with all your might. You know this because you have tried to drag yourself out of pain and misery in the past—and failed. We offer you an alternative.

Let's return to the boulder for a moment. To move it successfully, your best bet would be to slide a board under it, place a smaller rock halfway between you and the boulder, creating a fulcrum, and then push down on one end of that fulcrum in order to lift up the boulder at the other end.

The same principle—which we call the "fulcrum theory"—applies to moving yourself out of the victim stage. By adopting attitudes and pursuing activities that are incompatible with victimhood and keep you from feeling like a victim, you will stop seeing yourself as one and thus acting out the same old helplessness script. You can start by attempting to pay more attention to aspects of yourself and your life other than your pain and misery.

Taking Off Your Victim Blinders

While keeping your energy and attention focused on what is missing from your life, life itself passes you by. While trapped in the victim stage, the only time you stop staring at the damage done by your painful past experiences is the time you spend frantically searching for and indulging frenetically in the substances or activities you hope will make you feel whole again. In the meantime, you completely forget that there is more to life than pain and suffering, that there is fun, laughter, love, productivity, and adventure. Wearing your victim stage blinders, you simply cannot see the gold ring you could grasp if you reached for it, and therefore you do not reach out at all. And that is a choice.

"You can choose to be grateful or ungrateful, positive or negative, to forgive or not to forgive," asserts Philip H. Friedman, executive director of the Foundation for Well-Being, as quoted by columnist Darrell Sifford in the *Philadelphia Inquirer* (January 9, 1989). "You can be grateful even for adversity, because adversity, in some ways, forces you to grow.

"You choose beliefs and attitudes," Friedman continues. "When you make a choice to be positive, positive things start to happen. What you focus on expands your life. What you radiate, you attract."

Although this concept may at first seem simplistic or magical, to see its validity you need only consider what you have been doing while living like a victim. You have been radiating pain and misery—and getting *more* pain and misery. You have been acting out a victim script that has ended the same way every time and will continue to end that way. So why not try something new? You have nothing to lose but your pain.

Making Room for a Positive Outlook: A Visualization Exercise

Before you can adopt a more positive outlook, you must make room for positive input. Your circuits are overloaded with negativity, and they must be cleared, at least temporarily, for incoming messages of gratitude, optimism, and encouragement. The following visualization, recommended by Philip H. Friedman, is a must for those of you in the victim stage and is also beneficial for anyone at any point in the healing process.

> Relax, shut your eyes, and visualize a hot-air balloon that is attached not to the customary basket, but to a garbage can. The balloon is tethered to the ground at the moment. Imagine yourself walking over to it, lifting the lid off the garbage can, and dumping all of your emotional garbage into it. Fill the garbage can with your old injuries and injustices, and your resentments and self-deprecating statements, your helpless, hopeless feelings. Tear off your victim label and toss it in. And while you're at it, remove your blinders and trash them, too.
>
> Then replace the lid, untether the balloon, and watch it float away, taking your victim thoughts, feelings, and behaviors with it. Watch it until it is no more than a speck high in the sky, repeating to yourself, "I release my hurts."

While working your way out of the victim stage, try to use this visualization every day. You can continue to use it as needed throughout your healing process, conjuring it up whenever you notice yourself feeling like a victim.

Of course, visualizing your emotional garbage floating away in a trash can does not actually heal your old wounds. But it does allow you to let go of the pain for a few minutes, hours, or days at a time, and that leaves you open to the possibility of moving on. It also makes room for you to develop what people in twelve-step recovery programs refer to as "an attitude of gratitude."

The Gratitude Exercise

While entrenched in your own victimhood, you will no doubt find it difficult to feel grateful about anything. In fact, with your victim blinders on, you will not even notice anything to be grateful for. You see only what you do *not* have and that the little you do have does you little good. Consequently you may resist doing the following exercise, but we urge you to try it anyway. It won't take anything from you, and it may give you a more optimistic outlook than you've had in a long, long time.

> Beginning with your toes and working up through the rest of

your body, *say* that you are thankful for each and every part of your body. Repeat to yourself, "I am grateful for my toes. I am grateful for my feet. I am grateful for my ankles [legs, knees, thighs, and so on]." You do not have to *feel* grateful yet. By saying that you are, you are merely acknowledging the possibility that one day you really could be. Express your gratitude for every part of your body regardless of its imperfections. Your body does not have to be perfect to be appreciated. You may hate your thighs or wish you had a different nose, but where would you be if you didn't have them at all?

Then move on to *things* that you have or own, and again do not concern yourself with quality. Say that you are grateful for your car and your apartment, even if it is not the greatest car in the world or the apartment you would like to have. Cover as many things as you can think of—your bed, sofa, sneakers, job. If you have it, acknowledge it.

Do the same thing for the people in your life, imperfect as they too may be. Finally, express your gratitude for *anything* that you have accomplished during the preceding twenty-four hours, beginning with getting out of bed in the morning straight through to falling asleep at night.

Run through your list of gratitudes daily if possible, but at least three times each week. The time you spend doing this is time you do *not* spend focused on what is lacking from your life. But more important, it helps you recognize that your life, although not necessarily the way you would like it to be, has more in it than you thought it did.

Once you get used to listing gratitudes, you must start looking for new things to be grateful for. Every day try to notice three not previously listed people, events, or interactions that are positive—and being not as bad as you expected them to be counts. These things need not be earth-shattering. For instance, you could be grateful for not getting stuck in traffic for as long as you usually do, a waiter who brings you a glass of water without being asked more than once, a friendly convenience store clerk, the picture your child drew for you at kindergarten, or weather that is sunny or unseasonably warm. Believe us, when you start looking for positives, you *will* find them. They have been there all along.

Unvictim Behaviors

While stuck in the victim stage, you can develop considerable skill and expertise in victim behaviors, from wallowing in self-pity to indulging in junk-food binges. You leave victimhood behind you by applying the same diligence to constructive, self-enhancing unvictim behaviors.

Unvictim activities are those that enhance self-esteem, expand your world, improve your physical condition or emotional state, and keep you from feeling like a victim at least while you are engaged in them. They include "positive addictions" and ongoing efforts to improve overall wellness, such as regular exercise, a healthy diet, hobbies, gardening, crafts, adult education courses, counseling or participation in a support group, quiet time to relax or meditate, and so on. They can also be the little things that you do for yourself periodically or for short stretches of time, like walking in the woods, taking a bubble bath, playing with your children, going to a concert or a museum, having a romantic candlelit dinner with your spouse, or anything else that makes you feel good and takes your mind off your problems for a while.

Although we will go into more detail and offer more strategies for overall wellness in the final chapter of this book, take some time now to list a dozen unvictim behaviors that you could add to your life right away. Then do them, in spite of the excuses the victim part of you makes. Every moment you spend on them is a moment that you spend not being or feeling like a victim.

Getting Your Needs Met—Constructively

As we mentioned earlier, many of your unhealed wounds and much of your unfinished business can be traced back to unmet needs, things you wanted but did not get when you were hurt or after you were hurt. From your victim stance, you may believe that since you did not get those things originally, you have to live without them forever. But that simply is not true. You *can* fulfill your needs, whatever they may be, once you give up the myth that Daddy, Mommy, or whoever hurt you is the only person who can meet them and once you stop making futile attempts to satisfy them yourself—with victim behaviors.

First you must identify your unmet needs. Ask yourself, "What needs are my victim behaviors trying to satisfy? Am I looking for love, acceptance, belonging, being cared about or cared for, closeness, safety, security, intimacy, encouragement, an identity, or something else?''

Clarification Strategy Number 8:
Needs Identification

Down the left-hand side of a sheet of paper, list the needs you have been trying to fulfill in one way or another ever since you were hurt. Leave several lines between each need that you list.

Of course, for many of you, the real issue has never been the unmet need itself, but rather *whom* you expected to meet it. Much of your pain and certainly your inability to forgive is connected to the fact that the people who hurt you withheld something that you desperately wanted from them. So ask yourself, "Who failed to meet that need when and in the way I expected them to (or wished they would)?''

Next to each need you have listed, jot down the name, initials, or description of the person or people who did not satisfy that need when they could or should have.

Divide the remainder of the page into three columns. Title the first column "Things I Have Done," then think about the wallowing, self-indulgent, or intolerant things you have done. What were you trying to get by engaging in those behaviors? Match your actions to your needs, noting the various ways you have attempted to fulfill each need you have listed.

For instance, hoping to meet your need for love, you may have sought other people's sympathy, telling and retelling your tale of woe, complaining, playing the martyr, and so on. Or *to make up for* an unmet need, you may have consoled yourself with food, alcohol, gambling, drugs, sex, or *not* cleaning the house or taking care of yourself. Really put some thought into this part of the exercise. It can give you enormous insight into how and why you have acted like a victim in the past and are acting like one now.

Still working on this column, circle all of the behaviors you continue to do today. Put an asterisk (*) beside each one that has actually satisfied your need *without* hurting you or anyone else. Chances are that you will not be drawing many asterisks.

Title the second column "What I Could Do Instead" and try to come up with at least one *constructive* alternative to meet each need. For instance, if you need recognition, you could do volunteer work, get involved with a community theater group, chair or join a committee, run the PTA bake sale, coach a Little League team, or be more active and visible in other ways at work or in your community. If you need guidance, support, or encouragement, you could get counseling, join a support group, get involved in a twelve-step recovery program, or listen to the suggestions that the people already in your life have to offer. Please do not try to come up with the "perfect" alternative. Such a thing does not exist, and waiting for it is one of the reasons you are stuck.

Finally, label the last column "Whom Can I Turn To?" At least for the time being, accept that your needs simply will not be met today by the people who did not meet them in the past. You must look elsewhere. Ask yourself, "Who are the people in my life right now who could give me at least some of what I need? Who else [a therapist, support group members, new friends, old friends you've lost touch with, and so forth] could meet some of the needs I've been trying to take care of all by myself?" Across from each need, write the names, initials, or descriptive titles of people who could help you fulfill that need today. It is unrealistic and unhealthy to expect any one person to meet all your needs or even to entirely satisfy just one need, so try not to designate one person as your savior. Instead create a potential support *network* in which a number of different people contribute what they can so that you can get more of what you need.

With your responses to this strategy as a foundation, you can immediately take steps to obtain *real* comfort through friendships, counseling, support groups, community involvement, journal writing, accomplishments, and so on.

The Bottom Line

Self-esteem is the bottom line for healing and forgiveness. Without it, you will most likely continue to hurt yourself, expect little of yourself, and believe that you do not deserve to feel better or be better off than you are now. Your self-esteem has sustained a great deal of damage over the years. It was damaged when you were hurt and damaged again when denial sent you down one dead-end street after another. It was decimated by self-blame and plummeted to an all-time low as a result of the helplessness and hopelessness you felt while in the victim stage.

Fortunately self-esteem can be repaired and restored. Just as you learned *not* to like yourself, you can learn to like yourself again. You will have to work at it, however. You will have to take risks, be productive, and model your own behavior after people who demonstrate higher self-esteem than your own. You will have to look at how you are different from other people as a reflection of your own uniqueness instead of evidence that you are not good enough. You will have to exercise your personal power by making choices instead of merely reacting to circumstances, and you will have to connect with supportive people.

Each of these self-esteem building blocks will be explored in more detail later in this book, but that does not mean you have to wait so much as one more second before beginning to rebuild your self-esteem. By taking even one step—no matter how small—out of the victim stage, you automatically feel better about yourself. Anything, and we do mean anything, feels better than being a victim.

Of course, the victim part of yourself will never be gone entirely, and as was true for the other stages of the forgiveness process, you can expect to return to the victim stage from time to time.

But at least you now know that victimhood is a choice—*your* choice. You can choose to stop indulging the wallower, self-indulger, or meaner inside of you and step out into the light any time you want.

Unquestionably the fastest way to get out of the victim stage is to get angry about what happened to you. Anger supplies all the energy you did not have in the victim stage and then some. It also sends you from the frying pan into the fire as you enter the indignation stage of the healing process, which is discussed in the next chapter.

CHAPTER EIGHT

THE INDIGNATION STAGE

"My father really screwed me up," Mark declares, uttering words that he repeated over and over again while in the victim stage. But now those words sound different. Mark does not whine or snivel or seem weary and downtrodden when he says them. Instead he states his case firmly, authoritatively, and emphatically, adding forcefully, *"And he had no right to do that."*

"My parents were drunks who destroyed my childhood," Marcy asserts. There are no tears in her eyes now. Her lower lip does not quiver. Her gaze is not directed at the floor. No, Marcy stares right at us. In fact, she glares. She is outraged. Indignant. Furious. "They were supposed to be responsible for us," she says. "They were supposed to take care of us, and they blew it. Now my dad is dead and my mom is sober, and that's supposed to make everything okay. Well, it's not okay. I'm angry, and I won't pretend I'm not. *I've pretended long enough!"*

Mark and Marcy have reached the *indignation stage* of the forgiveness process. This stage, like the ones that came before it, has its drawbacks, but there is no denying that *being indignant is a far cry better than being a victim.*

Once we reach the indignation stage, we stop feeling helpless and hopeless. We may not know *how* to improve our life, but we once again believe that we can. We finally realize that we *deserve* to

145

be free of the pain and misery, to dump our excess baggage and move on unencumbered.

In the indignation stage, we also experience a resurgence of old anger that can make us feel like a ticking time bomb. And sometimes we do explode. Because we may not have learned how to use and express anger in a healthy, constructive way, we run the risk of doing and saying things that we will not feel proud of and which may actually do more harm than good.

You see, the indignation stage, like all of the stages that preceded it, is a double-edged sword. The very things that can get you moving in a positive direction can also get you stuck. However, if you *can* avoid the various pitfalls of the indignation stage, you will grow closer to healing and forgiveness than you ever have been before—and that is what we hope this chapter will help you do.

The Good, the Bad, and the Ugly of the Indignation Stage

"I refuse to allow this to go on affecting my life," Terry assures us. Although our conversation takes place over the telephone, we can practically see her setting her jaw and stomping her foot as she declares her independence from the unhealed wounds and unfinished business that have ruled her life ever since her grandfather first molested her. You may recall that convincing herself (and everyone else) that incest had not affected her was what Terry did while she was in the denial stage. But now, driven by righteous, justified anger that is appropriate in light of what she has been through, and directed at the source of her pain rather than at the nearest available target, Terry brings her grudges and resentments out into the open instead of digging a deep hole and burying them. And you will, too.

In this stage, you finally stand up for yourself and state clearly and emphatically what is and is not acceptable to you. Like Terry, in the indignation stage, you realize that you do not want to and do not have to be victimized for one second more by the hurt others perpetrated.

Your indignation has the potential to be *the motivating force that drives you to change for the better*. When you finally say, "I don't like this and will no longer accept it," you also find the inner strength to declare, "I am going to change this," and mean it.

"I finally figured out what I was doing to myself when Steve came back into my life," Melinda explains. "I ran into him at a seminar given by a professional organization I belong to, and we went out for a drink afterward.''

That was when Melinda learned that Steve had married the young woman he had been seeing when his relationship with Melinda ended. ''He said his marriage was a mistake,'' Melinda continues. ''Which I suppose was exactly what I wanted to hear. He said he was miserable, and of course by then I was an expert on taking care of miserable men. Maybe I saw my chance to 'be there' for him the way he said I wasn't the last time. I don't know. But we ended up having an affair.''

That affair lasted for almost a year, until Melinda spotted Steve's wife at a shopping mall. ''She was very pregnant,'' Melinda recalls. ''And I was shocked because Steve had never said a word about that. I felt thoroughly ashamed of myself for about two seconds, and then I got furious. It was pretty obvious that Steve's marriage wasn't as miserable as he said it was and crystal clear to me that if it ever came down to choosing between us, he would choose her again. I wanted to strangle him with my bare hands. He'd already devastated me once, and I refused to let him do it again.''

Melinda ended the affair and spent very little time mourning her loss. ''After all, I had already done that,'' she says. ''I had been doing it for years.'' Instead, she took a cold, hard look at herself and the life she had been leading. She finally realized that she did not want the kinds of relationships she had been having since she was first rejected by Steve.

''It won't happen again,'' Melinda proclaims. ''No more men on the rebound. No more wounded birds whom I nurse back to health so they can leave me. No more building up my hopes about some guy I don't even know, getting bent out of shape when he doesn't live up to my fantasies, and then settling for sex with whoever gives me a second look. I'm sick and tired of rejection and insecurity and pain. Steve started it, but *I'm going to get rid of it once and for all.*''

Although much of Melinda's outrage and indignation is aimed at what she herself did because she was hurt, she is not berating or punishing herself the way she did in the self-blame stage. Her anger is directed outward and allows her to *set limits for how she wants to be treated in the future.*

With outrage, instead of shame or self-pity, while in the indignation stage, you too declare that you are sick and tired of feeling, thinking, and acting under the influence of your painful past experiences. ''Never again,'' you proclaim loudly and clearly, establishing your personal bottom line—the treatment that you simply will not accept any longer. If you use your indignation constructively, you will actually be able to stick to that bottom line and stop repeating your old, self-destructive behavior patterns. Indeed, you may begin with a vengeance to clear various obstacles from your path.

Propelled by the energy anger provides, many of you will make dramatic life changes during this stage. You will quit dead-end jobs, extract yourself from unsatisfying or abusive relationships, embark upon diet and exercise programs, go back to school, finish projects you started years ago, or finally seek professional help to work through your unfinished business.

However, some of you may *not* use your indignation constructively. Instead you will spend a significant amount of time and energy wanting to—and sometimes attempting to—punish the people who hurt you, wishing that harm would come to them, hoping that they suffer as much as you have, and reminding yourself that they owe you an apology or should somehow pay for what they did to you. Indignation, although healthy and necessary in and of itself, is frequently *expressed* in unhealthy ways—like the endless games of one-upmanship that Harriet played. "Something snapped," she told us when her daughter compared her with her ex-husband, suggesting that she might be happier living with a father who paid attention to her than with a mother who was depressed and distracted most of the time. For months after that dinner table confrontation, Harriet was as angry as she had been depressed.

"I wanted to know how he got to be the good guy," Harriet says, recounting the thoughts that ran through her mind. "He had betrayed me, cheated on me, lied to me, and then blamed it all on me. I had exhausted and humiliated myself while he went right on with his affair. He was the one who started the custody battle that was draining me dry financially and emotionally, too, since I lived in constant fear that I would lose my kids.

"I was absolutely furious. I did not want him to have a moment's peace or happiness ever again."

Driven by her anger and a nearly insatiable desire for revenge, Harriet took action immediately. She successfully limited Larry's visitation rights on the grounds that his efforts to win his children's affection frequently included keeping them out late on school nights and taking them out of school altogether for vacations and long weekends. This move of course escalated the custody battle. Then, because she was now determined to win the war, Harriet turned around and did exactly what Larry had been doing, catering to her children's every whim and trying to buy their love and loyalty by giving them expensive gifts that she, unlike Larry, could not afford.

Harriet could no longer be in the same room with Larry or speak to him on the telephone without sniping at him. And even though she did not say belittling or critical things about him directly to their children, Harriet did "bad-mouth" Larry to her friends and relatives while the kids were nearby, and they could not help but hear her. Sometimes she even called his apartment late at night and hung up when he answered the phone.

Harriet was not proud of her behavior during this period of her healing process. In fact, there were many times when she hated herself for the way she was feeling and acting. Inner peace definitely did not describe her state of mind; pain from the past was still dictating how she lived her life. As new anger was heaped on top of the old, Harriet ran the risk of getting stuck with her indignation and the pain that fueled it—which is the ever-present danger of the indignation stage.

"But I Don't Do Anger."

For many of us, the indignation stage will be the most difficult stage of all, because it forces us to *get in touch with the anger* that our painful past experiences generated—anger that we have worked overtime to keep underground ever sense we were hurt. By feeling that anger now, by coming to understand the other, often more threatening emotions hidden behind it, and by finally expressing it in a *healthy* manner, we clear the way to solving the problems that we buried along with it.

Getting in touch with and working through that anger is an absolutely essential step in the healing process. But it is also very scary and extremely confusing, providing yet another breeding ground for internal conflict and emotional turmoil. In fact, it can be so threatening to your already shaky self-concept that you may try to avoid this stage of the healing process altogether, as Suzanne can tell you.

There came a time—numerous times, actually—when my counselor suggested that perhaps I had indulged the victim part of me long enough, that perhaps it was time to get in touch with my anger. For the most part, I ignored her advice. You see, I did not think I had any anger to get in touch with. I didn't express anger. I didn't recognize when I was feeling it, and I was pretty sure I had never felt it. I would sit in my incest survivors' group and listen to other people talk about how angry they were, but I truly could not relate to what they were going through. "This does not apply to me," I thought. "I'm never angry."

The truth of the matter was that I was too terrified by anger to get angry. Because my father was a very angry man who could and often did fly into violent rages, I had witnessed firsthand the devastation that anger could cause. More than once I had been a victim of that rage. I could vividly recall one particular incident, remembering in frightening detail being eight or nine years old and playing indoors on a rainy day. Ingeniously—or so we thought at the time—my sister and I tied a rope between our bedroom doors to make a swing, and my sister, who was smaller and lighter than I, tried it first. The rope broke. My sister fell, hitting her head against the wall and beginning to bleed profusely.

Hearing my sister's screams, my father came running, saw her lying there bleeding, and became furious at me. He picked me up and threw me against the wall. When I landed, he picked me up and threw me again. He continued to do this for what seemed like an eternity, and to this day I believe that had he not remembered that my sister needed medical attention, he would have gone right on doing it until he had killed me. Anger and death were permanently welded together in my mind, so much so that I wholeheartedly believed that if I got angry, I would hurt someone as badly as my father hurt me or, worse yet, kill them. So I did not do anger. I did not do it at all. Ever.

The attitude that Suzanne adopted—that anger was not and indeed should not be a part of her emotional repertoire—is quite common and may closely resemble your own point of view. Like Suzanne, you may not "do" anger because you are afraid of its power and the damage you could do if you did unleash it, or because:

- You still see yourself as a helpless victim or are still stuck in self-blame and believe that you do not have the *right* to be angry about things that are your lot in life or were your fault in the first place.

- Your role models during childhood expressed anger passively or manipulatively rather than assertively, or you grew up in an alcoholic or otherwise dysfunctional family where displaying negative feelings of any kind was against the "house rules."
- Feeling anger toward certain people leaves you feeling guilty and ashamed.

For any or all of these reasons, you came to believe that anger was simply too dangerous to deal with. To avoid losing control because of it or suffering the consequences of it, you stopped "doing" anger and, like Suzanne, often stopped recognizing when you were *feeling* it as well.

But the one you don't do, you get stuck with, I learned. Although I sincerely believed that I never felt angry, I was mistaken. I dug a deep hole and buried my anger, suppressing it before I even recognized that I was feeling it. But it did not want to stay buried. Indeed, it rumbled around inside of me, showed itself in subtle and not-so-subtle ways, and seeped out like toxic gas, poisoning my system and preventing me from truly letting go of pain from the past.

Suppressing Your Anger

Because you or the people who hurt you behaved badly while feeling anger, or reacted badly to your own expressions of anger, you may have labeled anger a "bad" feeling and learned to avoid it. However, even though indiscriminately, thoughtlessly, abusively, and endlessly venting anger is indeed dangerous and destructive, feeling anger is neither good nor bad but rather a *natural reaction* that occurs whenever you, your self-esteem, or your pride are hurt or threatened.

Frequently accompanied by physical reactions like muscle tension and enormous surges of energy caused by adrenaline rushing through your body, anger is automatic, instinctive, and necessary. It is a signal that something is wrong, that you are in physical danger, or that a vital psychological need is not being met. Anger provides the energy you need to protect yourself from those threats or to escape them. When used constructively, it prompts you to take action to stop or counteract whatever is hurting you.

When you don't "do" anger at all, or when you encounter situations in which it is inappropriate or impossible to express your anger, which was often the case when you were hurt in the past, you bury it instead. You suppress your anger, sometimes before you are consciously aware that you are feeling it. However, because the energy generated by anger is extremely difficult to contain, suppressed anger constantly clamors to be set free and in fact.breaks loose and comes out in many self-destructive ways.

For instance, Elise has been angry at her sister Megan since the day Megan was born. "But getting angry at Mommy and Daddy's little darling or even complaining about her was out of the question," Elise insists. If she did express her anger, Elise's parents got angry at her, paying even less attention to her because they were too busy consoling the "injured party"—Megan. As a result, Elise learned to bury her outrage and indignation, but she did not forget it. Indeed, she kept a running tally of all the injuries and injustices she sustained because of Megan and acted out her resentments in countless ways. As a child, Elise ignored and excluded Megan whenever she could, and when Megan did "tag along" behind her, Elise would not discourage her friends' taunts and teasing. In fact, she subtly encouraged them. As an adult, Elise intentionally picked out cheap, useless gifts to give Megan at Christmastime and for her birthday frequently bought items of clothing that were not only ugly, but also several sizes too large. Then Elise would say to her appearance-conscious sibling, "I'm sorry. But you did look like you put on weight."

Of course, Elise's suppressed anger did the most damage to Elise herself. With resentment coursing through her veins, Elise worked herself up into such a state at every family gathering that she ended up with a migraine headache and had to spend the next twenty-four hours in bed. When anyone so much as mentioned Megan's name, it could ruin Elise's entire day. She would snap at her children, criticize her husband, sulk, and indulge in her victim behavior of choice—taking several Valium and plopping down in front of the TV to watch soap operas.

Your suppressed anger, like Elise's, can turn into resentment that festers inside you. It is why you hold grudges and become tense or irritable in certain situations or when in the presence of certain people. What's more, suppressed anger feeds on itself until it explodes.

"My first real relationship was with one of my college professors," Terry recalls. "He definitely got off on having a young coed as his lover and cast himself as Professor Higgins molding Eliza Doolittle into the perfect lady." But Terry's lover went overboard, criticizing almost everything she did or said. He called her stupid and childish, crude and unsophisticated. He told her what to wear and how to act. If she did not "perform" up to his standards, he would berate and belittle her mercilessly. Not thinking much of herself to begin with and an expert at denying her true feelings, Terry took his verbal abuse stoically until he crossed her bottom line. "I don't even remember what he did, but I was enraged," she says. "I screamed at him and pounded on his chest—and he just laughed at me." When he did, all of Terry's pent-up anger burst loose. She picked up an empty champagne bottle and hit her lover over the head with it, creating a gash that took six stitches to close. As you might expect, Terry made sure not to "do" anger ever again.

When suppressed rage erupts, the sheer power of it is liable to terrify you, and like Terry, you will work even harder to keep your anger buried. You may even end up directing it at yourself so that you are constantly racked by guilt or chronically depressed. In addition, your bottled-up rage can lead to low self-esteem, withdrawal and isolation, difficulty maintaining friendships, suicidal thinking, sexual dysfunctions, migraine headaches, colitis, ulcers, high blood pressure, and substance abuse.

But even more important, because other emotions that you must deal with before you can move on hide behind your outrage and indignation, *you cannot heal*. You simply cannot let go of your pain until you let go of your anger. And as you can see, you do not let go of it by digging a hole and burying it.

Doing Damage While Doing Anger

Once you reach the indignation stage and get in touch with your anger, you will indeed express it. Unfortunately, much of what you do to discharge anger and "clear the air" will not work to your benefit. But it will be familiar. After all, you have seen anger expressed in destructive ways throughout your life.

As children, you observed adult role models, including your parents, express their rage loudly, explosively, violently, and unpredictably. You may have been physically or verbally abused by angry adults who would not let you express your own anger at them. You probably watched your mother end a telephone conversation with her mother and immediately find a reason to yell at you; saw your father come home angry about something that happened at work and yell at your mother; or stood by while other adults vented their outrage at bank tellers, sales clerks, and "Sunday" drivers who did nothing to warrant the treatment they received.

What did you learn from all this? Well, for one thing you were left with the impression that anger could take over at any time and that it made you do things that you would not normally do. You might feel bad about your behavior after the fact, but because you were angry, you really couldn't help yourself and therefore should not be held accountable for your actions. From your adult role models you learned to inflict pain when you felt angry, especially on people who were smaller or weaker than you and unable to defend themselves. Finally, you learned that it was okay to feel angry at one person but take out your anger on someone or something else.

These general impressions are reinforced by the media, which give us countless headlines sensationalizing violent crimes of passion and revenge. John Wayne movies, Rambo, and even Saturday morning cartoons reinforce the notion that when someone hurts you, you must "make them pay." In film and fiction, no wrongdoing goes unpunished, and that punishment generally includes hurting the "bad guys" at least as much as and preferably more than they hurt you.

What's more, in recent years various "pop" psychology books and "instant awareness" seminars have glorified getting anger out of your system in any way you can—including venting your outrage whenever you feel it. We do not doubt that this advice was well intended, and we certainly are not trying to tell you that you should *not* express your anger. However, "blowing off steam" and angrily dumping a long list of grievances in someone's lap—especially when you are "seeing red" and have adrenaline pumping throughout your body—invariably hurts or terrifies the person on the receiving end of your rage and anyone else in the immediate vicinity as well. You may think you are clearing the air and preventing ulcers, high blood pressure, or heart attacks, but in reality you are stirring up additional conflict and hostility as well as making messes that you rarely stick around to clean up. This will not enhance your healing process.

Clarification Strategy Number 9:
Anger You Know

Are *you* doing damage while "doing" anger? Why not take a moment to find out? Here is a list of some of the unhealthy, destructive, or simply ineffective ways to express anger. Some were done *to* you or in your presence by other people, and you were hurt or frightened by them. Check the ones that fit the description. Some you use to vent your own angry feelings. Mark those with an *X*.

__pounding fists on tables
__"peeling rubber"
__shouting
__kicking or hitting a wall or a pet or a person
__spanking
__put-downs
__battering
__name calling
__hanging up the phone
__other:

__slamming doors
__throwing things
__cursing
__dumping: airing grievances without allowing the other person to respond
__going for the jugular: aiming verbal attacks directly at another person's sore spots
__making threats

Perhaps you've noticed that much of what was done to you you now do to others. Like pain, destructive methods for expressing anger are passed on from generation to generation.

Clarification Strategy Number 10: Anger You Don't Know

The next list of inappropriate ways to express anger should be of particular interest to those of you who believe that you do not "do" anger. They are *passive-aggressive* behaviors that are motivated by the anger you do not express openly and may not even know you are feeling. They allow you to get your own way, make other people "pay," or act out your resentment *without* having to acknowledge or take responsibility for your anger. They generally infuriate other people, who end up acting out your anger *for you,* while you play the innocent bystander who would "never hurt anyone."

Again use an *X* to mark the ones you do and check the ones you have been on the receiving end of.

__lateness
__sarcasm
__"put-down" humor
__doing things that you know

__banging things around or making more noise than a task requires
__"accidentally" breaking

annoy someone and then saying (for the three-hundredth time), "I didn't know that bothered you."
—looking "through" people instead of at them
—sulking
—"pained" smiles
—not paying attention
—other:

soiling, or losing something that belongs to someone else
—embarrassing people or drawing unwanted attention to them
—silence
—gossip
—causing disturbances
—"forgetting"

Since you have been on both the giving and the receiving end of many destructive and passive-aggressive expressions of anger, you are probably well aware of the fallout they leave in their wake. Because they cause more discord, starting another round of the battle instead of ending the war, these ways of "doing" anger do not help you heal or forgive. In fact, each time you "lose your temper" or commit a vengeful act, you add to your already abundant supply of guilt and shame, as Suzanne has done.

> When I finally got in touch with my anger, I attempted to cut my father out of my life completely. I had no contact with him for almost three years, even though during that time he was gravely ill and in and out of the hospital.
> My father was dying, and I did not care. In fact, I was hoping that he would die. If he did, my problems would be over. My pain would finally end. But all the while I was thinking this, I was adding to my own pain. I felt guilty and ashamed. I did not see myself as someone who lacked compassion for a sick man, no less a dying one who was also my father. Yet that was precisely how I was acting.

In addition to creating new problems and dealing another blow to your self-esteem, explosive, violent, abusive, or otherwise destructive outbursts of anger—as well as passive-aggressive behaviors—block communication. When you are on the receiving end of them you feel hurt, frightened, and confused. You may want to end the confrontation by placating, conceding the point, changing the subject, or leaving the room. Or you may get in a few licks of your own, protecting yourself from anger with more anger and launching a counterattack. If you are the person venting anger, you are unlikely to pay much attention to what you are saying, you may not even mean most of what you say, and you probably are not considering the effect your words and actions have on the other person. You are too busy discharging your angry energy, energy that distorts your perceptions and leaves you in no mood to hear or give credence to the other person's point of view.

Finally, unhealthy expressions of anger do not solve problems. The unmet need behind your anger does not get met. Indeed, many of the things you are seeking—love, acceptance, encouragement, closeness, and so on—are harder than ever to come by after you vent your fury or inappropriately release your rage. What's more, while ranting, raving, sniping, or sulking, you are incapable of generating alternatives, negotiating compromises, resolving conflicts, or doing anything else that might *really* clear the air and solve your problems.

Again, we are not suggesting that you should stuff or suppress your anger and never express it at all. We are merely sharing our unshakable conviction that *how* that anger is expressed often does more harm than good and takes you farther away from healing and forgiveness instead of closer to it. In fact, your rage, attempts at revenge, revival of old conflicts, character assassination, and determination to keep the people who hurt you in prison virtually guarantee that you will get stuck with your old problems, your old pain, and your newfound indignation.

Getting Stuck in the Indignation Stage

As you now know, when you enter the indignation stage, you get in touch with your anger. Then to get out of this stage, you must let go of that anger. Most of us do not know how to do that. Consequently, instead of using the energy of the indignation stage to move you forward toward healing and forgiveness, you plant your feet squarely in this stage and refuse to budge. You get stuck and wreak havoc on your life and the lives of others.

When you get stuck in the indignation stage, you go from being angry at the people who hurt you and outraged by what they did to you to being angry at the world. You are constantly ready for a fight. Indeed, you may even look for opportunities to vent your anger.

But although your behavior may resemble that of the "meaner" victim, there is a subtle but significant difference. The meaner feels

victimized rather than angry. She is reacting to her own powerlessness
and pain in the only way she knows how—by passing it on to others
with her meanness. If you are stuck in the indignation stage,
however, you know that what you feel is anger, and your feelings are
likely to be justified. People and circumstances really do thwart you,
fail to meet your needs, cross your bottom line, and step on your
toes. The problem is that, while stuck in the indignation stage, you
are constantly on the lookout for these things, and you find them
everywhere you turn. And because you are determined to stand up for
yourself and make sure people pay for the damage they do, you
frequently and flagrantly let anyone and everyone know how angry
you are.

Your rage consumes you. It consumes time and energy as you
stew about your painful past experiences, internally curse the people
who hurt you, and plot ways to get even. Your anger calls the shots in
your life, making it difficult to concentrate on immediate tasks and
problems and taking the joy out of joyful occasions.

"For weeks before my wedding, I spent every waking moment
going over all the times my father 'went nuts' at weddings and other
social gatherings," Mark comments. "And when I wasn't thinking
about what he did in the past, I was coming up with worst-case
scenarios of what he could do to make my wedding day miserable. Of
course, those fantasies always included what I would do to him if he
did get out of line. I was absolutely convinced that he would ruin
things for me, but I was going to be ready for him this time. This
time I was going to make sure he got what he deserved."

As it turned out, Mark's wedding day *was* ruined, and he was
every bit as miserable as he thought he would be—but not because of
his father's behavior. "My father was a perfect gentleman," Mark
explains. "He didn't do any of the things I expected him to do, and I
was furious about that. I was furious because I had wasted all that
time worrying and having anxiety attacks. But most of all, I was
furious because I *wanted* him to pull one of his stunts. I wanted to be
able to tell him off once and for all—and he didn't give me the
chance."

Mark got stuck with all of the angry energy he had been
prepared to unleash on his father, and he wound up dumping it on his
new bride. "Our honeymoon started with the biggest fight we ever
had or ever would have again," he says. "We had a night of passion
in the bridal suite all right. We were passionately angry, passionately

yelling at each other, and passionately throwing things. It was a nightmare.''

When Mark's father ''behaved himself'' at the wedding, Mark could have been relieved. He could have relaxed and enjoyed himself, reminded himself of the love he felt for the woman he was marrying, or looked forward to the future they would have together. He might even have considered the possibility that his father did not have the power to ruin things for him anymore; that he was an adult and in charge of his own life. But his anger blocked all of this—and as long as Mark stayed stuck in the indignation stage, it always would.

Holding on to your anger makes it impossible to forgive the people who hurt you, even when they have changed and want to make amends. ''Now she wants to be my mother,'' Marcy seethes as she explains how her mother, now recovering from alcoholism, has been trying in every way she can to get back in Marcy's good graces. ''She offers to baby-sit so my husband and I can have a night out. She cooks meals and puts them in my freezer so I can just microwave them when I have to work late. She clips articles she thinks would interest me. Wants to take me out shopping. You name it.''

In these and other ways, Marcy's mother has tried to become involved in her daughter's life—which is precisely what Marcy longed for as a child and has ever since, right up until she got stuck in the indignation stage. Now she says, ''It's too little too late. Nothing she can do can make up for what she didn't do back then.'' And this is the paradox of the indignation stage. While in it, you want and often demand that ''they'' make up for what they did or did not do in the past. But they can never do enough to satisfy you—so you stay angry. You refuse to heal or forgive.

You do this because you *believe that you are justified in doing so* and have earned the right to say so whenever and in whatever way you want to. Acting upon your right to be right may be doing you more harm than good, and you must begin to ask yourself:

- Why am I right? Is my point of view *really* the only way to look at this situation?
- What do I gain by being right? Is it making me feel more powerful? Is it justifying actions that I might otherwise feel guilty about? Is it keeping me in the driver's seat?
- What does it cost me? Is it keeping me from getting my needs met, hurting the people I love, messing up my relationships,

making me feel guilty or regretful, increasing the stress in my life?
• Is what I gain worth the price I am paying?

The answer to that last question is always "no," yet you are likely to continue giving in to your indignation and venting your rage anyway. You see, while stuck in the indignation stage, you live out the true meaning of cutting off your nose to spite your face. Because you are constantly listening to the voice of your anger ("I'll show you who's boss. I'll teach you!") and acting accordingly, you not only insure that your needs go unmet, you also end up lonely, isolated, stressed out, unsupported, and in constant conflict with the people around you. You suffer these and other consequences because you'd rather be right than be happy—and that is no way to live your life or heal your wounds.

"But I want to be happy," you say. "I want that more than anything. I want to let go of my anger, but it just keeps coming back." Indeed it does and for a very practical reason—it is protecting you from something else. The late author James Baldwin, in *Notes of a Native Son,* put it this way:

> I imagine one of the reasons people cling to their hate so stubbornly is because they sense, once hate is gone, they will be forced to deal with the pain.

We wholeheartedly agree with Baldwin and have learned that anger protects people not only from pain, but from any facts or feelings that threaten them in any way. Anger keeps other people at a distance, protecting you from ridicule or rejection. By walking around with your dukes up and venting your rage frequently and indiscriminately, you compensate for feelings of powerlessness and ward off all those debilitating emotions that were part of the victim stage. In other words, while you are busy being angry, you do not hurt as much and are not as afraid of being hurt again as you would otherwise be.

As a result, you are unwilling to let go of your anger. You are afraid to give it up because you are afraid that you would not survive without it, that you will have to change, that you will have to face, and make amends for, everything you have done because you were hurt, and worst of all that you will feel powerless and victimized again.

Moving Out of the Indignation Stage

While stuck in the indignation stage, you want your hate *and* your peace of mind. But you cannot have both. You have to choose. You can keep your anger and give up inner peace. Or you can let go of anger and heal your wounds at last.

The key to getting through and getting out of the indignation stage is learning to feel your anger without permitting it to consume or control you. If you can do that, your indignation will help you rather than hurt you. You will be able to harness the anger and use it to empower you, to move you forward toward healing and forgiveness.

To begin to do that, you must gain new insights about anger. The one that works for us, and the one that turns the indignation stage into a fruitful and productive part of your journey to forgiveness, is the one we learned from Thomas Gordon, who created Parent Effectiveness Training and other effectiveness training programs that have helped millions of people get more of what they want out of life.

Gordon describes anger as a *secondary emotion*. It is triggered by and dramatizes some *underlying feeling*—fear, hurt, frustration, embarrassment, grief, shame—which you find more threatening or more difficult to cope with than indignation. Thus when you encounter painful or frightening situations, anger will rise to the surface before other emotions, but it does not actually replace those underlying feelings. Consequently, venting anger alone does not heal your real wounds or resolve your real issues. Indeed, if you do not look beyond the anger that often acts as a shield to protect you from your primary emotions, you may cause additional damage to your self-esteem and to the people around you.

For instance, you may have witnessed what most often happens when a young child wanders away from his mother in a department store. When the mother realizes that her five-year-old is missing, she panics. A wave of fear washes over her as she imagines that her child has been kidnapped, lured away by a child molester, climbed into an empty refrigerator and suffocated, or met with some other horrifying fate. Heaping guilt on top of her fear, she blames herself for not keeping her eye on him and searches frantically amid the racks, shelves, and display cases. She rushes over to the customer service desk, and they make an announcement over the public address system. Pacing, wringing her hands, and fighting back tears, she waits—thinking that she could not possibly survive if she lost this child whom she loves dearly.

But what does this mother do when her child is turned over to her by a security guard who found him wandering through the women's wear department, looking for his mommy and crying? She does *not* tell him how scared she was, how bad she felt about not hanging on to his hand, or how much she loves him and how terrible she would feel if she lost him permanently. No, because anger—activated by fear, guilt, and the pain of a possible loss—surfaces first, it is what she expresses. She vents her anger by smacking the child's bottom, grabbing his arm, and dragging him with her as she storms away, saying, ''How many times do I have to tell you not to leave my side when we're shopping? You'll never learn, will you? When you get home, you're going straight to your room and staying there for the rest of the day!''

What a difference it would have made if that mother had told that child that she loved him and would suffer if he was not in her life, if she had apologized for reacting angrily and acknowledged that she felt scared the whole time he was missing. Certainly the child, who was probably terrified and in need of some tenderness, would have had his sense of safety and security restored instead of threatened further by a parent who was so obviously unhappy to have him back at her side. And at the very least, the mother would not have felt ashamed of herself for handling the situation the way she did.

If you have done this, or something similar, it will not help the healing process for you to feel inordinate guilt. We've all expressed our angry feelings at times when we were not in touch with, or too afraid to express, our more painful, more vulnerable, primary feelings. We were trained to do that. But we can train ourselves now to be more in touch with, and more comfortable with, our primary emotions.

Clarification Strategy Number 11:
Anger Dialogue

Take some time now to figure out what your anger is most likely to dramatize, to identify the feelings and circumstances that stir up angry energy and push your anger to the surface. A creative way to do this is to *ask your anger* why it appeared when it did.

Think of recent or typical situations in which you became angry and then write a dialogue between yourself and your anger. You can ask what your anger really means, what it is hiding from you, or why it exploded with such force at that particular time. You can even discuss the role you would like your anger to play in the future. Here is an example contributed by a forgiveness seminar participant:

ME: Okay, old buddy, old pal, I know you're in there, and you have some explaining to do.

ANGER: *Don't tell me you're feeling guilty again. I'm getting pretty sick of this routine. First you ask me to help you and then you get bent out of shape by what I do.*

ME: But you aren't helping me. You're getting in my way.

ANGER: *What a wimp. I didn't hear you complaining when I reduced your ex-wife to tears.*

ME: Why did you do that, anyway?

ANGER: *Don't you remember? You wanted to hurt her.*

ME: I think that's what *you* wanted. I just wanted to make sure she didn't hurt me, just like I want to make sure other women don't get close enough to hurt me.

ANGER: *Brilliant insight, pal. But what's your problem? I make sure those things don't happen, don't I?*

ME: But you go overboard.

ANGER: *I only do what you let me do. I admit that if you give me an inch, I'm going to try and take a mile, but you're the one who just sits there and lets it happen. . . .*

As you can see, this seemingly innocuous exercise can give you valuable insight into the issues and feelings that are masked by your anger. It also helps you realize that anger is a *part of you* rather than an alien force that invades your body and forces you to behave the way you do. What you do with your anger is very much up to you, and we would like to offer the following guidelines for handling your anger constructively.

"Doing" Anger Constructively: A Prescription

Step One: Discharge the angry energy. When someone or something instigates indignation and you feel anger rising to the surface, the very first thing you must do is ask yourself, "Am I in charge?" Much of the time, you will not be. This is because anger's physical side effects as well as its emotional "charge" create energy that clamors to be released. The rush of adrenaline and the surge of energy must be discharged before you attempt to do anything about the situation that is making you angry. Here are some *healthy* ways to release that energy:

- going for a brisk walk
- biking
- throwing rocks into a pond
- chopping wood
- pounding a pillow
- crying
- singing loudly
- getting a massage
- throwing darts
- finding someplace no one will hear you, perhaps in the car with the windows rolled up, and screaming at the top of your lungs
- writing out your anger in a journal
- talking it out with a friend
- running or other forms of exercise
- throwing bottles at the dump
- vacuuming
- hitting a punching bag
- going to a counseling session
- dancing
- taking a shower

Although not all of these alternatives may work for you, at least one will. You will be able to get the angry energy out of your system *without hurting or frightening anyone,* as well as have an opportunity to clear your head and regain your perspective.

Step Two: Look underneath the anger. The underlying feelings, the fear, hurt, frustration, shame, and embarrassment, that your anger is dramatizing are frequently the result of wanting or needing something that you did not get or that was taken away from you. Whether you lost or did not get love, acceptance, pride, credit for something you did, anonymity, help with the housework, or anything else, "doing" anger is often an attempt to at best get that back or at least get something in return—like revenge. In order to "do" anger constructively and actually get something other than guilt and pain for your trouble, you must ask yourself, "What do I want or need right now? What am I hoping to achieve?"

If you are stuck in the indignation stage, your first answer to these questions is likely to be "I want to make him pay, I want him to suffer, to make up for what he did, to apologize, or to hurt as much as I hurt." If those are the answers you come up with, ask yourself the questions again, this time adding, "Can I realistically expect to achieve that goal? Will it really make me feel better?" Then ask yourself, "What else do I want?"

Harriet, for instance, at first believed that she wanted "Larry to never have a moment's happiness or peace as long as he lived." Her vengeful acts allowed her to achieve that goal to a certain extent. But they also left her feeling worse instead of better and escalated the custody battle, which was one of the underlying issues that fueled her anger. By delving deeper, Harriet recognized that what she *really* wanted was to "resolve the custody issue so I no longer have to live in fear of losing my kids." Once she realized that was what she wanted, she also realized that she could not get it if she continued doing what she had been doing.

Step Three: Consciously decide what to do. You take this step by asking yourself, "What can I do to get what I want or need without hurting myself or other people?" The first decision you must make is *not* to express your anger and other emotions in destructive ways. As you consider your options, check them against the list of ineffective and passive-aggressive expressions of anger in the strategies on page 154. If your option appears on the list, eliminate it as a possibility.

There are many productive ways to get your needs met, including meeting your own needs or turning to other people or other activities to give you what you have not gotten from someone who hurt you. But more often than not, and especially with immediate, here-and-now issues, you will probably want to express your feelings to the person who hurt you. If you choose to do this, you must act responsibly.

We suggest reviewing what you learned in step two and using that information to complete sentences that resemble the following:

I feel _____ when you (unacceptable behavior)
and I would prefer that you (alternative behavior).

Think of or write several versions of this sentence (and several alternative behaviors for each). Try to imagine how actually saying these words will affect you *and* the person who will be receiving your message.

For instance, one of Harriet's sentences read: "I feel angry because you are trying to steal my children away from me, and I wish you would just stop using them to hurt me." She soon realized that actually saying this to Larry probably would not deescalate the custody battle. Another version read: "I feel terrified when I think about losing custody of the kids and panic whenever you tell me you are going ahead with the custody suit. I wish we could discuss this rationally and find a way to negotiate a compromise." Although saying this did not guarantee that Harriet's problems would be solved, it did increase her chances of getting what she wanted without making matters worse.

Although you will not express your feelings and wishes by reading your statements word for word, you too must choose the approach that is most likely to meet your needs while doing the least amount of damage to the other person or your relationship.

Unfortunately, no matter how carefully you choose your words, letting people know that they hurt you or behaved in a way that is unacceptable to you is likely to create some conflict and confusion. Asking people to change their behavior in any way is likely to bruise their egos and hurt their feelings. Therefore it is unfair and unreasonable to speak your mind and walk away. Before you decide what to do, you must ask yourself: "Am I willing to stick around to clean up any mess I make?"

If you are not willing to spend some time discussing the issue or negotiating a compromise, or if you do not want to hear what the other person has to say to explain his or her behavior and definitely do not want to take any responsibility for the situation, then you are not yet ready to and probably should *not* express your feelings directly to the person who hurt you. You may still need to express yourself, however, and we suggest talking about and attempting to work through your anger with someone other than the person who hurt you.

In fact, whenever you feel angry and unsure of how you will react in the presence of the person who got you angry, we recommend that you first talk things over with your counselor, a support group member, a friend, a clergy person, or someone else not directly involved in the situation. This allows you to release some more of your angry energy, identify more underlying feelings or issues, and rehearse how you will express your feelings once you are ready to do so.

Although this may seem like an arduous, time-consuming process, it probably took longer to read about it than it will ever take you to do it. "Doing" anger constructively is simply a matter of thinking about what you will do *before* you do it rather than unleashing your rage and thinking about what you did wrong *after* you've done it.

Using this prescription is particularly beneficial for effectively handling immediate, here-and-now anger. However, to let go of anger generated by your unhealed wounds and unfinished business, you may have to go further and work on:

- recognizing that when you feel testy, edgy, impatient, irritable, or disgruntled, old anger and indignation may be rumbling around inside of you;
- realizing that this is most likely to occur when you are overtired, frustrated, nervous, rushed, or worried;
- doing something about *that* situation, including taking a nap, going for a walk, releasing tension through physical activity, talking with a support person, writing in a journal, soaking in a hot bath, or having a good cry.

In addition, you must continue to work on yourself and your self-esteem. As you make your life better, you will have less to be angry about and you will also have less proof that the people who hurt you deserve to be punished. In fact, you will become strong enough and healthy enough and big enough to consider unlocking the prison gates and releasing the people who hurt you. But first you must release yourself, setting yourself free by relinquishing your victim label and replacing it with a neon sign announcing that you are a survivor.

CHAPTER NINE

THE SURVIVOR STAGE

My father's health continued to deteriorate, but the fact that he might die before I made peace with him was not enough to get me to speak to him. As you might imagine, my mother considered my behavior to be inexcusable.

"Your father is dying," she would say during frequent phone calls. "You don't write. You don't call. The sicker he gets, the less you seem to care. Why are you doing this? After all, what have we ever done to you?"

This question was begging to be answered. Each time I heard it, I felt as if a knife had been plunged into my heart. Finally I did what I believed to be the only self-respecting thing I could do. I told my mother my awful secret.

I wrote her a letter and explained that although she herself had done nothing and I did not blame her, incest had occurred in our home. I can only imagine the shock she must have felt when she read that. After all, I was telling her that her husband, whom she had lived with, trusted, and loved for almost forty years, had molested her daughter. In fact, had molested both of her daughters. To tell you the truth, I did not expect to be believed.

The letter did hurt her, but she also believed the disclosure it contained. Within days she flew from Florida and we met at my sister's house. We talked and cried, hugged and kissed. It was the first real support I felt I had ever gotten from my mother, and it was a great relief to have finally told her about the incest. That was the good part.

But then, as my mother was preparing to leave us, she said, "We mustn't let your dad know this happened." Quite shocked, I assured her that he had to know. He was the one who did it. But she believed he had blocked it from his mind, and since I had done that myself, I did nothing to stop her from making up a story to tell him when she got home. I did tell her, however, that should he call, I would not confirm her story. I would not actively participate in another cover-up. But as it turned out, I was never asked to.

When my mother returned to my father, he was back in the hospital. She walked into his room but did not go over to kiss him, which was how she always greeted him. He sensed that something was wrong and asked for an explanation. And although she had fully intended to keep the information from him, she told him exactly what we had told her.

Finally, the truth was out in the open! I suppose I thought that would make everything okay again or at least pave the way for our unfinished business to be resolved before my father died. That was *not* what happened.

My father denied all of it; called us liars, said he wanted to have nothing to do with such despicable daughters, and disowned us.

My mother was torn. She did not know whom to believe. My brother stepped forward and told her to believe us because *it had happened to him, too*. My father simply disowned him as well.

There were several things Suzanne could have done at this point. She could have *denied* the impact of being disbelieved and disowned, shrugging her shoulders and declaring, "I said what I had to say, and it didn't work out the way I wanted it to. But it's no big deal. It doesn't bother me."

Suzanne could have *blamed herself* for the chaos and conflict that followed her disclosure, examining her own behavior under a magnifying glass while thinking, "If only I had handled things differently, our lives would not be such a mess right now."

Suzanne could have returned to the victim stage, whining, wallowing, and descending to new depths of helplessness and hopelessness. "Of course, nothing worked out the way I wanted it to," she could have said. "Nothing ever does."

Or she could have given free rein to her *indignation* and anger, vowing not to speak to her father as long as he lived and to spit on his grave when he died.

Yes, Suzanne could have reacted in any or all of these ways, but she did not.

> I was stunned by my father's response, although I should have been prepared for it. I was disheartened, but because I was moving forward in my healing process, I was not devastated, and I wasted very little time blaming myself for an outcome I could not control. Under the circumstances, I had done the best I could do—and what a powerful revelation that was. It enabled me to consider the possibility that I had been *doing the best I could all along*.
>
> Yes, I was disappointed, hurt, and angry, but I was also released from the expectation that I could ever get what I needed from my father, which freed me to look elsewhere and to myself to meet my needs. I took advantage of every resource I could find. I read books, attended lectures, went to workshops, and continued to get counseling and participate in an incest survivors' group. I started taking care of myself physically as well, jogging and improving my eating habits. I wallowed less and did more to get my life in order. Five years after my journey began, I had made it to the survivor stage of my healing process.

The Survivor Stage

Upon arrival in the *survivor stage,* we proudly proclaim, "I made it! I'm here! I survived!" And what precious, powerful, and important words those are. When we can say and fully believe them, we feel a cloud lifting from our soul. For the first time since we were hurt, we see a brighter future, realize that it is within our grasp, and reach out to embrace it.

You reach the survivor stage when you are ready and not one moment sooner. There are no magic words, no magic potions, that can bring you to this stage more quickly or guarantee that you never slip back into the more painful and self-defeating stages that came before it.

There is one and only one way to become a survivor, and that is by surviving—surviving the injuries and injustices you sustained, surviving the denial stage and all of the damage you did on the dead-end streets you used to travel, surviving the self-punishment of the self-blame stage, and wallowing and self-indulgence of the victim stage, and the rage that consumed you while you were in the indignation stage. Kicking, cursing, crying, struggling, but also learning every step of the way, you move through those stages according to your own needs and your own time frame.

And it all seems worth it when you reach the survivor stage, because knowing what you went through to get there makes this stage all the sweeter. You realize that you have *earned* the right to call yourself a survivor and to declare

> *I am alive.* I was hurt, and what I did because I was hurt made a difference in my life. I do not deny it, but I did live through it, and I've learned much from it.
>
> *I am okay.* I now know that I was not responsible for the hurtful things other people did to me and that I do not have to go on beating myself over the head for the things for which I *was* responsible.
>
> *I am back in the driver's seat.* I may have been powerless at the time I was hurt, but I am not powerless now. I was victimized, but I am not a victim. I am an adult, and I can steer my life in the direction that I want it to go.
>
> *I am better than I've ever been.* I am strong enough to face life without using indignation as a shield to protect me. I can feel angry, but I am not a slave to my anger.

Yes, these are the statements that survivors make, and they are full of power, pride, and dignity. Read them aloud and you will hear how vastly different they are from the sounds you made in other stages. Indeed, it feels so good to say these things—and mean them—that once you get a taste of the survivor stage, you never forget it. You may slide back into the earlier stages from time to time. All of us do. However, because you remember what it feels like to be a survivor and want to feel that way again, you do not stay down for long. You do whatever you need to do to get back to the survivor stage.

Under the Circumstances, You Did the Best You Could

> *Every single human being, at every moment of the past— when the entire situation is taken into account—has done the very best he or she could do, and so deserves neither blame nor reproach from anyone—including the self. This is in particular is true of you.*
>
> —Harvey Jackins
> *Quotes*

"I used to believe that being sexually abused by my grandfather did not affect me in a negative way," Terry wrote in response to a forgiveness seminar exercise. "But now I know that it influenced me every day of my life and was behind a lot of the self-destructive stuff I did over the years. I'm not proud of those things. If I could do it over again, I'd do things differently. But now I know that, under the circumstances, I was doing the best I could do."

Even though Terry spent nearly two decades going back and forth between "promiscuous phases" and relationships that lasted exactly as long as her grandfather's abuse had, and even though she contracted sexually transmitted diseases, had abortions, found herself in truly dangerous situations, jeopardized her career, and hurt her long-term lovers, Terry really was doing the best that she could. She lacked the *insight* to do better.

It may be difficult to believe that an intelligent woman who held a responsible position in a helping profession and was well educated about human behavior could be unaware of the self-destructiveness of her own behavior, but that was indeed the case. Terry did not recognize the connections between her past experiences and her present-day circumstances. She did not see that she was repeating certain patterns like clockwork. Terry's powerful denial defense mechanism blocked these realities from her conscious awareness and kept her from feeling the full impact of her own actions. Without that awareness, she could not change her behavior. She simply did not know enough about *why* she was doing what she was doing to act differently—and neither did you.

"I used to believe that I had to figure everything out on my own and handle everything all by myself," wrote Darlene. "But now I know that I am not in charge of the entire universe, that if I give other people a chance, they can be trustworthy and won't always let me down."

What Darlene used to believe and what she did because of it ensured that she would constantly feel overwhelmed and resentful. Her controlling behavior irritated and aggravated the people around her. Her job performance evaluations always included comments like "Does not delegate responsibility" or "Is not a team player," and she did not get the promotions she believed she deserved. Since no one else showed their appreciation, Darlene rewarded herself for "doing so much for so many" by bingeing on sweets and junk food. But compulsive overeating only compounded Darlene's problems. When we first met her, she was more than one hundred pounds overweight and had recently been diagnosed as a diabetic.

Yet, like Terry, Darlene had been doing the best she could. She did not have the *resources* to do better. As you may recall, Darlene was hurt when her parents got divorced and her father repeatedly failed to show up for visits. Circumstances that could be expected to hurt any child hurt Darlene more because she experienced them at a time when divorce was relatively uncommon. Darlene had no one to answer her questions or help her understand her feelings. There were no books to read or TV movies of the week to watch. In fact, Darlene was well into her teens before she even met another child from a broken home. Believing that she was the only person in the world who felt the way she did and because there really were no resources available to her while she was growing up, Darlene did indeed have to figure everything out on her own. With little information and few options, Darlene figured things out to the best of her ability and then acted accordingly—and so did you.

"I used to believe that anger and violence were the same thing," wrote Caryn, another forgiveness seminar participant. "I used to think that as long as I did not get angry, I would never do to other people what my mother did to me. But now I know that bottling up my rage caused my downfall and that I was destined to repeat my past until I learned from it.

"But I did learn from it," she continues. "I learned how I took over the role of the oppressor and abused myself with alcohol and drugs. I learned that being under stress while being out of touch with my feelings meant I was bound to explode eventually. I even learned about the horrible guilt and shame my mother must have felt after she battered me—because I felt it the day I nearly strangled my daughter, who was only three at the time. That was three years ago, and although there is no excuse for abusing a defenseless child and I am not justifying what I did, I do know that given what I had to work with, I was doing the best I could."

The incident Caryn refers to frightened her so badly that she immediately sought professional help. She no longer drinks or takes drugs and never again abused her son. But even when she was doing those things and had reached the lowest, most destructive point in her life, Caryn was still doing the best she could. She lacked the emotional support and *nourishment* to do better.

As a child Caryn was beaten severely, often, and for no comprehensible reason by her mother, whose grave mental illness was denied or ignored by everyone around her. Caryn's father did nothing to protect her or stop the beatings, even though he was often at home when they occurred. Caryn's grandmother, whom Caryn calls "the only bright spot in my childhood," was also a victim of Caryn's mother's abuse and in fact had been battered by her husband throughout their marriage. Although she gave Caryn the only unconditional love and acceptance she would ever receive, Caryn's grandmother was a role model of passivity and victimhood. "Just try not to get her angry," was her advice—and it did not do much good since Caryn's mother beat her daughter because "the voices" told her to and not because of anything Caryn did. What's more, because her mother and later Caryn herself lied about the origin of broken bones and bruises, teachers, neighbors, nurses, and doctors who might have intervened on Caryn's behalf did not get the chance to.

Throughout her childhood, Caryn needed someone to stand up for her, someone to protect her and tell her that what was happening to her was not okay. She needed guidance and encouragement, comfort and reassurance that she was more than her mother's punching bag. But Caryn did not get these things. In fact, she received virtually no emotional nourishment as a child or as an adult. And until she started getting some positive input, she had nothing to work with but her pain, no examples to learn from but the negative ones she'd observed during childhood and too little emotional maturity to exert control over her destructive impulses. Those were the facts of her life, and although they do not excuse her behavior, they do explain why what she did—although not good enough—was the best that she could do at that time.

Like Terry, Darlene, and Caryn, each and every one of us did the very best we could with the insight, resources, and emotional nourishment available to us. If we had *more* conscious awareness of what made us tick, *more* information and alternatives available to us, *different* life experiences and *more* love, support, and encouragement, we could have done better. And we would have.

Once you accept this as a truth about your own life, you gain admission to the survivor stage and make a major breakthrough in your healing process. You move even closer to forgiving yourself— by letting go of guilt, feeling less ashamed, and focusing less attention on the regrets that keep you grounded in pain from the past.

Letting Go of Guilt, Shame, and Regrets

Guilt is an immediate reaction to things that we do wrong or that go wrong. Guilt sets boundaries to protect us from our own excesses. When we cross that boundary—as Darlene did, for instance, when she ate the cupcakes intended for her daughter's birthday party, as Harriet did when she called Larry late at night and then hung up as soon as he answered the phone, or as Bruce did when he went into debt to support his cocaine habit—we feel guilty, and it is appropriate to feel that way because what we did or what happened was indeed our fault. In fact, a good deal of what you may have done to block out, compensate, and make people pay for your pain falls into that category.

You may have developed addictions and given in to compulsions that not only damaged you, but also hurt other people. You may have lied, lost jobs, gone into debt, neglected the people you loved, and even stolen to support your dependency on alcohol, drugs, food, or gambling. Chances are that you caused physical and psychological pain with your self-indulgences and meanness while in the victim stage and by indiscriminately venting your anger during the indignation stage. You may have strained and damaged your relationships with your children, spouses, friends, co-workers, and family members. As you enter the survivor stage, you are acutely aware of your own wrongdoing—and you feel guilty.

Fortunately, this sort of guilt—which is focused on specific behaviors that you can do something about—can be productive. If you feel guilty about something you have done or failed to do, you can apologize, make amends, learn from your mistakes, choose not to make those same mistakes again, change your behavior, and move on.

"Sometimes this horrible feeling of doom washes over me," says Alison, who spent years blaming herself for her father's suicide and trying to make amends by making people happy no matter what it cost her. "It starts in the pit of my stomach, just this strange hollow feeling. But then it gets stronger, like waves pounding the shore, a wave of anxiety, a wave of fear, a wave of terror, until I just want to curl up into a ball, squeeze my eyes shut, and disappear. And underneath it all is the shame. The shame of having a father who killed himself and knowing I couldn't stop him from doing that. The shame of all the things I've done since then, the ridiculous lengths I went to in order to 'fix' things for everyone and usually making a bigger mess than there would have been if I'd just let things happen the way they were supposed to happen. The shame of marrying a man who had the same mental illness my father had. You name it, I can feel ashamed of it, and it's an awful, awful feeling.''

Indeed it is. *Shame* is the reflection of guilt that has piled up and been incorporated into your identity—and as such is far more difficult to let go of. Unlike guilt, which evaluates a specific behavior or attitude as wrong or bad and motivates you to change that aspect of yourself, shame makes a statement about who you are as a person. Somewhere along the line you stopped thinking, ''I *did* something that I now realize was stupid,'' and started thinking, ''I *am* stupid, and I am ashamed of myself for being stupid.''

As you might expect, shame has its roots in the self-blame stage of the healing process. Assuming responsibility for wrongs that were not your fault—which is what you did in that stage—leaves you feeling guilty about circumstances that were, in reality, beyond your control. Since it was someone else's behavior and not your own that caused the problem in the first place, there was nothing you could do to actually relieve your guilt, no amends you could make, no productive way to change yourself or the situation so that you could learn from it and avoid making the same ''mistakes'' again.

However, shameful feelings can come back to haunt you long after you leave the self-blame stage. Bombarding yourself with the negative messages you originally received from other people, you may feel ashamed of yourself for being the lazy, ignorant, incompetent, worthless person that they let you know you were. This negative self-image, this constant sense of being ashamed of who you are, makes it extremely difficult to believe that you *deserve* more than you are already getting out of life and therefore creates a major obstacle to healing and forgiveness.

Finally, your *regrets* reflect your genuine sorrow over opportunities that you missed or things that you failed to say or do in the past. You can regret everything from missing your children's early years because you were a workaholic to being unable to make peace with a parent before he or she died. Yet no matter what they are about, all regrets have two things in common. First, you cannot rewind your life like a videotape, going back in time to do things differently.

Second, wishing that you could keeps your gaze trained on the past—so much so that you are likely to miss the opportunities that present themselves today. In short, you accumulate more regrets.

Like that traveler dragging fifty pounds of excess baggage through the train station, your progress toward healing and forgiveness is slower and more of a struggle while you are weighted down by guilt, shame, and regret. You simply must let go of it. Fortunately, the revelation that admitted you to the survivor stage helps you do just that.

Once you accept that you did the best you could with the insight, resources, and nourishment that you had, you can finally stop brooding about everything that went wrong and that you did wrong in the past. Instead you take tangible steps to repair your relationships, make amends for the wrongs you have done in the past, and change your behavior so that you do not make the same mistakes in the future. Whittling away at shame and letting go of it bit by bit, you begin to home in on what you do have instead of seeing only what you lack. You unload that excess baggage, developing new attitudes and soaring to new heights.

New Attitudes

Old Slave's Prayer

> *Oh God, I ain't what I ought to be,*
> *And God, I ain't what I want to be,*
> *Dear God, I ain't what I'm gonna be,*
> *But thank you, God—I ain't what I used to be!*
>   —Anonymous

"I want this," Terry thought, while sitting on the patio of a friend's home in the hills north of San Francisco. Her friend Amanda sat nearby, bouncing her eight-month-old son on her knee and watching her three-year-old daughter dig a hole in the lawn. In addition to two beautiful children, Amanda had a terrific husband, a happy marriage, a thriving private psychotherapy practice, a home, friends, roots, and, it seemed to Terry, no insecurities whatsoever.

"I want this," Terry said aloud, and was shocked by Amanda's response.

"You'll never have it at the rate you're going," Terry's friend replied sharply. "You don't build a relationship by sleeping with every man you meet on the remotest chance that one of them might be Mr. Right. If you keep doing what you're doing, you're going to get what you've always gotten—a lot of loneliness and a lot of pain.''

Stunned, Terry tried to explain away Amanda's remarks. ''I tried to convince myself that the baby had kept her up all night and she was too tired to know what she was saying,'' Terry recalls eighteen months later. ''I thought that she might have been irritated because I had spent so much time dumping on her about my latest relationship breakup. And of course, I told myself that Amanda had always been prone to exaggeration and that I really didn't sleep around *that* much.'' Indeed, the only explanation Terry did not try on for size was that Amanda had decided it was finally time to confront her with the truth. Yet that was precisely the thought that kept popping back into Terry's mind. For the first time in her life, Terry's well-honed denial defense mechanism failed her, and for the first time in years, Terry cried.

''We spent the rest of the day and most of the night talking about me and what a mess I'd made of my life,'' Terry reports. ''Amanda already knew all the surface details. I told her those years ago. But this time around, she made me talk about what they meant and how I really felt and why I kept doing the same stupid things over and over and over again. Once I said those things to her, there really was no way I could go back to completely denying them.''

From that moment on, Terry made a concerted effort to peel away the layers of denial and examine the realities of her life. She returned to therapy, joined a support group, read books, attended personal growth workshops, kept a journal, and had many a long, honest conversation with Amanda as well as with other friends. As a result, she gained new insights about herself and her self-defeating behavior patterns. Then she emerged in the survivor stage and began to change those patterns.

''I'm in phase three,'' she explains with a smile that is genuine and far different from the one that was permanently painted on her face while she was in the denial stage. ''In phase one, I did stupid things without thinking about what I was doing or caring about the consequences. In phase two, I still did stupid things, but I felt rotten about them afterward. Then I got depressed and did more stupid stuff so I wouldn't have to think about the pain. Now I don't give in to the urge to go out and get picked up as often as I used to. When I do, I still feel rotten about it, but instead of beating up on myself, I try to figure out *why* I did what I did, and I look for other, better ways to take care of myself when I'm feeling lonely or insecure or unappreciated.''

Increased awareness of the reasons behind your actions and a willingness to try new, self-enhancing rather than self-destructive behaviors is what distinguishes survivors from victims. The goal, of course, is to eliminate those self-defeating habits altogether, and in the survivor stage you develop a positive yet realistic perspective on your progress toward that goal.

You can do this because as you rise above pain from the past, *everything looks different*. Instead of expecting perfection and berating yourself for falling short of that standard, you set reasonable goals and appreciate how far you have come already. "I'm getting there," you say. "I've made strides, and soon I'll make more."

"There are still things I want but don't have yet," Terry explains. "A healthy relationship is one of those things. But at least I now know what a healthy relationship is—and I'm even beginning to believe that I deserve one." In the survivor stage you too will come to believe that you deserve something more or better than you have gotten in the past. And that attitude change enables you to stop repeating the past and start moving full speed ahead toward a brighter future.

For years you may have approached new relationships and situations with the conscious or subconscious desire to "get it right this time around," but you got new pain and disappointment instead. Once you reach the survivor stage, however, you realize that, given the conditions and raw materials you had to work with, you actually "did it right" the first time—even if you did not do it very well. As a result, you no longer need to or want to reenact your painful past experiences in your present-day relationships or continue repeating patterns that net you the same sort of pain you felt in the past. Instead of playing the same scenes with new actors standing in for the people who once hurt you, you are free to write new scenes and follow a new script that can indeed end with everyone living happily ever after.

In earlier stages of your healing process, everything was black or white, good or bad, right or wrong. You were either absolutely perfect or a complete failure. The people who hurt you were either totally despicable because of what they did or they were saints whose hurtful actions had to be "explained away" with denial or self-blame. Because you could not or would not see the shades of gray, you felt threatened and baffled each and every time real life and real people did not conform to your image of the way things were supposed to be. Now, in the survivor stage, you are able to *tolerate life's ambiguities*. As Suzanne did, you can say, "You never really know how things will turn out," and add, "But that's okay. That's how life is."

You can even laugh at life's absurdities because in the survivor stage, you *find the sense of humor* you lost when you were hurt or never really had because of the injuries and injustices you sustained early in life. In fact, you realize that the people you wanted to throttle for saying, "One day you'll look back on this and laugh," were right. In retrospect, many incidents from your past do seem funny— including scenes that once seemed too humiliating to think about, much less find amusing.

For instance, several years after Harriet attended a forgiveness seminar, her perspective on the demise of her marriage had changed drastically. Seated across from us in the hotel lounge outside the ballroom where we were scheduled to present a workshop, Harriet reminisced about events that once brought bitter rather than mirthful tears to her eyes and laughed so heartily that she had to gulp for air between sentences. "That scene in the bank," she sputtered. "Can you imagine what that must have looked like? A jilted wife in designer jogging suit dumping her unfaithful husband's clothes on his mistress's desk? How melodramatic can you get? I'm surprised no one called the men in the white suits to carry me away."

Yes, in the survivor stage you smile, chuckle, even belly laugh easily and often. And that laughter is not the nervous, forced laughter of the denial stage. Nor is it the derisive laughter that accompanies the sarcastic, biting, "put-down" humor of the victim and indigna-tion stages. No, the smiles and laughter of the survivor stage are genuine—because all the pain and misery you have already been through keeps daily living in perspective. As actress Ethel Barrymore once said, "You grow up the day you have your first real laugh—at yourself," and you have indeed grown up enough to do that.

"Some of the things I did to try and hang on to Larry just crack me up now," Harriet continues. "Like parading around in sexy lingerie, fish-net stockings, and spiked heels. Believe me, I looked more like a centerfold for *Mad* magazine than for *Playboy*. And heaven only knows why I thought pretending to be the Happy Hooker could save a marriage that had been disintegrating for years. Counsel-ing, maybe, or a Marriage Encounter™ weekend, but sexy lingerie? How absurd!"

In addition to your sense of humor, as a survivor you rediscover your sense of *compassion*. Because you are no longer focusing all of your attention on *your* pain and *your* powerlessness and *your* problems, you can feel for other people who are struggling to work through their pain. Eventually that compassion is also extended to the people who hurt you.

Finally, because you now know that limited insight, resources, and nourishment were the reasons doing the best you could was not enough to heal your wounds and improve your life, you renew your commitment to increase all three so that you can do and be better in the future. As a result, you conduct your life differently than ever before.

New Behaviors

"I took the advice you gave us at that forgiveness seminar," Bruce explained when he met us for dinner before we went to a Broadway show and he headed for an AA meeting. "I made a list of all the things I needed to do to be physically, emotionally, and spiritually healthy. Then I added those things to my life one at a time. I'm halfway through the list, and I've never felt better in my life."

Bruce certainly looked healthier than ever. Thanks to daily workouts at a health club and a diet that was far different from the candy bars and coffee he once lived on, a year after he attended that forgiveness seminar Bruce's body was lean and well toned rather than painfully thin. His once pasty, pale skin glowed, and his blue eyes sparkled. He had given up cigarettes. He had attended numerous hotel management training seminars, developing new skills and impressing his superiors with his motivation and self-discipline, so much so that he had received several promotions and a transfer to corporate headquarters in New York City. He had even begun to conduct training seminars of his own, teaching other hotel managers the time management and organizational techniques he had learned and put into practice. In addition, Bruce continued to attend AA and Narcotics Anonymous (NA) meetings and recently began meditating as a way to reduce stress.

"I look at myself and my life now," Bruce said, "and I go, 'Who is this guy? He can't be the same guy who used to hang out in bathrooms snorting cocaine or puking his guts out from drinking too much Scotch.' And then when I realize that I am the same guy, I think about how far I've come and go, 'Okay, what next? Come on, world. I'm ready for you.' "

It is indeed hard to believe that this optimistic, self-confident young man is the same person who would do just about anything *not* to face reality or take responsibility for his own life, who once took no risks whatsoever because he was convinced that he was completely inadequate and perpetually doomed to fail. Yet, as difficult as it may be to accept while you are in the denial, self-blame, victim, or indignation stage, the survivor stage not only promises this sort of turnaround, but delivers it as well.

For one thing, in the survivor stage you spend more and more time *looking ahead toward health instead of back toward your pain*. This does not mean that you deny that you were hurt or minimize the impact that your painful past experiences had on your life.

"Yes, it was horrible," you admit.

"No, I wouldn't want to go through it again," you acknowledge.

"But since I did," you add, "I am going to make something from it. I am going to use it to put more joy, meaning, and purpose into my life."

Although you may have *thought* this before, in the survivor stage you actually *do* it. After years of merely responding to the people and circumstances that you happened to encounter, you take back the reins that you handed over to fate and play an active role in determining your own destiny. You become an actor instead of a reactor, a player in the game of life rather than a spectator watching from the sidelines while life passes you by.

Instead of acting out of habit, giving in to your compulsions, or simply drifting any way the wind blows, as a survivor *you make choices*. As Suzanne did when she decided to reveal the incest to her mother, you ask yourself, "What is the self-respecting thing to do in this situation?" You thoughtfully consider your alternatives and explore both the positive and negative consequences of each option. Then you choose the course of action that is best for you, that you can feel proud of and can act upon without hurting yourself or anyone else.

One of the choices you make in the survivor stage is to stop committing systematic suicide. You discontinue self-defeating and self-destructive pursuits, taking giant steps forward in your recovery from alcoholism, addictions, co-dependency, or compulsive overeating. You give up habits that hurt you, replacing them with new, healthier habits like:

- regular exercise;
- watching what, when, and how much you eat;
- managing your time and using more of it to play, relax, and replenish your energy supply;
- developing and maintaining friendships;
- organizing and adding some beauty to your home or work environment;
- injecting new romance and excitement into your marriage or love life.

Whether or not you have reached the survivor stage yet, you can start to make those sorts of changes in your life right away. The following strategy can help you identify your own systematic suicide behaviors and come up with some alternatives that will move you in the direction of overall wellness.

Clarification Strategy Number 12: Systematic Suicide

You are committing systematic suicide each time you:

- light a cigarette;
- drive your car without fastening your seat belts;
- have sex with someone whose sexual history you do not know;
- eat red meat or fried foods even though your cholesterol count is high;
- go on a crash diet, lose ten, twenty, or thirty pounds, and then gain it all back again;
- put off going to the gynecologist even though you are overdue for a Pap test;
- work twelve hours a day and worry about work during all other waking hours;
- do anything else—no matter how small—that jeopardizes your physical or emotional health or leaves you feeling guilty or ashamed of yourself.

Think about your own behavior. How do you commit systematic suicide? What do you eat, drink, swallow, or smoke that you would be better off without? What do you do that increases tension and stress? What don't you do that you should do in order to feel physically and mentally healthy?

Take out a sheet of paper, draw a line down the middle of it, and list ten of your own systematic suicide behaviors. We do not think you will have trouble coming up with ten examples, but if you do, you can consult the Clarification Strategy Number 1 on page 68 of chapter 4.

Choose five that you really feel rotten about and would like to change. Rank order those five, giving the one you would like to work on first an "A" rating, the one you want to change next a "B," and so on.

Then, realizing that the behavior you want to give up is probably fulfilling a need, try to determine what that need is. For instance, do you reach for a cigarette when you feel anxious or run to the refrigerator when you are bored? Do you eat high-cholesterol foods because they "fill you up" or because you have never developed a taste for healthier foods? Do you work twelve hours a day because you have trouble managing your time? Try to find the *reason* behind your systematic suicide behavior because it provides a clue about *what you can do instead.*

Brainstorm a list of alternative behaviors for each of your five lettered items, perhaps asking for suggestions from friends and colleagues. Appropriate options are those that fulfill the need that your systematic suicide behavior is currently meeting—but are productive rather than destructive. For example, instead of eating when you are bored, you could do a crossword puzzle, call a friend, write in your journal, read a book, garden, paste snapshots into a photograph album, write letters, play with your kids, or take a bubble bath—to name just a few alternatives. Similarly, if giving up cigarettes is likely to leave you jumpy and irritable, you must build into your life-style anxiety-reducing activities like exercise, walks in the woods, massage, hobbies and crafts that keep your hands busy, and meditation.

Keep the entire brainstorm list for future reference. But to get started on your effort to change, choose the three most appealing alternatives for each of your lettered systematic suicide behaviors and list them on the right side of the page opposite the items they will replace.

Finally, make a commitment to give up your self-destructive habits one at a time, beginning with the "A" behavior. Actually write out a contract with yourself that states what you will stop doing and what you will do instead. Then sign it, date it, and *do it*.

By giving up systematic suicide behaviors and pursuing overall wellness, you do much more than improve your physical health, although that is certainly part of what you do. The new habits that you develop also fulfill your emotional and spiritual needs, expanding your horizons and adding new dimensions to your life—which used to have only one dimension, the one defined by pain from the past.

More Signs of Survival

In the survivor stage, you no longer go to extremes. You change your life dramatically, but you make those changes wisely—taking them one step at a time rather than attempting to do a complete overhaul overnight. This is an important point, because should you try to do too much too quickly, you will overwhelm yourself and the people around you. If you approach healing with the same obsessiveness that you had for your self-destructive pursuits, change becomes an all-or-nothing proposition: if you don't get everything you want as soon as you want it, you give up trying to get anything at all and slide back into one of the earlier stages of the healing process. So please pursue wellness with energy and determination, but also with moderation. Fanaticism is dangerous even when it is focused on things that are good for you.

To approach change sensibly, but also because you can bump into pain from the past at any time as well as experience new injuries and injustices, you must build a support network and use it. This network might include counselors, members of a self-help group or a recovery program like AA, friends, relatives, your spouse, or people you meet at workshops or seminars and keep in touch with by writing letters and making telephone calls. The members of your support network are people you can laugh and play with as well as people who are able to help you solve problems, brainstorm alternatives, take stock, and take the risks that will expand your horizons and give you a whole new world to explore. They should *not* be people who, as psychologist Hanoch McCarty, of Cleveland State University, puts it, "massage your neurosis," wallowing with you and encouraging you to indulge yourself.

Few of you will reach the survivor stage *without* this kind of support. Because you know that the insight, resources, and nourishment these people can provide will help you heal and grow, once you are in this stage you continue to build and reach out to your support network. When you hit a rough spot, instead of withdrawing from the human race the way you used to do, you turn to people who can comfort, encourage, and advise you.

In addition, as a survivor you *give* support as well. As May Sarton, author of *At Seventy,* put it, you "take your anguish and set out." You use your newfound compassion and what you have learned while going through your own healing process to help other people who are struggling with theirs. For instance, Suzanne, who survived incest, now leads Incest Survivor Support Groups at the University of Massachusetts. Because she has grown, she can help others grow. She does this without getting down and wallowing with others, as she would have in the victim stage, or encouraging vindictiveness and a "screw the bastard" attitude, as she would have in the indignation stage. Similarly, some of the most effective substance abuse counselors are recovering addicts and alcoholics who have not only achieved sobriety, but have also come far enough along in their own healing process to compassionately and open-mindedly guide other people through that process. When you reach the survivor stage, you are able to (and you just may want to) do this too.

A New Lease on Life

> *I'm a survivor. . . . Being a survivor doesn't mean you have to be made out of steel, and it doesn't mean you have to be ruthless. It means you have to be basically on your own side and want to win.*
>
> —Linda Ronstadt

As a survivor, you experience the healing power of being a person like other people in spite of having been hurt.

When my father disowned me, I did not abandon my quest for inner peace. If anything, I worked even harder to find it. My commitment to healing took me to Amherst, Massachusetts, in July of 1981 for a personal growth workshop conducted by Dr. Sidney B. Simon. Yes, the same Sid Simon who is now my husband and co-author of this book. At the time I knew him only as a man whose books on values clarification I had used in my classroom. I had no idea how he and that five-day workshop would change my life. Everyone in that workshop had been hurt, too. They all wanted to get beyond that hurt so that they could grow. I finally began to feel less alone.

I also began to recognize that there might be more to me than the fact that my father had abused me sexually. Although I defined myself as the product of incest and nothing else, the people I met at that workshop saw more, and they said so. They told me that I was a good listener, that I was insightful, articulate, intelligent. They validated qualities that my total attention to the pain had kept me from seeing, and their messages got through. It was possible to finally see myself as more than the damaged and abandoned remnant of a horrible experience that had happened long ago.

As Suzanne's comments reflect, one of the hallmarks of the survivor stage is the realization that you do have positive attributes and admirable personality traits, that your identity is made up of more than your flaws, failures, and pain. What's more, as you begin to appreciate your own strengths, talents, and accomplishments, your entire outlook changes. Your life is now defined not by what is missing from it, but instead by what you do have and want more of. You even begin to recognize that you actually gained something from your painful past experiences, including unique skills and abilities that you can use to your advantage now and in the future.

For instance, we recently received a letter from Marcy, who, ever since we met her at a forgiveness seminar several years ago, has been sending us periodic cross-country updates on her life and her healing process. "I was just offered the job of my dreams," she informed us, going on to explain that she would be heading up an important research project, and that the position met every one of her criteria right down to having a day care center on the premises.

"My old boss recommended me for the job," Marcy wrote. "He said that I had an uncanny ability to see the 'big picture,' to anticipate problems and always have a contingency plan so that I could cut a crisis off at the pass. When the interviewer told me that, I nearly fell off my chair—because it describes to a tee what I used to do as a child. And it suddenly dawned on me that I had gotten more than pain from being an ACOA [adult child of an alcoholic]. What I did to survive back then was actually beginning to work to my advantage now. I never thought I would say this, but some good came out of the hell I lived through."

As a survivor, you too will see the good that grew out of the "hell" you went through, both when you were hurt and throughout your healing process. If you are an incest survivor, for instance, you may have a built-in "sixth sense" that enables you to tell a great deal about people from even the most subtle body language. For your own protection and survival, you *had* to develop that skill. Now you can use it positively—to make you a sensitive parent or lover, an effective helping professional, or even to tell if your sales pitch is winning over a potential customer. Regardless of how you were hurt or what you did to survive, there was indeed gain as well as pain, and in the survivor stage you can take some time to give yourself a well-deserved pat on the back for the adaptability, courage, creativity, and other strengths you developed.

This new awareness of your strengths and unique talents along with your new attitudes and new behaviors enables you to see yourself in a positive light, quite possibly for the first time since you were hurt. As the old feeling that there is something inherently wrong with you begins to fade, you begin to sense that you are, in fact, a good person. You are less likely to keep people at a distance so that they do not discover your secrets and imperfections. In fact, thinking, "If you got to know me, you'd really like me," you are open to and even actively seek out new relationships. What's more, your new relationships as well as many of your existing ones will be better than they have ever been before.

Once you reach the survivor stage, every step you take—from making choices to improving your relationships—enhances your self-esteem. And the first rumblings of positive self-worth feel so good that you want more. To build upon your new foundation of positive self-esteem, you can:

- Look for mentors and models, people you know or know about who seem to like themselves. Observe their behavior and attitudes, and incorporate what you can into your own approach to daily living.
- Take risks. Open your mind to new ideas, challenge yourself physically, and take emotional risks, too—especially those that help you conquer your fears about letting other people get close to you.
- Get involved in activities that give you recognition and a sense of belonging. Do volunteer work, join clubs, committees, professional organizations, or a bowling league. Be part of the world and you will not feel apart and alienated from it.

- Be productive. Take courses, develop new hobbies, finish old projects, get organized, and plan to accomplish something—no matter how small—every day.
- Take advantage of self-esteem-building resources.

When you combine these pursuits with the decision-making power, a sense of your unique talents and positive attributes, and a connection to a support network—all of which are elements of the survivor stage—your self-esteem flourishes. You believe in yourself. You believe you deserve inner peace and a better life. With each passing day you become more confident that you can indeed achieve the goals you set for yourself and create a brighter future.

Moving On

Autobiography in Five Short Chapters
I.
I walk down the street.
There is a deep hole in the sidewalk.
I fall in.
I am lost . . . I am helpless . . . It isn't my fault.
It takes forever to find a way out.

II.
I walk down the same street.
There is a deep hole in the sidewalk.
I pretend I don't see it.
I fall in again.
I can't believe I am in the same place again, but it isn't my fault.
It still takes a long time to get out.

III.
I walk down the same street.
There is a deep hole in the sidewalk.
I see it is there.
I still fall in . . . it's a habit.
My eyes are open . . . I know where I am. . . . It is my fault.
I get out immediately.

IV.
I walk down the same street.
There is a deep hole in the sidewalk.
I walk around it.

V.
I walk down another street.
—Portia Nelson

In the survivor stage the present becomes more powerful than the past, and you are less interested in looking back at how you were hurt and what you did because you were hurt. Pain from the past is no longer playing the starring role in your life. However, you have not yet let go of it. You see the hole in the sidewalk and you walk around it, but you are not yet walking down a different street. To do that, you must finally unlock the prison gates and allow the people who hurt you back into the human race.

True healing and forgiveness become possible once you put your painful past experiences in perspective and realize that you no longer need to use them as an excuse, to define your identity or to protect you from being hurt again. When you figure out that *not* forgiving no longer serves you in any healthy way, you let go of pain from the past and get on with your life. You also enter the next, and final, stage of the healing process—integration.

CHAPTER TEN

INTEGRATION

"It all began when I bought a pair of running shoes," Warren chuckles, and we once again notice how different he is from the grim, guarded man who once attended our forgiveness seminar only because his wife insisted upon it. He walked away from that seminar more determined than ever to hang on to his grudges and resentments. But three years later, as he drives us from an airport to the site of a conference sponsored by his church, Warren no longer looks as if the weight of the world rests on his shoulders. Indeed, he smiles warmly and laughs frequently as he tells us how forgiveness "snuck up" on him while he wasn't watching.

As you may recall, Warren's father treated him like "the invisible kid" even though Warren tried valiantly to earn his love and attention. Acknowledging that he was still furious about that when he left the forgiveness seminar, Warren says, "As far as I was concerned I'd given my father all the chances he was going to get. It was over between us."

But of course it wasn't. For one thing, Warren's father, who had recently survived a heart attack and wanted to establish a relationship with his estranged son and grandchildren, continued to call Warren's home on a regular basis. Although Warren would still not speak to him, Warren's wife did, unable to comprehend how her husband could be so unyielding.

During the arguments between him and his wife that inevitably followed, Warren railed against "the bastard" who had made his life miserable, while his wife pleaded with him not to let his vindictiveness deprive their children of a grandfather. "But I wouldn't give in," Warren reports. "I couldn't pass up this opportunity to get even, to reject him the way he used to reject me. And she would drop the subject until the next time he called."

During this same period of time, Warren's construction business went into a slump. To cut costs, he reduced his staff and attempted to do their jobs in addition to his own. He worked twelve-hour days and frequently spent his evenings locked in the den going over his accounts. After midnight on one such evening, he walked through the door of the den and immediately tripped over a large brass trophy. "My son had been named Most Valuable Player on his Little League baseball team," Warren recalls. "My wife explained that he wanted me to know, but knew better than to bother me when I was working.... I felt lousy about that, and when I realized I hadn't made it to a single one of his games that season, I felt even worse."

Slowly, as the arguments between Warren and his wife increased in frequency and intensity and his children tiptoed around the house trying to stay out of his way, it dawned on him that his own family was beginning to resemble the one he had grown up in. "But I didn't know what to do about it," Warren sighs. "Everything seemed completely out of control."

And that was when the running shoes entered the picture. When Warren went for his annual physical examination, his doctor suggested he take up jogging. "He told me exercise would help me relax *and* give me more energy," Warren explains. "Which made absolutely no sense to me, but I knew I had to do something, so I went out and bought a pair of running shoes and started to jog every morning."

Warren began to feel better physically, and after several months of jogging by himself he asked his son if he would like to jog with him. Father and son got to know each other well during the hour they spent together each morning, and the trust between them grew to the point where Warren's son felt free to say that he wished his parents wouldn't argue as much as they did. As a result, the next time Warren's wife suggested it, Warren agreed to go with her to see a marriage counselor. The couple's relationship grew stronger and more loving. Together and separately, Warren and his wife added new and positive experiences to their lives. Warren got into individual therapy and hired a consultant who helped him reorganize his business and taught him stress and time management techniques. Sunday became family day, and each week a different family member chose an activity they could all do together. It was Warren's wife's idea to spend one of those "family days" with Warren's father at his country club.

"She asked me to give my dad a chance," Warren remembers. "She said that if things didn't work out, I could always go back to hating him the next day." But things did work out. In fact, Warren saw his father in a whole new light. "He was very relaxed and interested in my work. He had a great sense of humor. He donated his time to work with sick kids at a clinic in the worst part of the city, and he played a mean game of golf. I never knew any of that, because I never wanted to know it. The man I had hated all those years was not the man he is today . . . and neither was I."

When that visit was over, Warren's wife asked him if he was glad that they had gotten together with his father. "And I was," he says.

So Warren, who never actually intended to forgive his father, began to do just that. He bought a pair of running shoes and jogged into the survivor stage. Then, with each step he took to improve his life circumstances and self-esteem, Warren's hatred for his father decreased automatically. It simply was not as important to him as it once was.

With little fanfare, Warren slipped into the *integration stage* of the healing process, unloaded the last of his excess baggage, and severed the last of his ties to pain from the past. And each of you, in your own way and according to your own internal timetable, will do that, too. You will *integrate* your painful past experiences, putting them into perspective, letting go of the intense emotions attached to them, and yes, even forgiving the people who hurt you so that you can truly get on with your life.

The Integration Stage

Human pain does not let go of its grip at one point in time. Rather it works its way out of our consciousness over time. There is a season of sadness. A season of anger. A season of tranquillity. A season of hope. . . .
　　　　　　　　　—Robert Veninga
　　　　　　　　　　Gift of Hope: How We Survive
　　　　　　　　　　Our Tragedies

Every healing journey involves a gradual awakening to new possibilities, including the possibility of forgiving the people who hurt you. As Warren's story so clearly demonstrates, everything you do, including something as seemingly simple as buying a pair of running shoes, contributes to that awakening. Although your giant leaps forward may be followed by several steps backward and you will sometimes stand still for what seems like an eternity, every success and even every setback moves you closer to forgiveness. Your mistakes and misadventures in the denial, self-blame, victim, and indignation stages, as well as the ''smart'' choices and positive behavior changes you make in the survivor stage, all help you heal. And eventually the jigsaw puzzle pieces you have been collecting from the moment you were hurt fall into place and fit together. When they do, you enter the integration stage of the healing process.

Your entry into this stage will not be nearly as dramatic as your entry into the survivor stage. It is fascinating, and perhaps fitting, that the inner peace you have worked so long and hard to attain arrives peacefully. However, even without sirens blaring or neon signs flashing, you know when you reach the integration stage because:

- you no longer bristle or cringe when someone brings up the topic of abuse or divorce or alcoholism or anything else that once hurt you;
- hearing about the person who hurt you no longer ruins your day or compels you to go on a tirade about what a rotten, lousy scumbag that person is;
- the intense emotions associated with your painful past experiences seem to have slipped away;
- you still have feelings about those experiences, but those feelings do not overwhelm you. You no longer worry that your tears will never end or that your anger will rage out of control.

In the integration stage, we come to understand how our painful past experiences fit into the *whole* of our lives. We acknowledge that they were part of our lives and recognize how they shaped our lives. But we also realize that pain and heartache were not the only things we experienced and that our painful experiences were not the only ones that made us who we are today.

Of course, none of this means that we forget what happened to us or that what happened was not important and did not affect our lives. It does mean that once we reach the integration stage, those old injuries and injustices are less emotionally charged. We can think about them without going into a tailspin, and when we do think about them, we are less likely to dwell on them. As a result, forgiveness does—as Warren put it—"sneak up on you when you aren't watching."

In fact, it sneaks up on you *because* you are not watching, because you are no longer staring at and wallowing in pain from your past but instead looking ahead and moving forward toward wellness and a brighter future. You see, the changes you made and the new direction you took in the survivor stage opened the door to the integration stage and paved the way for forgiveness.

Paving the Way for Forgiveness

"It's okay to identify yourself as an adult child of an alcoholic," Indiana University professor Robert Ackerman advised his audience at a recent conference on alcoholism. "That is what you are. But do not stop there, because you are more than that." Ackerman then went on to inform the conference participants that if they introduced themselves to him as adult children of alcoholics, they should expect him to look at them and say, *"And . . . ?"*

How would you answer that one-word question? Who are you *besides* the damaged or healing remnant of some past injury or injustice? Are you also a parent, a spouse, a friend, a supportive person, a creative thinker, a jogger, a gardener, or a gourmet cook? How many different endings can you write for a sentence that begins with the words *I am*? Take out a sheet of paper and write those sentences now. Chances are that you will be pleasantly surprised by how many different facets of your identity you can list.

You have always been more than a victim of pain from the past. Earlier in your healing process, however, the hurting, hating, grudge-holding part of yourself was the single most important aspect of your identity. Pain from the past and resentment toward the people who hurt you played such a vital role in your life that you would not have known what to do or who to be without them. Even after you traded in your victim label for one with "survivor" written on it, your old wounds defined who you were. You were a survivor *of something*. If you forgave that "thing" or let go of the intense emotions attached to it, you also gave up a piece of yourself, a fundamental part of your identity.

Fortunately, while in the survivor stage the new attitudes and behaviors you adopted, as well as the positive sense of self-worth you developed, enabled you to rediscover the parts of your identity that were not defined by or connected to your painful past experiences. In the integration stage you go one step further, realizing that other parts of yourself—being a parent, a spouse, a student, a teacher, or even an amateur oil painter—are just as important as and perhaps even more important than the part of your identity that developed because you were hurt. You would still have an identity even if the hurting, hating, grudge-holding part of you ceased to exist. And when that dawns on you, *letting go of the pain, giving up your resentments, and forgiving the people who hurt you becomes possible.*

What's more, as your health, self-esteem, relationships, and decision-making skills improve, you no longer need your unhealed wounds and unfinished business as excuses. Because you discontinued your systematic suicide behaviors during the survivor stage and adopted new habits (like regular exercise, a healthy diet, using a support network, and managing your time), you have no reason to point to pain from the past and say, "Don't expect much from me. Considering what I've been through, I'm lucky to be keeping my head above water."

Since you are moving steadily forward toward wellness and even getting glimpses of inner peace now and then, why would you *want* to get bogged down in pain from the past? The fact of the matter is that you don't. In the integration stage you recognize that hanging on to your painful past experiences and not forgiving the people who hurt you *no longer serves you in any healthy or useful way.* Indeed, the injuries and injustices that were such handy excuses and justified your self-indulgent or self-destructive behaviors in the past become obstacles at this point in your healing process. With each passing day, the prospect of getting rid of those obstacles becomes more appealing, *even if it means that you must let the people who hurt you "off the hook."*

Finally, in this stage you fully acknowledge that nothing you have done to punish *them* has helped *you* heal. Whether you have actually done things to make sure that the people who hurt you suffered at least as much as you did; restricted yourself to revenge fantasies and wishing harm would come to them; or brooded and fumed while you waited around for them to somehow make up for what they did to you, *not* forgiving the people who hurt you has drained *your* energy, consumed *your* time, and kept *you* living in pain from the past. The question is, how long do you intend to go on doing that? Because you are committed to healing and well on your way to achieving that goal, in the integration stage you answer, "Not one moment longer."

Unfortunately there is a rather large gap between recognizing that we would be better off if we forgave the people who hurt us and actually doing it. Bridging that gap, actually letting go of pain from the past, and letting the people who hurt us back into the human race requires understanding, acceptance, and ultimately a leap of faith.

Crossing the Threshold to Forgiveness

> *The function of freedom is to free someone else.*
> —Toni Morrison

In addition to receiving the first building blocks for improving self-esteem, the personal growth workshop I attended in the summer of 1981—and one strategy in particular—paved the way for eventually forgiving my father. Sid asked us to find a partner, pretend that partner was someone who had hurt us, and say to them, "I know you did the best you could. If you could have done better, you would have."

But I could not get those words to come out of my mouth. They bunched up in my throat. I did not believe them, and I did not want to say them without meaning them or feeling them. I thought that if I really tried, I could be sincere in saying that my mother did the best she could. But even that seemed beyond my capabilities at that time.

Suzanne had reached another turning point in her healing process. She had encountered the last major barrier to the inner peace she had been seeking for so long—her attachment to the unforgiven and seemingly unforgivable acts that had been dictating the storyline of her life ever since her father first molested her.

You too will encounter this obstacle. No matter how far you have gotten in your own healing process, merely considering the possibility that those words *might* be true is still likely to churn up feelings of anger, outrage, and cold, raw fear. "No way," you think. "There is no way on earth anyone is going to get me to believe that the son of a bitch who hurt me did the best he could. I'm not letting him off the hook so easily.''

Yet letting the people who hurt you ''off the hook'' is precisely what you must do in order to let *yourself* off the hook, too. What you resist persists, weighing you down and keeping you floored no matter how determined you are to spread your wings and fly off to explore new horizons. To let go and move on, you must try to understand and accept the people who hurt you in the same way that you have learned, throughout your healing process, to understand and accept yourself.

If the person who hurt you has a clearly identifiable problem, like alcoholism, for instance, mental illness, or a history of being abused, it is relatively easy to understand how that problem created circumstances or conditions that ultimately led to your pain. ''As they say at Al-Anon, alcoholism is a disease of the body, mind, and spirit, a form of insanity,'' Marcy comments. ''I tend to look at it as demonic possession, actually, because Lord knows a whole new personality inhabited my mother's body when she was drinking. Still, if she had known about AA, or hadn't had my dad as a drinking buddy or realized that alcoholism was a disease and not something she could control on her own, I really do believe she would have done something about her problem and been a better mother than she was.''

In other instances, there is not a clear-cut problem to point to or simply no way of knowing what prompted the actions of the person who hurt you. However, this does not prevent you from trying to understand the situation from the other person's point of view. ''Sometimes I try to put myself in her shoes,'' says Sandy, whose biological mother abandoned her soon after she was born. ''I imagine her being very young and poor and alone, not really knowing how to take care of a baby, not knowing whom to ask, maybe not even having the money to buy diapers or formula. I've been working with the homeless, and I've met a lot of young girls like that. I've helped some of them put their kids in foster care—and they do love those kids. So I really can believe that my mother loved me and tried to keep me, even if I'll never actually know for sure.''

And regardless of the circumstances, understanding that *you,* at every moment of your life, did the best you could with the insight, resources, and nourishment you had available to you, makes it possible to imagine that maybe, just maybe, the people who hurt you were doing that, too; that maybe they too would have done better and would not have inflicted that wound if, at that time, they had more insight, more alternatives, more support, or less devastating past experiences of their own. This comparison, as well as the realization that understanding someone's limitations is not the same as condoning their behavior, helped Suzanne take her leap of faith during the personal growth workshop she attended.

> Recognizing that I nccded to acknowledge the unfairness of what had happened to me, Sid suggested that I try saying, *"That was no way to treat a little kid,* but I know you did the best you could. If you could have done better, you would have.''
> That helped. The kind, unconditional acceptance I felt from my partner helped. I said those words about my mother. I meant them, and then I cried.

Of course, in Suzanne's case, as well as in Marcy's, Sandy's, and your own, acknowledging that what the people who hurt you did might have been the best they could do, in no way alters the fact that what they did was wrong, rotten, and *not good enough.* That is undeniable, and indeed you do not want to deny it. But you *do* want to forgive it, and understanding that a lack of insight, resources, or nourishment was the reason behind what happened does, in fact, make it easier to let go.

So does *accepting* the fact that there is nothing you can do to change the people who hurt you; no way that you can shame, manipulate, humiliate, subtly torture, punish, or hate them enough to make them make up for what they did to you. There is no form of revenge that can heal your wounds, and shutting a parent or a child or a friend out of your life does not take away your pain. Learning that the rapist or mugger or drunk driver who wreaked havoc on your life has gotten the maximum sentence for his crime provides a certain amount of satisfaction, but it does not restore the order and tranquillity to your life. The only way to do that is to work through the healing process and reach the point where you can say, ''Yes, it happened to me, but it is not me. I am more—and so is the person who hurt me.''

As Darlene put it, ''When I started feeling better about myself, I started feeling better about other people. It wasn't a goal I set for myself. I didn't say, 'I think I'll stop overeating and lose weight and quit trying to handle everything myself so that I can trust other people and have better relationships with them.' In fact, I didn't even think that was possible. But it happened. And it didn't happen because *they* changed. It happened because I did.''

As Darlene discovered, letting go of your need to change other people and accepting them instead is a natural outgrowth of changing yourself. This change in attitude often gets you thinking about reconnecting in some way with the people who hurt you, even though you may not have forgiven them yet and still may not be certain that you want to.

Reconciliations

> I cried through the remainder of the strategy, which involved writing what we would like to do with what we had learned from the role play. I cried for twenty minutes, which was how long it took me to write one sentence: ''I want to say those words to my father.''

If you were involved in any kind of relationship with the people who hurt you, those relationships were undoubtedly damaged and possibly discontinued when you were hurt or while you were working through your healing process. During the integration stage, while considering the *possibility* of forgiving the people who hurt you, you also think about rebuilding your relationship with those people. Like everything else that occurs in the integration stage, your renewed interest in seeing, spending time with, and possibly discussing the past with someone who hurt you is motivated by your own need to get on with your healing process.

For instance, Warren, whose hatred had diminished greatly as his self-esteem increased, agreed to spend a day at his father's country club because he needed to find out if ''I would hate him again once I saw him or if he or I or both of us had changed enough to treat each other differently.'' And Sandy decided to look for her biological mother because ''there had always been a missing chapter in my life. I didn't have a sense of my own history, and I felt like I needed that connection to the past if I was ever going to feel complete.'' Suzanne also chose to reconnect with her father for her own sake.

> I did not want to see my father in order to extract an apology from him or to grace him with my forgiveness so that he could

die in peace. At this point in my healing process, I was not even sure I had forgiven him. No, seeing my father again was something I had to do because I needed to prove to myself that I could come face to face with this man and not be crushed by the formidable, almost mystical power I had attributed to him since childhood. I needed to know that I could be in the same room with him and not self-destruct.

Of course, you may not be able to actually contact or reconnect with the people who hurt you. They may be dead now. They may be childhood playmates or high school sweethearts or former employers who truly have no role to play in your life today. Try as you might, you simply may not be able to find the father who abandoned your family or the mother who put you up for adoption. That's okay. You do not have to "work things out" with that person in order to work through your pain and let go of it.

And even when the people who hurt you are alive and available, some of you will not want to resolve your issues with them directly. That's okay, too. Reconciling your differences and reestablishing or changing your relationship is not required in order to heal your old wounds and complete your unfinished business.

If you do want to reconnect with someone who hurt you, however, and decide to actually take steps to repair the bonds between you, please be aware that this is likely to be a slow and difficult process. We advise you to proceed cautiously, to take the time to ask yourself, "What is the most self-respecting way to handle this?" and not to expect positive or dramatic results immediately. In fact, we recommend that you take the following steps *before* you actually approach the person who hurt you:

1. *Know what you* really *want*. Start by doing some serious soul-searching to determine the real reason behind your interest in reconciliation. By now you know that wanting to extract an apology or give the people who hurt you another opportunity to make it up to you as well as expecting them to fulfill the needs that they failed to meet in the past are the *wrong* reasons. Try to define the relationship you want in terms of how it could be now and in the future, not by how you wish it had been in the past.

For instance, if Harriet decided to make peace with Larry because she viewed rebuilding their relationship as a stepping-stone to getting back together as a couple, she would have been setting herself up for disappointments that would have perpetuated her pain.

Fortunately she did not do that. Indeed, because she approached Larry wanting to reconcile their differences so that they could get along well enough to end their custody battle and work cooperatively to raise their children, her realistic expectations netted positive results.

Similarly, when Marcy began accepting her mother's helpful overtures and talking with her mother about alcoholism's effect on both their lives, she did not want to be cared for the way she had not been during her childhood. Nor did she want to make her mother feel guilty or ashamed. "I wanted us to be friends, really—two adult women who had gone through a lot together and separately," she said. "And I wanted us to be able to share what that felt like and help each other through rough spots and maybe even have some fun together."

It is not easy to identify what you want from any relationship, much less one that has already caused you a great deal of pain. You can start this decision-making process by taking a close look at the state of your relationship right now. You can do this by completing these sentences:

> Right now, I am...
> You are...
> We are...

Then ask yourself how the relationship would be *in your perfect fantasy*. Describe the ideal outcome of your reconciliation by completing the following sentences:

> In my perfect fantasy, I would...
> You would...
> We would...

How does your fantasy compare with the state of your relationship right now? Chances are there are large gaps between your two sets of sentences. You can close that gap and set reasonable goals for your reconciliation by identifying a middle ground, represented by your response to

> Realistically, I could...
> You could...
> We could...

2. *Think about what you can do to reach your goal.* None of you will wake up one morning, decide to invite someone who hurt you back into your life, reconnect, and then rebuild your relationship before the end of the day. There are many factors to consider, including:

- how you will approach someone you have for quite some time punished overtly or within the confines of your own mind;
- what you want to say to that person and what, if anything, you want to ask of him or her;
- the various ways that person could respond to your overtures (and how each would affect you);
- your own fears or ambivalence about letting go of your resentments and grudges.

To deal with these complex and anxiety-provoking issues, you can *brainstorm* a list of alternative approaches and then identify the potential negative and positive consequences of each one. This method usually reveals the best way to initiate a reconciliation, although it will not be perfect, and thus you must be prepared to deal with less-than-perfect results.

You can *visualize* the interaction—getting yourself into a relaxed state, shutting your eyes, and imagining yourself carrying out the approach you have chosen. Many people find it soothing to picture the other person surrounded by white light. If you find yourself envisioning the worst possible outcomes, stop the visualization, relax again, and start over, modifying your approach to account for the obstacle you encountered. Getting "worked up" each time you visualize the situation means one of two things, either you are not yet ready to make this move or you have chosen the wrong approach. Put the reconciliation on the back burner for a while and then begin again by reviewing your options.

You may want to *rehearse* your reconciliation, asking your counselor, spouse, or a friend to "sit in" for the person who hurt you. This is a particularly effective way to get a reading on how your words sound to someone else and even choose better ones if the ones you chose originally get a strong negative reaction. Rehearsing also allows you to get some sense of how you will feel during the actual conversation and how you will react if the other person responds to you in certain ways. You can even ask your role-play partner to say the words you least want to hear, preparing you for the worst should it occur.

Or you may want to write a *letter*. Seeing your thoughts in writing helps to clarify them. Indeed, the thoughts that flow onto the written page may even take you by surprise, getting to deeper concerns than the ones you originally thought you wanted to share with the person who hurt you. Although no one ever has to see this letter, some of you may choose to send it as a way of making the first move toward reconciliation.

3. *Get emotional support.* Letting someone who hurt you out of prison and back into your life is very scary because you do not know how your efforts will work out. Your indignation, the victim part of you, and even your vulnerable inner child will have something to say about this ''crazy notion'' of yours—and believe us, their words will *not* be the encouraging kind. What's more, if your attempts to rebuild your relationships do not live up to your hopes and expectations, you will feel new pain and disappointment along with the resurgence of old fears and self-doubt.

You simply cannot get through all that emotional turmoil on your own. Consequently we advise you not to attempt to patch things up with the person who hurt you *unless* you have adequate emotional support. Talk about your plans with your counselor, support group members, friends, or other nurturing people in your life. Let them know you will need them throughout this rebuilding process and actually take advantage of the guidance, encouragement, and caring they have to offer you.

4. *Remember that you cannot know in advance how things will turn out, and that no matter how they do—you did the best you could.* By following the steps we have recommended, you will be able to approach the situation with your eyes wide open and act with dignity and self-respect. This does not guarantee that you will get what you want, however. Suzanne learned that the hard way when she made her first move to reconnect with her father.

Three days after the personal growth workshop, I surprised myself by picking up the telephone and dialing my father's number. I lived through hearing his voice and said, ''Hello, Dad. This is Suzanne.'' His response was one you might expect from a man who had not spoken to his daughter in three years. He assumed something was terribly wrong and immediately asked if I was all right. I said that I was okay, but that I needed to talk to him.

''Can I put your mother on the extension?'' he asked, and I

did something I had never done to him before. I said, "No! I want to speak to you alone, and I don't want you to interrupt me."

He respected my request and listened as I told him, "Daddy, I want you to know that sometimes the memory of what you did to me hurts me a lot, and sometimes I don't think about it at all. Sometimes I blame all my problems on this, and sometimes my life feels wonderful and good. I'm growing and making progress and moving ahead with my life, and I want you to know that I know you did the very best you could; and if you could have done better, I'm sure you would have, because I know you loved us."

I knew he heard what I said to him, and I knew he felt the full impact of my words. He became upset and agitated, blurted out the words "I'm sorry," and said that he never wanted to hurt me. Then he hung up abruptly.

Suzanne was shocked, of course, and disheartened by her father's response. More often than not, your initial attempts to reestablish or repair your damaged relationships will fail to live up to your expectations. However, an unexpected or less than satisfactory outcome does not mean that you must give up all hope of ever having a healthy relationship with that person. Think of it as planting seeds. If you go back and check on them periodically, you may discover that they have taken root and, with a little additional effort on your part, can grow and flourish.

I persisted. I had set myself on a course of healing, and one of my goals was to have a father again. I wrote and I called, and finally after several months had passed, I got through. A year later, at Christmastime, he finally agreed to see me.

Our reunion took place in a hospital room, and the father I found there was not the menacing giant I remembered, but rather a shriveled little man, physically weak although not spiritually defeated. I had not rehearsed what I would say to him. But the instant I set eyes on him, it became clear that I did not have to say anything at all. The tears began to flow as I walked to his bedside. I hugged him and he hugged me. And that was all the communication either of us needed. I knew I had my father back in my life, and he knew he had his daughter back in his.

Of course, every reconciliation will proceed differently. For instance, after their initial face-to-face contact, neither Suzanne nor Warren discussed the past with their fathers. On the other hand,

Marcy and her mother talked at great length about the past—and still do. Harriet and Larry were able to resolve their differences only after they received help from a professional mediator, and Melinda decided, after several less than successful attempts, that she was better off having no contact with Steve at all.

What's more, Suzanne's journey did not end here, and should your attempts at reconciliation succeed, neither will yours. Reconciliation is not the same as forgiveness, and letting someone who hurt you back into your life is not the same as truly letting go of the pain.

Becoming a "Believer in Life"

Forgiveness is not an action. It is a discovery. Forgiveness is not a goal. It is the gift we receive because we have pursued other goals, including improved physical and mental health, positive self-esteem, more nourishing friendships, more fulfilling intimate relationships, greater insight into our own behavior, and much more. As Robert Caldwell put it in an article published in *Pathways* titled "Forgiveness . . . Choosing Between Getting Even and Getting Close," it is "an attitude, a stance inward and outward that grows naturally and inevitably from confronting one's hurts, discovering one's strengths, and understanding and accepting the other and oneself."

Once you have traveled far enough down that long, winding, often painful road we call the healing process, you will indeed find forgiveness and inner peace waiting for you. Your present will be more powerful than your past, and as a result you will not want to be held back or bogged down by old injuries and injustices. You will let go of them instead.

For the first time since you were hurt, you realistically assess any responsibility you did have for the hurtful things that happened to you. You fully accept that as a child you were blameless, especially when injuries were perpetrated by the adults entrusted with your care. However, you also realize that more often than not you did contribute in some way to the situations that caused you pain as an adult. Harriet, for example, did not pay as much attention to Larry as she did to her business during the years immediately preceding the demise of their marriage. Although this did not force Larry to have an affair, it did put a strain on the relationship that Harriet did not take as seriously as she might have. Similarly, Melinda "set herself up" for rejection each time she chose to become involved with married men or those on the rebound. And Darlene contributed to her own burnout and constant disappointment by repeatedly assuming other people's responsibilities before they had a chance to handle them themselves.

Because the intense emotions surrounding their experiences had subsided, Harriet, Melinda, and Darlene could view those experiences objectively. Without punishing themselves or going overboard to fix things that were, in reality, beyond their control, they determined what they could and would do differently in the future. You will do this, too. Whether you decide to create a healthier balance between your personal and professional life, as Harriet did; give more thought to what you need from your friendships and intimate relationships, as Melinda did; or delegate tasks and share responsibilities, as Darlene did—you will indeed learn from your painful past experiences and incorporate what you learn into your new, improved life-style.

You will also have a more balanced and objective perspective on life in general. You accept that bad things can and do happen; that people hurt each other; that no one gets through this life without experiencing some pain, sorrow, or misfortune. However, you are equally aware that good things happen, too; that people love, support, and show compassion toward each other; that life also provides countless opportunities for joy, success, and satisfaction. This new perspective is beautifully captured in the following excerpt from ''Comes the Dawn,'' a poem by an anonymous writer:

> So you plant your own garden and decorate your own soul,
> Instead of waiting for someone to bring you flowers.
> And you learn that you really can endure . . .
> That you really are strong,
> And really do have worth
> And you learn and learn
> With every goodbye you learn.

Long after your gaze turns away from the past and toward the future, long after the hate and hurt has made way for inner peace and forgiveness, you will still be learning. Among other things, you will learn to deal with new injuries and injustices . . . because healing the old wounds does not guarantee that you will not sustain new ones. All of us will be hurt again. That is one of the inevitable realities of living in a decidedly imperfect world. We may be lucky enough to sustain only a few bumps and bruises, or we may suffer some devastating losses. Regardless, the new injuries and injustices will send us back to earlier stages of the healing process. In fact, we will probably have to work our way through all of the stages again. This will be easier to do the second, third, or fourth time around, but it will never be painless. The best advice we can give you is to take advantage of the insight, resources, and support network you have developed and remind yourself of what it feels like to first survive and then forgive.

Realize too that your journey is a never-ending one. After you make peace with your past, you do not get a free pass to a brighter future. There is always more to learn, experience, and become. Ahead of you lies what reevaluation counselor Nancy Kline calls a "life of no limits," and because you have taken this healing journey, you do believe in your own ability to be joyful, productive, peaceful, and limitless. When you consciously chose to heal your wounds and complete your unfinished business, you committed yourself to making the most out of your life. All that remains is to go out and do it!

Where They Are Now

Eighteen months after I visited him in the hospital, my father died. It was July of 1984. Four years had passed since I made the fateful decision to stop denying that incest had affected me. My healing process had taken me through pain, shame, confusion, and self-doubt. It had led me to the depths of despair and powerlessness, where I had wallowed and paid attention to nothing but the pain for what seemed like an eternity. It had forced me to feel the anger that I found so frightening, and it had shown me what it meant to be a survivor. And yes, it had directed me to a place of inner peace, a place where I was indeed able to forgive.

I received the news of my father's death while I was in San Diego, co-leading a personal growth workshop with Sid. And it was during the flight east to attend my father's funeral that I realized I had truly forgiven him. On that flight, I did not give much thought to the ways my father had hurt me. My mind was too cluttered with pleasant memories, the joyful moments from my childhood as well as the highlights of time we spent together and telephone conversations we had during the months preceding my father's death. I knew then that my father was much more than the hurtful things he did to me. I took out several sheets of paper and wrote a eulogy, celebrating the good in a man I once believed to be all bad. I read that eulogy at my father's funeral to commemorate the end of his life and the continuation of my own journey.

And the journey did continue. I moved to Amherst, Massachusetts, and began counseling and facilitating support groups for incest survivors. Sid and I got married in September of 1985, and we continued to co-lead personal growth workshops and forgiveness seminars. I began giving workshops and keynote addresses on my own as well. I worked on my relationship with my daughter, who is an adult now and about to get married. I am still working on myself, and since my goal is to become more each day than I was the day before, that work will never end. I am willing to do the work because I have found some inner peace, and want even more.

That is where Suzanne is today. But what about the other people you read about throughout this book? Did they heal and forgive? Some of them did, and some of them are still trying to. Where did their healing journeys take them? Here is a quick update on those people, who have kept us informed of their progress.

"She may not have been much of a mother, but my mom is the world's greatest grandmother," Marcy wrote in her most recent letter. "And I don't mean that she spoils them. She's just good with them, not too easy and not too strict, very tuned in to their feelings. Watching her with my kids makes me even more sure that she would have been a terrific mom if she had sobered up sooner. She's got a really solid recovery going, too. I tease her about hanging out at AA meetings to meet men, but she knows how much I respect what she's doing."

Clearly, Marcy views her mother in a much more positive, yet realistic light, and over the past few years the two women have developed a relationship that is, according to Marcy, "really close. If we had been a normal mother and daughter when I was a kid, I don't think we'd have a relationship this good now. I'm telling you, going through hell really does have its benefits."

In addition to being closer than ever to her mother, Marcy's healing process has helped her to be an efficient—but also a more relaxed and compassionate—research project director. She no longer comes unglued because the rest of the world does not conform to her expectations or schedule, and although she still gets anxious when she makes mistakes, the anxiety does not turn to panic or send her into a crippling depression.

"I haven't been really depressed in ages," she concluded her letter. "With a job I love, a family I'm incredibly proud of and amazed by, connected to a mother again, and with a brand-new sense of humor, there just isn't any room for wallowing."

About a year ago, we received a formal invitation to the opening of Melinda's restaurant, and although we were unable to attend the official event, on our way to New York recently we did stop in to see her. There was a certain glow about her, a bounce to her walk that we hadn't noticed before, and an unmistakable air of confidence and serenity. "Dumping Steve and getting into therapy was the turning point for me," Melinda informed us. "Everything grew out of that, although I didn't pay that much attention to what was happening."

As it had for Warren, inner peace sneaked up on Melinda while she was busy doing other things, including changing her diet and learning more about natural foods, taking business courses at the state university, joining a volleyball team, traveling throughout the United States to visit natural-food restaurants, and finally opening a restaurant of her own.

"Actually it's not mine alone," said Melinda, her eyes twinkling and an impish grin appearing on her face—and we soon learned why. It seems that when Melinda decided that she was serious about having her own restaurant, she went to see an old college friend, a man named Paul whom she had kept in touch with sporadically for years. "He was always there to pick up the pieces after my relationships fell apart," she commented. Melinda and Paul became business partners and, according to Melinda, "spent every waking minute of every day together getting this business off the ground." And at some point during that hectic time in their lives, they fell in love.

"That sort of snuck up on me, too," Melinda said, laughing. "Yup, Mr. Right was in my life the whole time I was out looking for him. I was just too hung up on Steve and guys like him to figure that out." By working through the stages of the healing process, Melinda did figure it out. When we visited her she and Paul were engaged, and by the time you read this they will be married. "In a way, I have Steve to thank for that," Melinda concluded. "Finally getting fed up enough to realize that he wasn't who I wanted pushed me to learn what I did want from men and life in general. And then I got off my duff and did what I needed to do to get it.''

Harriet and Larry resolved their differences with the help of a mediator and agreed on a joint custody arrangement. For six months of every year their children lived with Larry during the week and visited Harriet on weekends. Then for the next six months they lived with Harriet and visited Larry. ''The first year was tough,'' Harriet acknowledged. ''But then we both loosened up and my daughter somehow wound up living with me most of the year while my son lived mostly with Larry. Everybody visits everyone else when they feel like it. Sometimes Larry and I even sit around drinking tea and talking about the good old days.''

In addition, Harriet's interior design business is flourishing, she is active in a support network for women business owners, and is dating a man who is ten years her junior. ''I wanted to explore new horizons—well, I'm definitely doing that.'' She shook her head in wonder. ''We do things like sky-dive and hang-glide, camp out under the stars, or see a Shakespearean play and then go to a rock concert on the same night. There's so much out there, and if I hadn't decided to get my act together, I might never have seen it.''

''On the surface, our relationship is the same as it always was,'' Mark explained. ''But I feel different about it. Actually it's more what I *don't* feel that's different. I don't feel angry at my dad anymore, and I don't get all worked up before I see him. I can't say I'm crazy about him or that I look forward to being with him, but I don't waste all that time and energy hating him, either. I've found some peace of mind.''

Mark left his job at the rehabilitation hospital and began working at a sports medicine clinic. Coming in contact with patients who were highly motivated to achieve and committed to being in peak mental and physical condition ''rubbed off'' on him, and Mark began taking more risks. He is currently in graduate school, does volunteer work as a counselor at a men's resource center, cross-country skis in the winter and hikes in the summer, and spends as much time as possible with his wife and infant son.

''Mostly, I'm working on forgiving myself,'' Bruce said during a recent phone conversation. ''I could spend an hour every day for the rest of my life making amends to the people I hurt while I was drinking and drugging. But that's okay. It keeps me on the straight and narrow, reminds me where I've been and how I don't want to be there again.''

Bruce recently celebrated his fourth year of sobriety and is an executive for a national hotel chain. His marriage did not fare as well as Bruce did, and soon after we first met him, he and his wife separated and then divorced. He remarried, however, and he and his new wife are expecting their first child. Bruce isn't sure if he has completely let go of pain from the past. "How can you forgive a school system?" he asked. "I've been doing my part to make sure what happened to me doesn't happen to other kids, though." He tutors children with learning disabilities and occasionally speaks on the topic of drug and alcohol abuse to students and parent groups.

Feeling that her best bet was to make a fresh start, Terry moved to San Francisco and took a job supervising several halfway houses for women recovering from drug and alcohol problems. She has not engaged in any promiscuous sexual behavior for over a year and attends a twelve-step program for people with sexual addictions and compulsions. "I'm going through a brand-new phase," she informed us. "Celibacy. It isn't so bad, although I don't think I'll adopt it as a permanent lifestyle." She recently began dating someone she likes quite a bit. "But I'm taking it real slow, which is also a novel approach for me."

"To tell you the truth"—Terry abruptly changed the tone of our conversation—"I'm in a rotten place right now. But I'm working my way through it."

With the help of a therapist and an incest survivor's support group, Terry had worked through her feelings about her grandfather and the sexual abuse itself. However, she recently slipped back into the indignation stage and is "stuck with all this anger toward my mother and grandmother." Terry went on to explain that she is having trouble forgiving them for what they did when they found out she was being molested by her grandfather. "They didn't say one word about it," she explained. "They just made sure I never spent any time alone with my granddad. They punished me without telling me what crime I'd committed."

During a recent visit to her hometown, Terry felt so resentful in the presence of her mother and grandmother, whom she refers to as "those hypocritical southern belles," that she packed her bags in the middle of the night and left without saying good-bye. "This too shall pass," Terry told us, and we have every confidence that it will, because in spite of her angry feelings, Terry has continued to both avoid her systematic suicide behaviors and take care of herself physically, emotionally, and spiritually.

The last time we saw Darlene, we barely recognized her. With the help of Overeaters Anonymous, a nutritionist, and daily laps in the community swimming pool, she had stopped binge eating and lost seventy-five pounds. Thrilled with her "new look," Darlene dressed more fashionably and was dyeing her hair to cover the prematurely gray strands.

We only got to speak to her for a few minutes, but we did learn that there had been more than physical changes in her life. She had learned to delegate at work, and her performance evaluations were much more positive. She was up for a promotion but did not know whether she really wanted it. "I'm trying to have fewer pressures and responsibilities in my life right now, not more," she explained.

Because of a crisis experienced by one of her children, Darlene and the other members of her family went into family therapy. "I learned so much about myself," Darlene said, "that I decided to get counseling for myself, too. We're tackling my problems one at a time and haven't gotten around to my dad yet, but I can already tell that my attitude toward him is changing. In fact, I just sent him a letter telling him that I'd like to get to know him again."

So there you have it—a quick summary of where some of the people you read about are right now. Now only one question remains: Where are *you* right now—and what is the next bold step you want to take?

At the end of our forgiveness seminars, we often ask everyone in the room to write what we call "the healing letter." Like other letters written in other stages of the healing process, this is not a letter that you will send to anyone. Instead it helps you get a clearer idea of where you are in your own healing process right now and what you want or need to do next. It is a fitting way to end a forgiveness seminar, because it helps participants take what they learned in that room and use it in the outside world. We encourage you to write a healing letter, too, so that you can determine how this book may have affected the journey you've been on throughout your healing process.

Back in the denial stage, you wrote a letter to yourself from someone who hurt you and owed you an apology. Your healing letter should be addressed to that person.

The opening line of your letter should read: ''I am on a healing journey, and you are my focus.''

Following that line, compose a three-part letter. Part one should describe how the injury or injustice used to affect you and what you used to do because of it. Part two should describe how the injury or injustice affects you now and what you do, think, or feel because of it now. And part three should describe what you need to and plan to do to heal that wound and get on with your life.

We would like to end this book with one of those healing letters, because we believe that it eloquently sums up what healing and forgiveness are all about and will encourage you to embark upon or persevere on a healing journey of your own.

The Healing Letter

Dear Dad,

I am on a healing journey, and you are my focus. . . . I used to think that eating chocolate made me feel better. Sometimes I ate it so fast—for fear of being caught in the act—that I didn't taste it or even remember eating it. My life was like those chocolate binges. I didn't remember living it.

I used to allow other people to obliterate me, and I used to believe that I was expendable, easy to overlook, too insignificant to be remembered, and certainly unworthy of anyone's respect, including my own. Of course I acted like I was better than everybody. That way they would never find out how inadequate I really was.

But I do not compare myself with other people anymore. And I do not use chocolate bars and chocolate bon-bons and chocolate ice cream to stuff down my feelings. Because now I believe that I matter and that I have something to offer.

I am just fine, thank you, and I plan to get even better. Although I may visit now and then, I do not intend to ever again live in the places my pain has taken me to. I have better things to do. I plan to keep moving forward out of the darkness and into the light. I want to leave the pain and anger and insecurity behind me—without forgetting what caused it or what I have learned from it. I want to forgive, and I believe that some day very soon I will. There's a world out there waiting for me, and I *will* explore it and be a part of it. Any day now, I'll open my arms and shout, ''Ready or not life, here I come!''

Your Daughter

Sid and Suzanne Simon conduct personal growth workshops on Forgiveness and other topics, including Getting Unstuck, throughout the world. For further information, please contact them at:

45 Old Mountain Road
Hadley, MA 01035

INDEX